Content

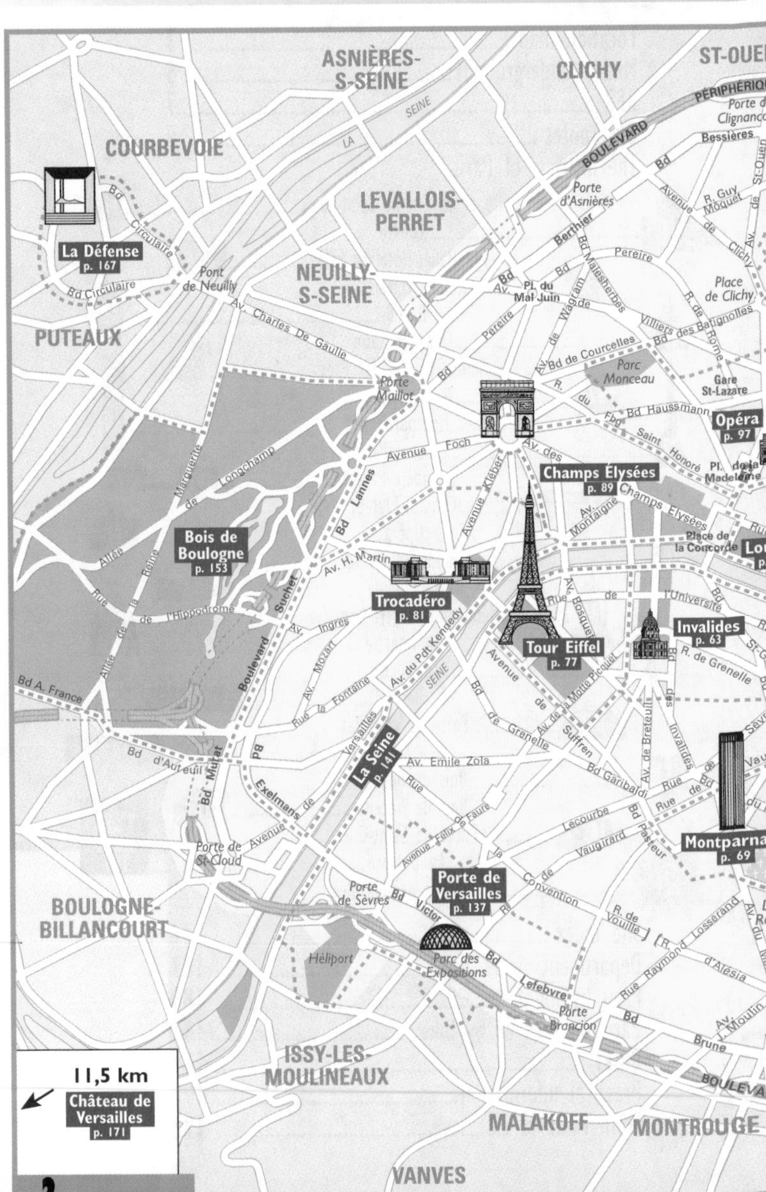

ASNIÈRES-S-SEINE
CLICHY
ST-OUEN
PÉRIPHÉRIQUE
Porte de Clignancourt
Bessières
SEINE
LA
COURBEVOIE
BOULEVARD
Bd
Porte d'Asnières
R. Guy Môquet
Avenue de St-Ouen
Avenue de Clichy
LEVALLOIS-PERRET
Berthier
Bd Malesherbes
Bd Circulaire
La Défense
p. 167
Pont de Neuilly
NEUILLY-S-SEINE
Pereire
Pl. du Mal Juin
Place de Clichy
Av. de Wagram
Villiers
des Batignolles
R. de Rome
PUTEAUX
Av. Charles De Gaulle
Bd de Courcelles
Parc Monceau
Gare St-Lazare
Porte Maillot
R. du Fbg Saint Honoré
Bd Haussmann
Opéra
p. 97
Avenue Foch
Av. des
Champs Élysées
p. 89
Pl. de la Madeleine
Allée de Longchamp
Marguerite
Bd Lannes
Avenue Kléber
Av. Montaigne
Champs Élysées
Rue
Place de la Concorde
Louvre
p.
Bois de Boulogne
p. 153
Allée de la Reine
Av. H. Martin
Trocadéro
p. 81
Rue de l'Université
Rue de l'Hippodrome
Suchet
Av. Ingres
Av. du Pdt Kennedy
Av. Bosquet
Invalides
p. 63
Tour Eiffel
p. 77
R. de Grenelle
Av. Mozart
Avenue de la Motte Picquet
Bd A. France
Allée de Longchamp
Boulevard
Rue la Fontaine
SEINE
Bd de Grenelle
Av. de Suffren
Av. de Breteuil
Bd des Invalides
Bd d'Auteuil
Bd Murat
Versailles
La Seine
p. 141
Av. Emile Zola
Bd Garibaldi
Rue de Sèvres
Rue de Vaugirard
Bd Exelmans
Avenue de
Rue
Avenue Félix Faure
Lecourbe
Bd Pasteur
Rue du
Montparnasse
p. 69
Porte de St-Cloud
Rue de la Convention
Porte de Versailles
p. 137
Porte de Sèvres
Bd Victor
BOULOGNE-BILLANCOURT
R. de Vouillé
R. d'Alésia
Av. du Maine
Héliport
Parc des Expositions
Rue Raymond Losserand
Bd Lefebvre
Porte Brancion
Av. J. Moulin
Bd Brune
ISSY-LES-MOULINEAUX
BOULEVARD
11,5 km
Château de Versailles
p. 171
MALAKOFF
MONTROUGE
VANVES

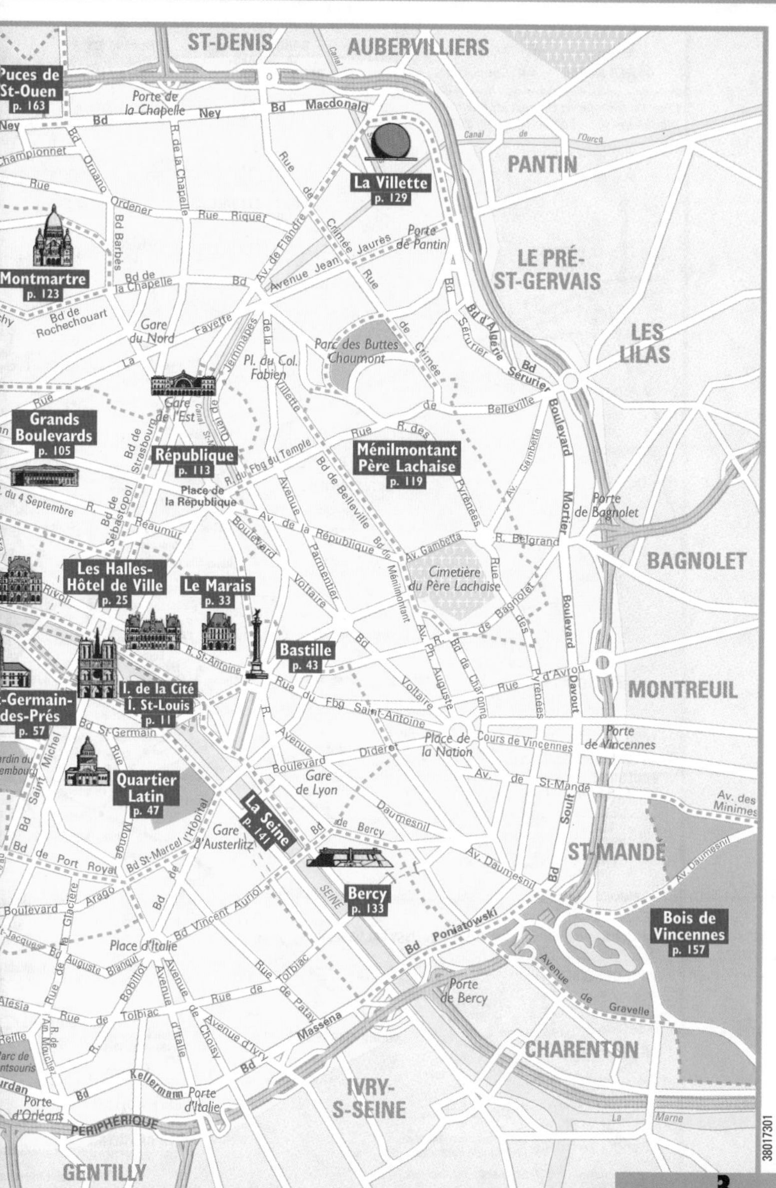
ST-DENIS
AUBERVILLIERS
Puces de St-Ouen p. 163
La Villette p. 129
PANTIN
Montmartre p. 123
LE PRÉ-ST-GERVAIS
LES LILAS
Grands Boulevards p. 105
République p. 113
Ménilmontant Père Lachaise p. 119
BAGNOLET
Les Halles-Hôtel de Ville p. 25
Le Marais p. 33
Bastille p. 43
-Germain-des-Prés p. 57
I. de la Cité Î. St-Louis p. 11
MONTREUIL
Quartier Latin p. 47
La Seine p. 141
Bercy p. 133
ST-MANDÉ
Bois de Vincennes p. 157
CHARENTON
IVRY-S-SEINE
GENTILLY
PÉRIPHÉRIQUE
38017301

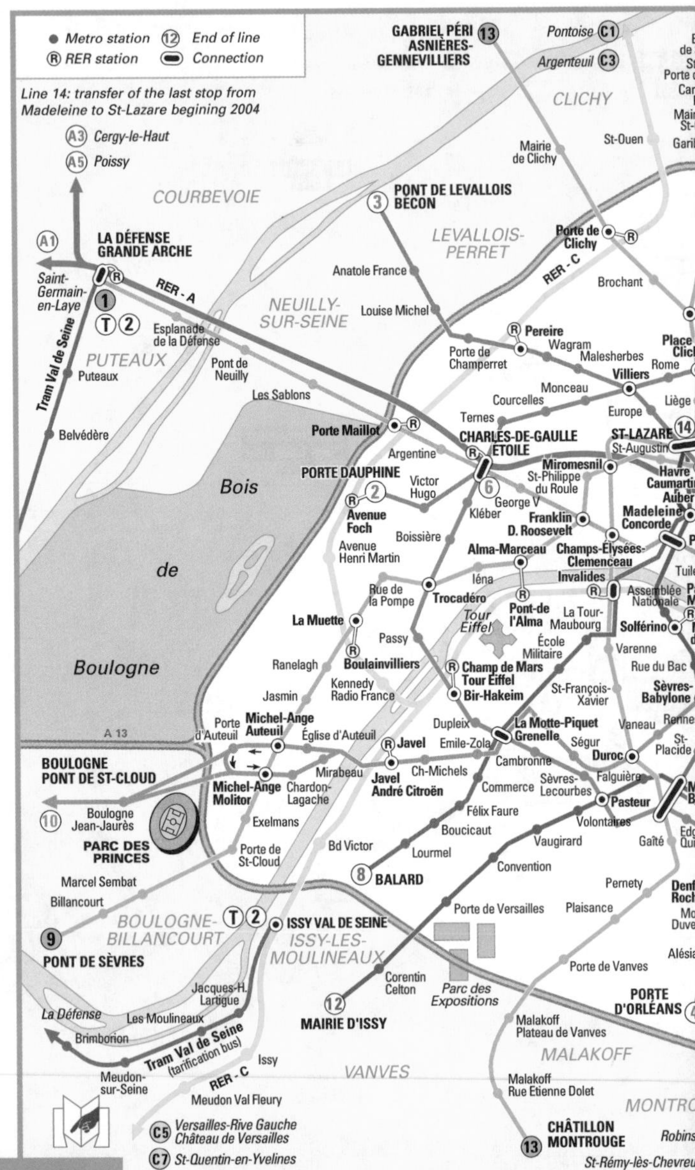

Metro station
End of line
RER station
Connection
Line 14: transfer of the last stop from Madeleine to St-Lazare begining 2004
Cergy-le-Haut
Poissy
COURBEVOIE
LA DÉFENSE GRANDE ARCHE
Saint-Germain-en-Laye
RER - A
Tram Val de Seine
PUTEAUX
Puteaux
Belvédère
Esplanade de la Défense
Pont de Neuilly
Les Sablons
NEUILLY-SUR-SEINE
GABRIEL PÉRI ASNIÈRES-GENNEVILLIERS
Pontoise
Argenteuil
CLICHY
Mairie de Clichy
St-Ouen
PONT DE LEVALLOIS BÉCON
LEVALLOIS-PERRET
Anatole France
Louise Michel
Porte de Clichy
RER - C
Brochant
Pereire
Wagram
Malesherbes
Porte de Champerret
Villiers
Rome
Place de Clichy
Monceau
Courcelles
Ternes
Europe
Liège
Porte Maillot
CHARLES-DE-GAULLE ÉTOILE
ST-LAZARE
St-Augustin
Argentine
PORTE DAUPHINE
Victor Hugo
Avenue Foch
Miromesnil
St-Philippe du Roule
Havre Caumartin
Auber
George V
Kléber
Franklin D. Roosevelt
Madeleine
Concorde
Bois de Boulogne
Boissière
Avenue Henri Martin
Alma-Marceau
Champs-Élysées-Clemenceau
Invalides
Tuileries
Iéna
Rue de la Pompe
Trocadéro
Assemblée Nationale
Tour Eiffel
Pont-de l'Alma
La Tour-Maubourg
La Muette
Solférino
Passy
École Militaire
Varenne
Boulainvilliers
Ranelagh
Champ de Mars Tour Eiffel
Bir-Hakeim
Rue du Bac
Kennedy Radio France
Jasmin
St-François-Xavier
Sèvres-Babylone
Michel-Ange Auteuil
Porte d'Auteuil
Église d'Auteuil
Dupleix
La Motte-Piquet Grenelle
Vaneau
Rennes
A 13
Javel
Emile-Zola
Ségur
St-Placide
Duroc
BOULOGNE PONT DE ST-CLOUD
Michel-Ange Molitor
Mirabeau
Chardon-Lagache
Javel André Citroën
Ch-Michels
Cambronne
Commerce
Sèvres-Lecourbes
Falguière
Pasteur
Boulogne Jean-Jaurès
Exelmans
Félix Faure
Volontaires
PARC DES PRINCES
Boucicaut
Porte de St-Cloud
Bd Victor
Lourmel
Vaugirard
Gaîté
BALARD
Convention
Marcel Sembat
Billancourt
Pernety
BOULOGNE-BILLANCOURT
ISSY VAL DE SEINE
ISSY-LES-MOULINEAUX
Porte de Versailles
Plaisance
PONT DE SÈVRES
Alésia
Porte de Vanves
Corentin Celton
Parc des Expositions
Jacques-H. Lartigue
PORTE D'ORLÉANS
MAIRIE D'ISSY
La Défense
Les Moulineaux
Malakoff Plateau de Vanves
Brimborion
Tram Val de Seine (tarification bus)
MALAKOFF
Issy
Meudon-sur-Seine
RER - C
VANVES
Malakoff Rue Etienne Dolet
Meudon Val Fleury
Versailles-Rive Gauche Château de Versailles
St-Quentin-en-Yvelines
CHÂTILLON MONTROUGE
Robinson
St-Rémy-lès-Chevreuse

Metro (underground)

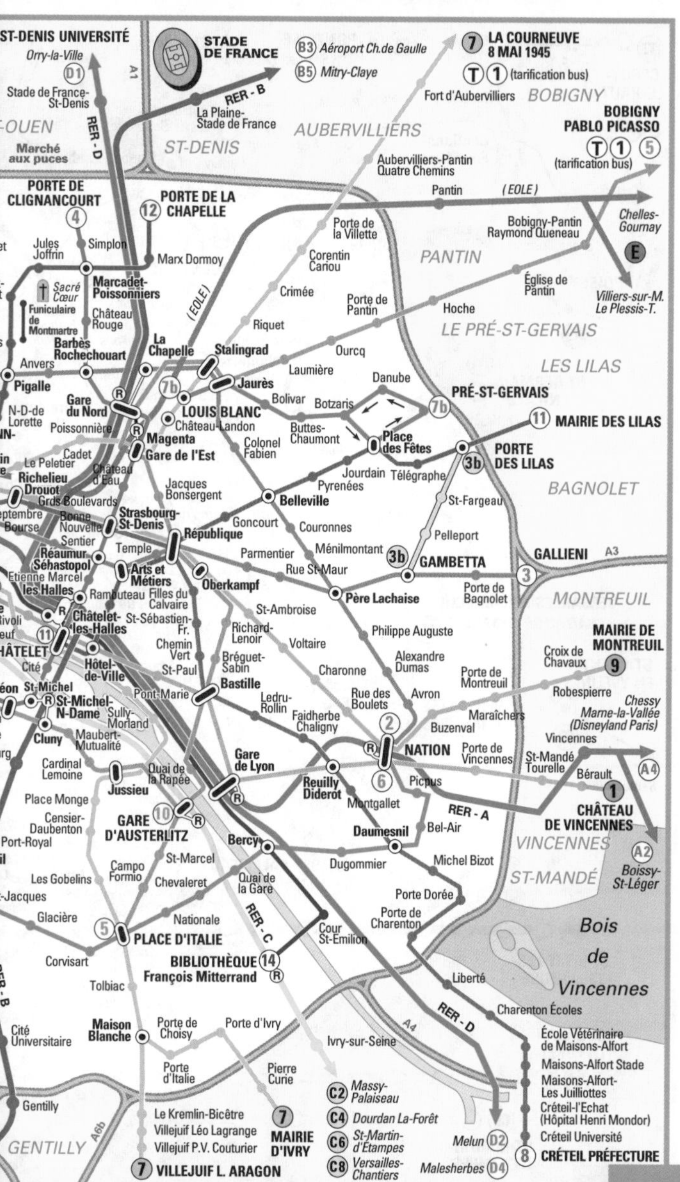

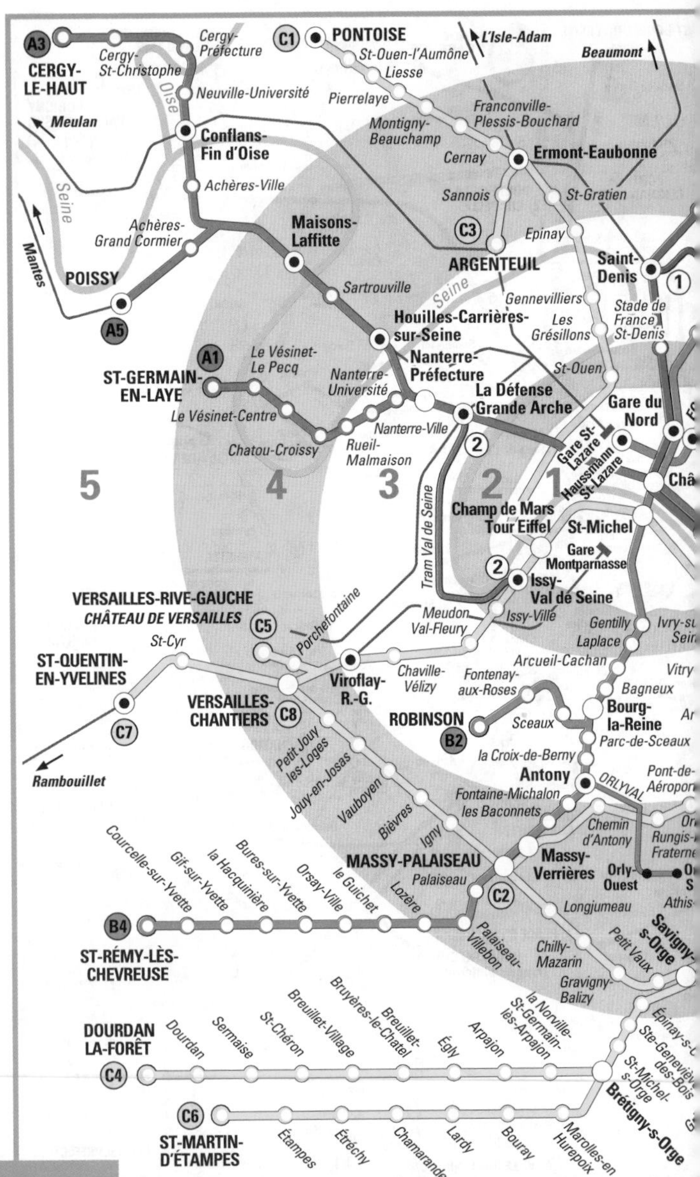
A3
CERGY-LE-HAUT
Cergy-St-Christophe
Cergy-Préfecture
Neuville-Université
Oise
Meulan
Conflans-Fin d'Oise
Achères-Ville
Seine
Mantes
Achères-Grand Cormier
POISSY
A5
C1
PONTOISE
St-Ouen-l'Aumône
Liesse
Pierrelaye
L'Isle-Adam
Beaumont
Franconville-Plessis-Bouchard
Montigny-Beauchamp
Cernay
Ermont-Eaubonne
Sannois
St-Gratien
C3
ARGENTEUIL
Epinay
Saint-Denis
1
Maisons-Laffitte
Sartrouville
Seine
Gennevilliers
Les Grésillons
Stade de France St-Denis
Houilles-Carrières-sur-Seine
Nanterre-Préfecture
St-Ouen
A1
ST-GERMAIN-EN-LAYE
Le Vésinet-Le Pecq
Nanterre-Université
La Défense Grande Arche
Gare du Nord
Le Vésinet-Centre
Nanterre-Ville
2
Gare St-Lazare
Haussmann St-Lazare
Chatou-Croissy
Rueil-Malmaison
5
4
3
2
1
Tram Val de Seine
Champ de Mars Tour Eiffel
St-Michel
Gare Montparnasse
2
Issy-Val de Seine
Issy-Ville
VERSAILLES-RIVE-GAUCHE
CHÂTEAU DE VERSAILLES
C5
Porchefontaine
Meudon Val-Fleury
Gentilly
Laplace
St-Cyr
ST-QUENTIN-EN-YVELINES
Viroflay-R.-G.
Chaville-Vélizy
Arcueil-Cachan
Fontenay-aux-Roses
Bagneux
VERSAILLES-CHANTIERS
C8
C7
ROBINSON
B2
Sceaux
Bourg-la-Reine
Parc-de-Sceaux
la Croix-de-Berny
Rambouillet
Petit Jouy les-Loges
Jouy-en-Josas
Vauboyen
Antony
ORLYVAL
Fontaine-Michalon
les Baconnets
Bièvres
Igny
Chemin d'Antony
MASSY-PALAISEAU
Massy-Verrières
Orly-Ouest
Palaiseau
C2
Longjumeau
Courcelle-sur-Yvette
Gif-sur-Yvette
la Hacquinière
Bures-sur-Yvette
Orsay-Ville
le Guichet
Lozère
B4
ST-RÉMY-LÈS-CHEVREUSE
Palaiseau-Villebon
Chilly-Mazarin
Petit Vaux
Gravigny-Balizy
DOURDAN LA-FORÊT
Dourdan
Sermaise
St-Chéron
Breuillet-Village
Bruyères-le-Châtel
Breuillet-
Égly
Arpajon
la Norville-St-Germain-lès-Arpajon
C4
C6
ST-MARTIN-D'ÉTAMPES
Étampes
Étréchy
Chamarande
Lardy
Bouray
Marolles-en Hurepoix
Brétigny-s-Orge

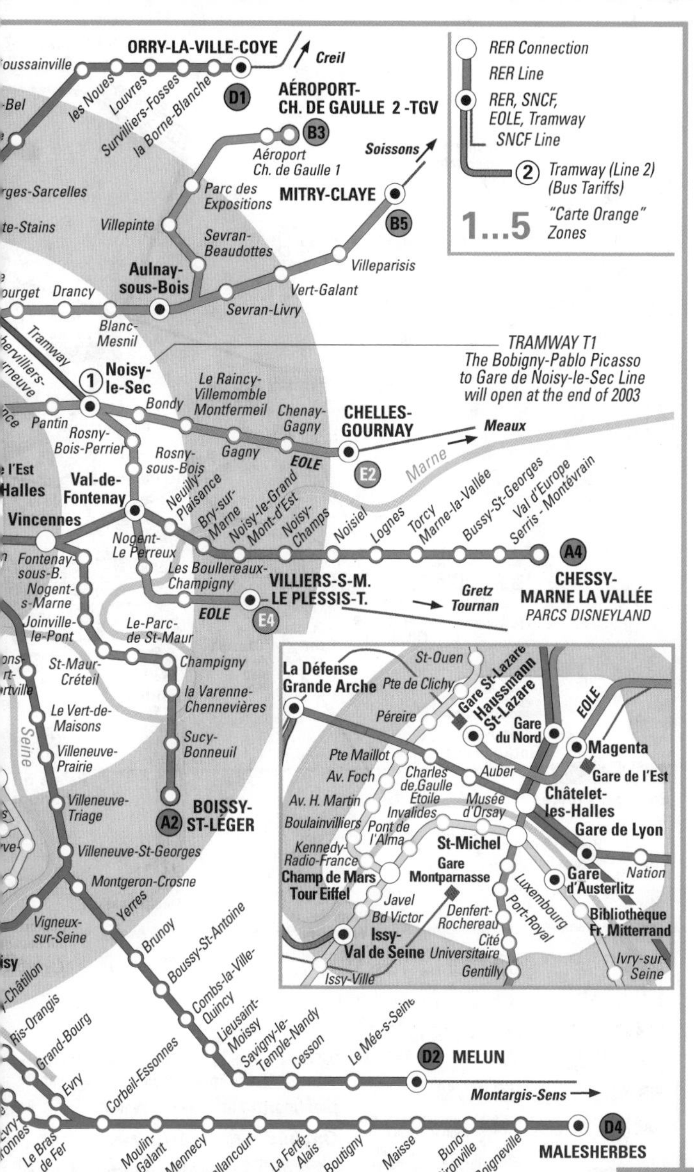
ORRY-LA-VILLE-COYE
Creil
D1
les Noues
Louvres
Survilliers-Fosses
la Borne-Blanche
AÉROPORT-
CH. DE GAULLE 2 -TGV
B3
Aéroport
Ch. de Gaulle 1
Soissons
Parc des
Expositions
MITRY-CLAYE
Villepinte
B5
Sevran-
Beaudottes
Villeparisis
Aulnay-
sous-Bois
Vert-Galant
Drancy
Sevran-Livry
Blanc-
Mesnil
Tramway
RER Connection
RER Line
RER, SNCF,
EOLE, Tramway
SNCF Line
2
Tramway (Line 2)
(Bus Tariffs)
1...5
"Carte Orange"
Zones
TRAMWAY T1
The Bobigny-Pablo Picasso
to Gare de Noisy-le-Sec Line
will open at the end of 2003
1
Noisy-
le-Sec
Le Raincy-
Villemomble
Montfermeil
Bondy
Chenay-
Gagny
CHELLES-
GOURNAY
Meaux
Pantin
Rosny-
Bois-Perrier
Rosny-
sous-Bois
Gagny
EOLE
E2
Marne
Val-de-
Fontenay
Vincennes
Neuilly-
Plaisance
Bry-sur-
Marne
Noisy-le-Grand
Mont-d'Est
Noisy-
Champs
Noisiel
Lognes
Torcy
Marne-la-Vallée
Bussy-St-Georges
Val d'Europe
Serris - Montévrain
A4
Nogent-
Le Perreux
Fontenay-
sous-B.
Nogent-
s-Marne
Les Boullereaux-
Champigny
VILLIERS-S-M.
LE PLESSIS-T.
EOLE
E4
Gretz
Tournan
CHESSY-
MARNE LA VALLÉE
PARCS DISNEYLAND
Joinville-
le-Pont
Le-Parc-
de St-Maur
St-Maur-
Créteil
Champigny
la Varenne-
Chennevières
Le Vert-de-
Maisons
Seine
Sucy-
Bonneuil
Villeneuve-
Prairie
Villeneuve-
Triage
A2
BOISSY-
ST-LÉGER
Villeneuve-St-Georges
Montgeron-Crosne
Yerres
Vigneux-
sur-Seine
Brunoy
Boussy-St-Antoine
Combs-la-Ville-
Quincy
Lieusaint-
Moissy
Savigny-le-
Temple-Nandy
Cesson
Le Mée-s-Seine
D2
MELUN
Montargis-Sens
Ris-Orangis
Grand-Bourg
Evry
Corbeil-Essonnes
Le Bras
de Fer
Moulin-
Galant
Mennecy
Ballancourt
La Ferté-
Alais
Boutigny
Maisse
Buno-
Gironville
Boigneville
D4
MALESHERBES
La Défense
Grande Arche
St-Ouen
Pte de Clichy
Gare St-Lazare
Haussmann
St-Lazare
EOLE
Péreire
Gare
du Nord
Magenta
Gare de l'Est
Pte Maillot
Av. Foch
Charles
de Gaulle
Étoile
Auber
Av. H. Martin
Invalides
Musée
d'Orsay
Châtelet-
les-Halles
Boulainvilliers
Pont de
l'Alma
Gare de Lyon
Kennedy-
Radio-France
St-Michel
Champ de Mars
Tour Eiffel
Gare
Montparnasse
Nation
Gare
d'Austerlitz
Luxembourg
Port-Royal
Javel
Bd Victor
Denfert-
Rochereau
Bibliothèque
Fr. Mitterrand
Issy-
Val de Seine
Cité
Universitaire
Gentilly
Ivry-sur-
Seine
Issy-Ville

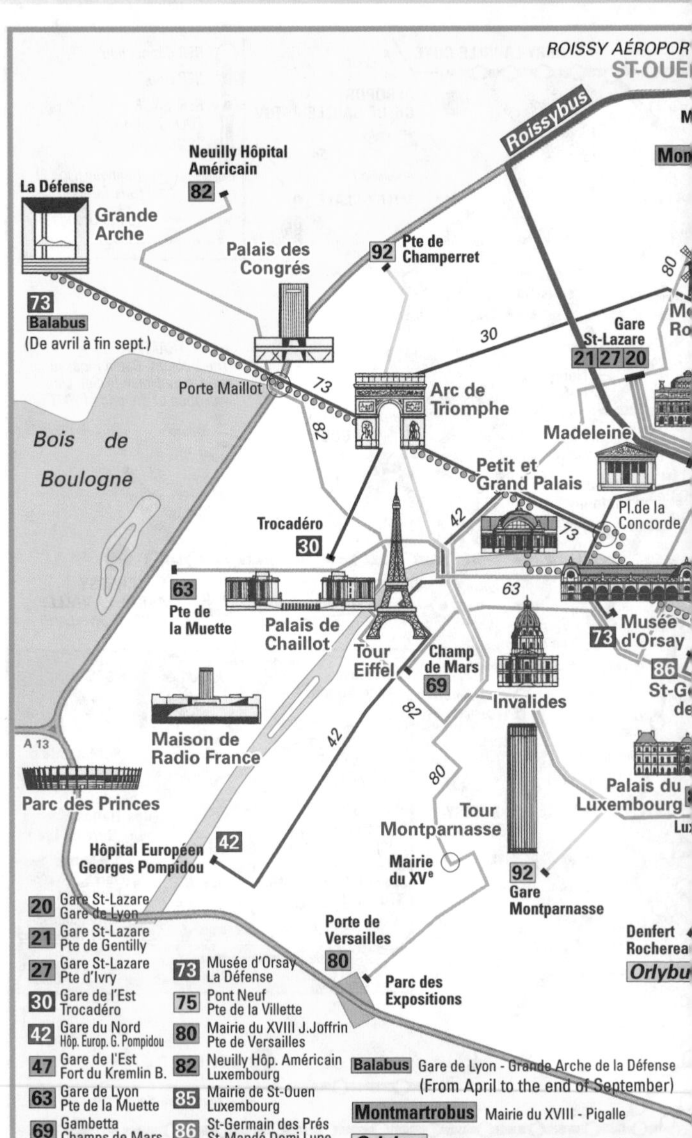

ROISSY AÉROPOR
ST-OUE
Roissybus
Neuilly Hôpital Américain
82
La Défense
Grande Arche
Palais des Congrés
92
Pte de Champerret
73
Balabus
(De avril à fin sept.)
30
Gare St-Lazare
21 27 20
Porte Maillot
73
Arc de Triomphe
82
Madeleine
Bois de Boulogne
Petit et Grand Palais
Trocadéro
30
42
Pl.de la Concorde
73
63
Pte de la Muette
63
Palais de Chaillot
Tour Eiffel
Champ de Mars
69
Musée d'Orsay
73
86
Invalides
82
Maison de Radio France
42
A 13
80
Palais du Luxembourg
Parc des Princes
Tour Montparnasse
Hôpital Européen Georges Pompidou
42
Mairie du XVe
92
Gare Montparnasse
Porte de Versailles
80
Denfert Rochereau
Orlybu
Parc des Expositions
20 Gare St-Lazare Gare de Lyon
21 Gare St-Lazare Pte de Gentilly
27 Gare St-Lazare Pte d'Ivry
30 Gare de l'Est Trocadéro
42 Gare du Nord Hôp. Europ. G. Pompidou
47 Gare de l'Est Fort du Kremlin B.
63 Gare de Lyon Pte de la Muette
69 Gambetta Champs de Mars
73 Musée d'Orsay La Défense
75 Pont Neuf Pte de la Villette
80 Mairie du XVIII J.Joffrin Pte de Versailles
82 Neuilly Hôp. Américain Luxembourg
85 Mairie de St-Ouen Luxembourg
86 St-Germain des Prés St-Mandé Demi Lune
92 Pte de Champerret Gare Montparnasse
Balabus Gare de Lyon - Grande Arche de la Défense (From April to the end of September)
Montmartrobus Mairie du XVIII - Pigalle
Orlybus Denfert Rochereau Aéroport d'Orly
Roissybus Opéra Aéroport Roissy Ch. de Gaulle

LES DE GAULLE
hé aux Puces
A 1
Stade
de France
ST-DENIS
85 Porte de
Clignancourt
80
bus
Porte de
la Villette 75
Cité des Sciences
et de l'Industrie
Sacré-Coeur
Cité de la Musique
75
Gare du
Nord
42
alle
30 47
Gare de
l'Est
éra
rnier
ybus
Palais
Royal
47
75
Gambetta
69
A 3
Centre
Pompidou
20
Cimetière du
Père Lachaise
sée du
vre
75
Place
des Vosges
69
Place de la Bastille
27
Notre-
Dame
86
86
Château de
Vincennes
Nation
63
Opéra Bastille
Seine
Porte de
Vincennes
20 63
Balabus (De avril à fin sept.)
Gare de Lyon
Panthéon
Gare
d'Austerlitz
47
86
St-Mandé
Demi-Lune
ervatoire
27
21
Place
d'Italie
Bibliothèque
Nationale
de France
Bois de
Vincennes
Porte de
Gentilly
21
27
Porte de Vitry
A 4
Orlybus
ÉROPORT
D'ORLY
A 6b
47 Le Kremlin Bicêtre

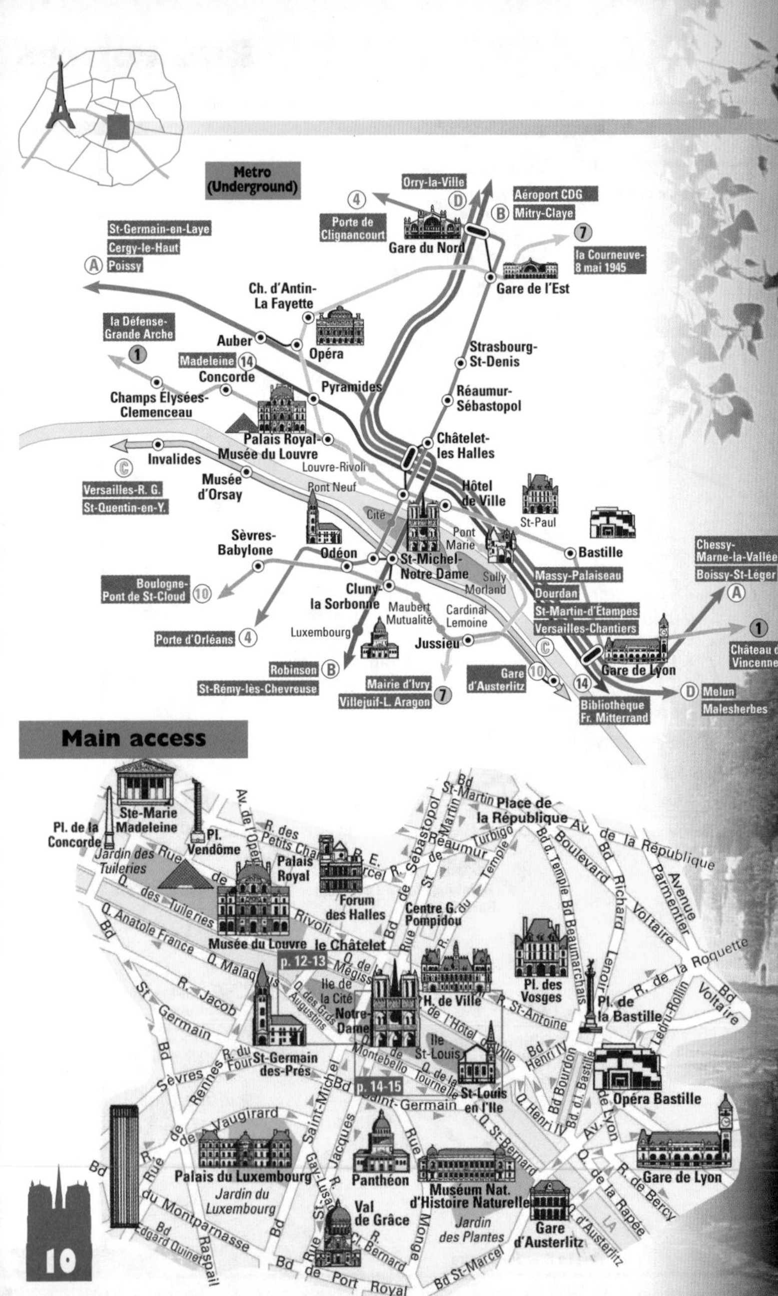

Metro (Underground)
Orry-la-Ville
Aéroport CDG
Mitry-Claye
Porte de Clignancourt
Gare du Nord
la Courneuve-8 mai 1945
Gare de l'Est
St-Germain-en-Laye
Cergy-le-Haut
Poissy
Ch. d'Antin-La Fayette
la Défense-Grande Arche
Auber
Opéra
Strasbourg-St-Denis
Madeleine
Concorde
Pyramides
Réaumur-Sébastopol
Champs Élysées-Clemenceau
Palais Royal-Musée du Louvre
Châtelet-les Halles
Invalides
Louvre-Rivoli
Musée d'Orsay
Pont Neuf
Hôtel de Ville
Versailles-R. G.
St-Quentin-en-Y.
Cité
St-Paul
Sèvres-Babylone
Pont Marie
Bastille
Odéon
St-Michel-Notre Dame
Chessy-Marne-la-Vallée
Boissy-St-Léger
Boulogne-Pont de St-Cloud
Sully Morland
Massy-Palaiseau
Dourdan
Cluny-la Sorbonne
Maubert Mutualité
Cardinal Lemoine
St-Martin-d'Étampes
Versailles-Chantiers
Porte d'Orléans
Luxembourg
Jussieu
Château de Vincennes
Gare de Lyon
Robinson
St-Rémy-lès-Chevreuse
Mairie d'Ivry
Villejuif-L. Aragon
Gare d'Austerlitz
Bibliothèque Fr. Mitterrand
Melun
Malesherbes
Main access
Ste-Marie Madeleine
Pl. de la Concorde
Pl. Vendôme
Jardin des Tuileries
Palais Royal
Forum des Halles
Centre G. Pompidou
Place de la République
Av. de la République
Musée du Louvre
le Châtelet
p. 12-13
Ile de la Cité
Notre-Dame
H. de Ville
Pl. des Vosges
Pl. de la Bastille
St-Germain des-Prés
Ile St-Louis
p. 14-15
St-Louis en l'Ile
Opéra Bastille
Palais du Luxembourg
Jardin du Luxembourg
Panthéon
Val de Grâce
Muséum Nat. d'Histoire Naturelle
Jardin des Plantes
Gare d'Austerlitz
Gare de Lyon

Île de la Cîté
Île Saint-Louis

Place Dauphine

This Square, so full of charm, was named after the Dauphin, the future Louis XIII. The surrounding land was sold to raise funds to build the Pont Neuf and to build thirty-two houses which have remained as they were, for the most part.

Square du Vert Galant

Like the prow of a ship, the tip of the island has faced the Seine's flowing waters since Lutecia was first built.

Île de la Cité

It was in the 4th century when the Roman prefec Julian l'Apostat was proclaimed emperor, tha Lutecia was named after its first inhabitants, th Parisii and became Paris. Spared by the Huns, besie ged by the Franks, it escaped looting and famin thanks to the benevolence of a young woman, wh later became Saint-Geneviève, the patron saint o Paris. In the 6th century, Clovis chose it for capita and built a royal palace. In the 9th century it wa attacked several times by the Norman. In th Middle Ages, as Notre Dame was being built, th city spread to both sides of the river. The Ile de l Cité was a maze of narrow and mudd streets until the 19th century when i was razed to the ground b Haussmann to make way fo public buildings.

Pont des Arts

Pl. de l'Institut

INSTITUT DE FRANCE

Sainte-Chapelle

It was quickly built under Saint Louis between 1241 and 1248 to house the relics of the Passion of Christ. This master piece of Gothic Art contains two chapels: the higher chapel, which was reserved for the king and his court and the lower chapel for the ser-

vants. The modest lower chapel look more like a crypt while the higher chapel is dazzlin and flighty. The stained glass windows, the oldest i Paris, depict biblical scenes and the Passion o Christ.

4 boulevard du Palais - 01 53 73 78 52

Everyday from 9.30 am to 6 pm

Admission: 5.5 euros – Reduced rate: 3.5 euros

21-27-38-85-96 and Balabus

0 250
0 5 mn

La Conciergerie

This old royal palace dates from the Middle Ages. It was abandoned by Charles V. Saint-Louis stayed there and built the Sainte-Chapelle. Philip the Beautiful extended it to put his administrative, financial and legal services. He also built a large hall, la salle des Gens d'Armes. The Conciergerie also housed a parliament which dispensed justice and a prison before being taken over by the revolutionary tribunal. Many prisoners were kept in its cells, including Marie-Antoinette, before being guillotined.

Boulevard du Palais - 01 53 73 78 50

Everyday from 9.30 am to 6 pm

Admission: 5.5 euros, Reduced rate: 3.5 euros

21-24-27-38-58-81-85 and Balabus

Marché aux Fleurs

Flowers and all kinds of plants are sold in an atmosphere reminiscent of tropical greenhouses. On Sundays it becomes a bird market.

Place Louis Lépine

From 8 am. to 7.30 pm.

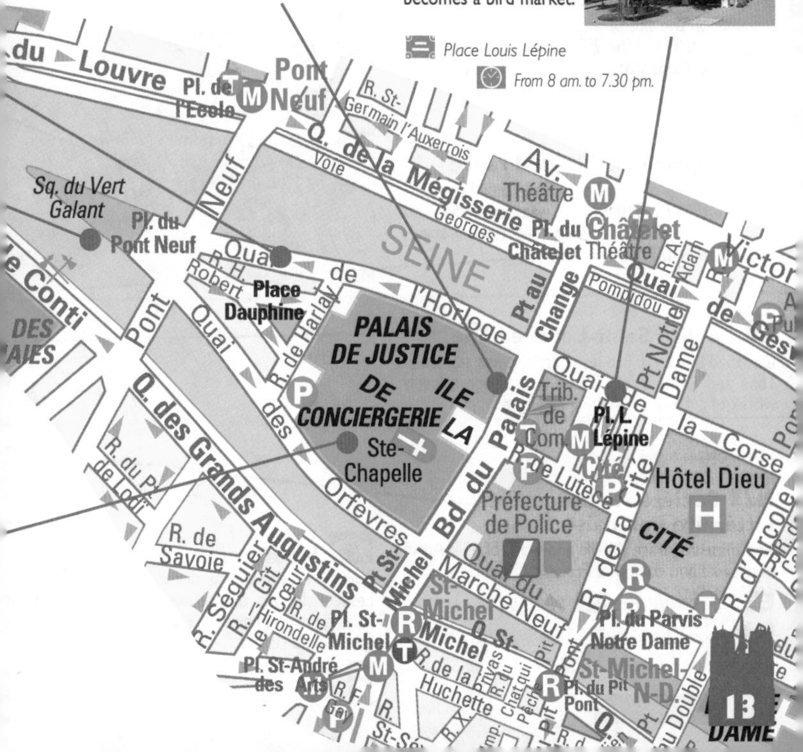

Hôtel-Dieu

The hospice, founded in the 7th century, was rebuilt in the 19th century after Haussmann cleared the island.

Square Jean XXIII

It stands on the site of the old bishop's palace destroyed in 1830. On the 2nd of November 1789, the Assemblée Constituante confiscated all the clergy's assets.

Square de l'Île-de-France

The western tip of the Ile de la Cité housed the morgue from 1864 to 1910 before it was transformed into a garden. The 'Memorial de la Deportation' stands right at the end.

Église Saint-Louis-en-l'Île

Designed by Le Vau in a Jesuit style, it was started in 1664 and finished in 1726. It houses some lovely works of art and interesting furniture.

Société Historique et Littéraire Polonaise

Two museums trace the life and work of poet Adam Mickiewicz and composer Frederic Chopin.

6 quai d'Orléans - 
01 43 54 35 61

Visits organised on Thursdays at 2, 3, 4 and 5 pm and by appointment

Admission: 4 euros - 
24-63-67-86-87

Île Saint-Louis

The Ile-aux-Vaches and the Ile Madame were used as pastures, together they became the Ile Saint-Louis. In the 17th century, the task of joining the islands to the banks of the river was trusted to an engineer, Christophe Marie. He planned the regular and perpendicular streets. Many wonderful houses were built at the time, some by Le Vau. The island has changed little since the 17th century.

Hôtel Lambert

Built by Le Vau, it was decorated by Le Brun and Lesueur. It was the setting of some memorable receptions given by Princess Czartoryski. The Hôtel is still in her family.

2 rue Saint-Louis en L'Ile

Île de la Cîté - Île Saint-Louis

Cathédrale Notre-Dame

The cathedral was built on the remains of a basilica and a church. It was started by Maurice de Sully in 1163 and finished in 1330. In spite of the length of time taken by the construction, the ravages of time, history and restorations, the building has retained its original unity and harmony. At the heart of Paris and its history, it saw Philippe the Beautiful's Etats Généraux (16th century), the coronation of Henri VI, the king of England, the trial of Joan of Arc (15th century) and the coronation of Mary Stuart. It was not spared by the French Revolution when many statues were broken and the spire destroyed. It narrowly escaped destruction and was returned to the church in 1802, just before Napoleon's coronation. It was Victor Hugo's novel Notre-Dame de Paris who raised awareness for the need to restore the cathedral. The work was trusted to Viollet-le-Duc and Lassus.

6 place du parvis de Notre-Dame

01 44 32 16 70

Everyday from 8 am to 6 pm

Visits of the towers: Admission: 5.34 euros, Reduced rate: 3.51 euros

20-29-65-69-96

Hôtel de Lauzun

It is such a pity that it is not open to visitors. Built by Le Vau in the 17th century and beautifully decorated by Le Brun, it was the meeting place of the 'Hachischin Club' whose members included Beaudelaire, Balzac and Théophile Gautier. It was bought by the city of Paris in 1928.

17 quai Anjou

01 43 54 27 14

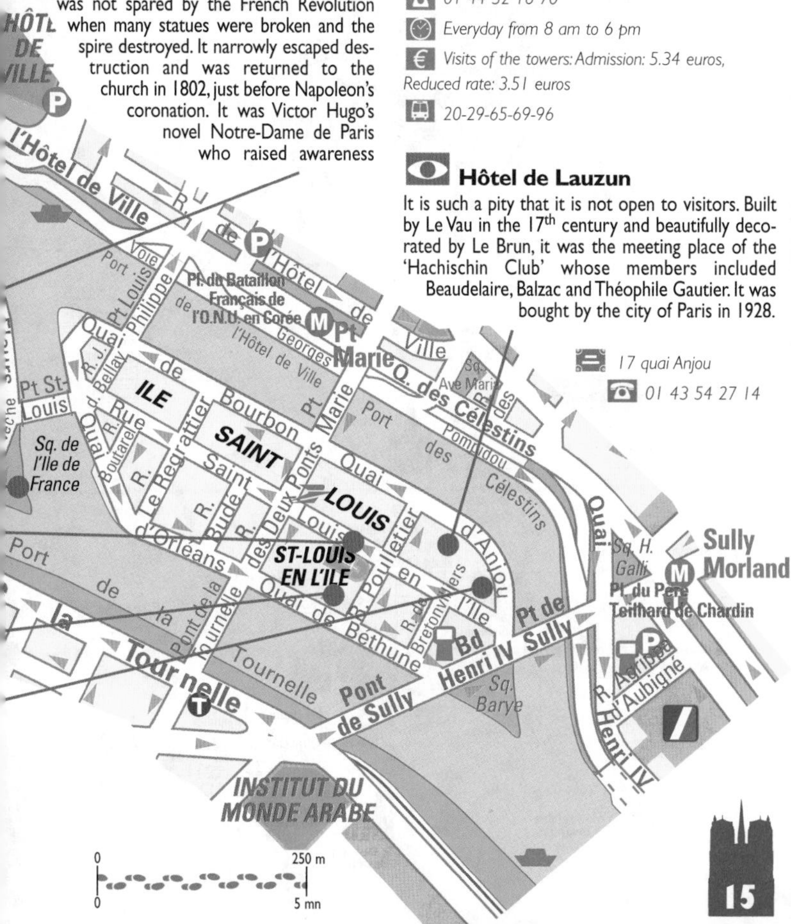

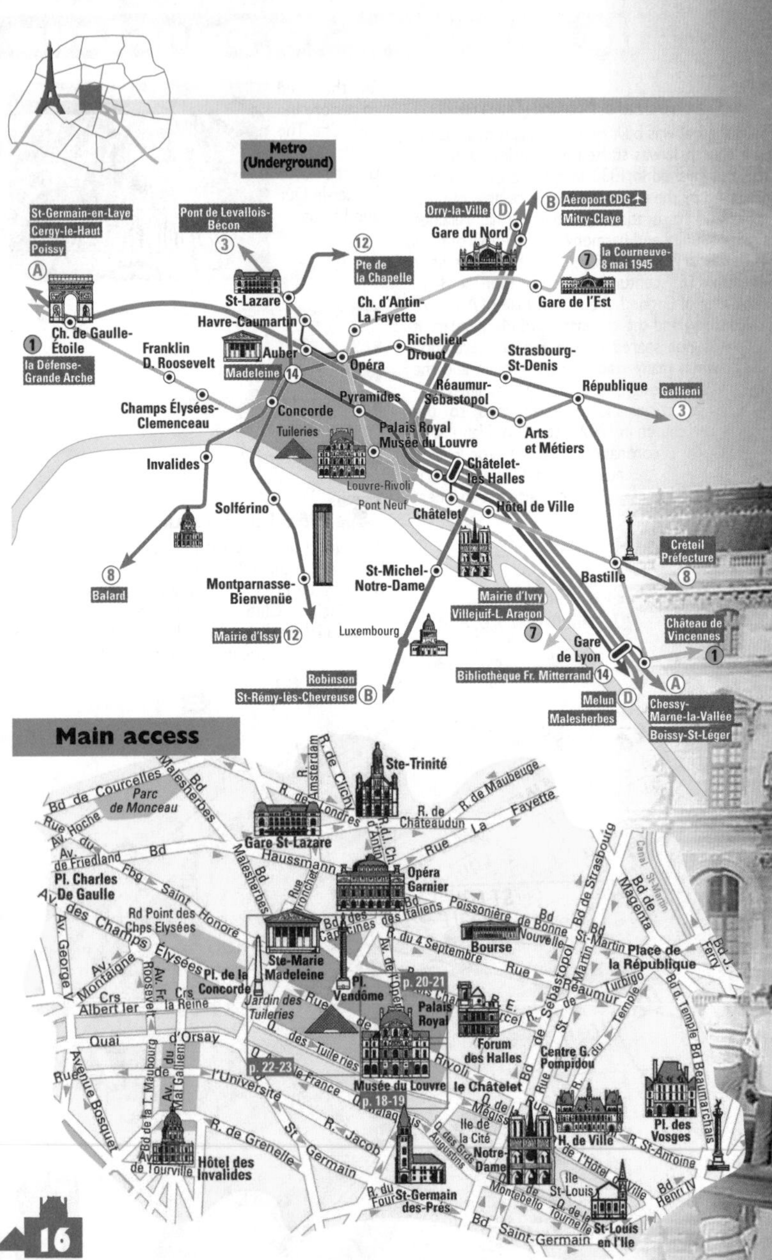
Metro (Underground)
St-Germain-en-Laye
Cergy-le-Haut
Poissy
Pont de Levallois-Bécon
Orry-la-Ville
Aéroport CDG
Mitry-Claye
Gare du Nord
Pte de la Chapelle
la Courneuve-8 mai 1945
Gare de l'Est
St-Lazare
Ch. d'Antin-La Fayette
Havre-Caumartin
Ch. de Gaulle-Étoile
Franklin D. Roosevelt
Auber
Opéra
Richelieu-Drouot
Strasbourg-St-Denis
la Défense-Grande Arche
Madeleine
Réaumur-Sébastopol
République
Gallieni
Champs Élysées-Clemenceau
Concorde
Pyramides
Tuileries
Palais Royal Musée du Louvre
Arts et Métiers
Invalides
Châtelet-les Halles
Louvre-Rivoli
Pont Neuf
Châtelet
Hôtel de Ville
Solférino
Créteil Préfecture
Bastille
St-Michel-Notre-Dame
Montparnasse-Bienvenüe
Balard
Mairie d'Ivry
Villejuif-L. Aragon
Château de Vincennes
Mairie d'Issy
Luxembourg
Gare de Lyon
Bibliothèque Fr. Mitterrand
Robinson
St-Rémy-lès-Chevreuse
Melun
Malesherbes
Chessy-Marne-la-Vallée
Boissy-St-Léger
Main access
Ste-Trinité
Bd de Courcelles
Parc de Monceau
Bd Malesherbes
R. Amsterdam
R. de Clichy
R. de Londres
R. de Maubeuge
R. de Châteaudun
Rue La Fayette
Gare St-Lazare
Bd Haussmann
Opéra Garnier
Av. de Friedland
Pl. Charles De Gaulle
Fbg Saint Honoré
Rue Tronchet
Bd de Strasbourg
Bd de Magenta
Canal St-Martin
Av. des Champs Élysées
Rd Point des Chps Elysées
Bd des Capucines
Bd des Italiens
Poissonière
Bd de Bonne Nouvelle
Bd St-Martin
Bourse
R. du 4 Septembre
Place de la République
Bd J. Ferry
Av. George V
Av. Montaigne
Ste-Marie Madeleine
Pl. de la Concorde
Pl. Vendôme
Av. de l'Opéra
p. 20-21
Palais Royal
Rue Réaumur
Turbigo
Bd Temple
Bd Beaumarchais
Crs Albert Ier
Av. Fr. Roosevelt
Crs la Reine
Jardin des Tuileries
Q. des Tuileries
Forum des Halles
Bd de Sébastopol
Centre G. Pompidou
Quai d'Orsay
Avenue Bosquet
Av. du Mal Gallieni
Rivoli
p. 22-23
Rue de l'Université
Musée du Louvre
le Châtelet
p. 18-19
Bd de la T. Maubourg
Ile de la Cité
Pl. des Vosges
R. de Grenelle
R. Jacob
St Germain
Q. des Grds Augustins
Notre-Dame
H. de Ville
R. St-Antoine
Av. de Tourville
Hôtel des Invalides
Ile St-Louis
Bd Henri IV
R. du Four
St-Germain des-Prés
Montebello
Q. de la Tournelle
Bd Saint-Germain
St-Louis en l'Ile

Louvre

Le Louvre

The Louvre started life as a fortress built by King Philippe-Auguste to defend Paris from the English invaders. Saint Louis, Philip the Beautiful and Charles V transformed it into a royal residence before it became, eight centuries later, the world's

largest museum.

François I had the dungeon destroyed and asked Pierre Lescot to extend the palace. Henri II also extended the palace and so did Catherine de Medici who also built the Palais des Tuileries. The wars of religion delayed the work. The Riverside and Small Galleries were only finished under Henri IV. But the palace was still not big enough and it was extended further under Louis XIII and Louis XIV by LeVau. The square court was also closed off.

Then Louis XIV decided to live in Versailles and it was not until Napoleon I that new projects were undertaken and a north wing built by Percier and Fontaine. The ambitious project was completed under Napoleon III and the Great Court to the north closed off..

Part of the palace was burnt down during the Paris Commune.

It was architect Leoh Ming Pei who added the final touch when he built the famous glass pyramid.

The museum's collection are unparalleled:

- Oriental and Islamic Antiquities: Works of art from regions extending from the Mediterranean to the Indus, from Mesopotamia (the Khorsabad Bull), Iran (Darius's Archers) and the Syrian-Palestinian coast.
- Egyptian Antiquities: The department was set up by Champollion. It is classified by themes (the large Sphinx, the sitting scribe and bas-relief from the tomb of Seti I)
- Greek, Etruscan and Roman Antiquities: Major statues (the Victory of Samothrace, the Venus de Milo), an important collection of Greek vases, Etruscan sarcophagus and busts of Roman emperors.
- Sculptures: Mainly French, from the Middle Ages to the 19th century displayed under the glass roofs of the Cours Marly and Puget.
- Paintings: European paintings from the 13th to the 19th centuries. They are classified by national schools. France (Georges de la Tour, Nicolas Poussin, Charles Le Brun, Jean-Antoine Watteau, Louis David, Eugène Delacroix, Jean-August-Dominique Ingres, Camille Corot), Italy (Fra Anglico, Ucello, Botticelli, Leonardo de Vinci, Rapahaël, Titian), Spain (El Greco), Flanders (Peter Paul Rubens, Antoon Van Dyck), Holland (Rembrandt, Harmenszoon Van Rijn, Johannes Vermeer), Great Britain (Joseph Mallord William Turner), just to name a few of the better known artists.
- Fine Art: In this department we find tapestries, furniture, gold works, jewelleries, potteries and porcelains from antiquity until the 19th century and the original apartments of Napoleon III.

There is also a Graphic Arts Department and a department devoted to Arts from Africa, Asia, Oceania and America.

Main entrance through Pyramid

01 40 20 50 50

Everyday except Tuesdays and some Public Holidays, from 9 am to 6 pm. Late opening until 9.45 pm on Mondays (short tour) and Wednesdays.

Admission to museum and temporary exhibitions 7.50 euros before 3 pm, 5 euros after 3 pm and all day Sunday. 7 euros for exhibitions in the Hall Napoleon. All inclusive 11.50 euros before 3 pm and 9.50 euros after 3 pm and Sundays.

21-24-27-39-48-68-69-72-81-95

Web *www.louvre.fr*

Avenue du
Pont Royal

0 250 m
0 5 mn

Arc de triomphe du Carrousel

Built by Napoleon I to celebrate his great Army's victory at Austerlitz, it finds its inspiration in Roman arches.

Musée des Arts décoratifs

It houses a collection of furniture, pottery, glass, gold and silverware, wall papers, tapestries, paintings, sculptures, toys and drawings illustrating the art of living from the Middle Ages to the 20th century.

Musée de la Mode et du Textile

Over an area covering 2000 m^2, the permanent exhibitions are renewed every 6 months chosen from an extensive collection containing tens of thousands of costumes and accessories, and fabrics dating from the 18th century until today. There is also a restoration workshop and a documentation centre.

Musée de la Publicité

Most collections were donated to the museum. The 100 000 posters dating from the 18th century until today, the press ads and the 20 000 advertisement clips come from the four corners of the world.

The UCAD (Union Centrale des Arts Decoratifs), regroups 3 museums (the Decorative Arts, the Fashion and Textile and Publicity) and has a single entry ticket for the three.

105-107 rue de Rivoli - 01 44 55 57 50

Tuesdays to Fridays from 11 am to 6 pm. Late opening, Wednesdays from 11 am to 9 pm. Saturdays and Sundays from 10 am to 6 pm. Closed on Mondays

Admission 7 euros, Reduced rate 4.5 euros

21-27-39-48-68-72-81-95

www.ucad.fr

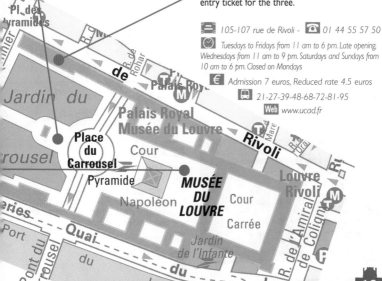

Église Saint-Roch

The first church dates from the middle of the 17th century and its classical design is the work of Jacques Le Mercier. Several chapels were added later: Our Lady's Chapel in 1705 by Jules Hardouin-Mansart, then the Communion Chapel and the Calvary Chapel by Etienne-Louis Bouclée in 1760 which was rebuilt in the 19th century. It is richly decorated inside and many personalities are buried there (Corneille, Le Nôtre, Diderot). In 1795, the church square was the scene of a struggle between Bonaparte and royalist supporters opposing the Convention.

24 rue Saint-Roch - 01 42 44 13 20

21-27-68-69-72-73-81-95

Web *www.saint-roch.org*

Rue Saint-Honoré

Although overshadowed by the rue de Rivoli, its luxury boutiques have made its reputation.

Comédie Française

From the very start, great classical plays were performed on its stage. The tradition is still perpetrated by the actors of the world's oldest theatre company.

1 place Colette - 01 44 58 15 00

21-27-39-48-67-68-80-91-95

Web *www.comedie-francaise.fr*

Fontaine Molière

Designed by Visconti, it was built in 1844 as a tribute to the playwright who died on 17 February 167 at No 40 rue de Richelieu.

Avenue de l'Opéra

Built in 1876 to link up the Opera to the Palais Royal district. It is still a very lively street.

Louvre des Antiquaires

This 19th century building was once the 'Grands Magasins du Louvre'. It was taken over by 250 antique dealers who offer in their luxury galleries a great variety of antiques for rich and keen amateurs.

2 place du Palais Royal

01 42 97 29 86

2167-69-72-81

Web *www.louvre-antiquaires.com*

Palais Royal

Built in the 17th century by Richelieu, it was first called the Palais Cardinal. When he died he left it to Louis XIII and it took its present name. In 1763, it was almost destroyed by fire. It was restored by Victor Louis and new houses added and the galleries built. In 1781, another fire destroyed the theatre and the right wing. It was later replaced by the Theatre Français which became the Comédie Française, and the Theatre du Palais Royal. After the revolution, it became the ideal place for gallant meetings and games. Napoleon I housed his administration there. During the Paris Commune, it was damaged by a third fire. It was restored again in 1873, before the State Council moved in. Since 1953, it has also housed the Constitutional Council.

39-48-69-95

Web *www.palais-royal.org*

Galerie Véro-Dodat

This glass roofed lane dates from the 19th century. It is lined with beautifully quaint boutiques.

Oratoire du Louvre

Built by Le Mercier and Métezeau for the Oratorian order at the beginning of the 17th century, it was used as a royal chapel until the 18th century before being turned into a Protestant temple in 1811.

4 rue de l'Oratoire

01 42 60 21 64

Balabus-72-81

0 250 m
0 5 mn

Galerie du Jeu de paume

The 'jeu de paume' is the ancestor of tennis. This hall was built by Napoleon III. It housed impressionist paintings before they were moved to the Musée d'Orsay in 1986. It is now the venue for temporary contemporary art exhibitions.

1 place de la Concorde - 01 42 60 69 69

Tuesdays to Fridays from 12 noon to 7 pm.
Late openings Tuesdays until 9.30 pm.
Saturdays and Sundays from 10 am to 7 pm.

Admission 6 euros, Reduced rate 4.50 euros.
Free for children under 13

24-42-52-72-73-84-94

Musée de l'Orangerie

It was built at the same time as the Jeu de Paume gallery. For a long time, it was reserved for Monet's 'Nymphéas'. Since 1984, it has also housed collections gathered by Paul Guillaume.

1 place de la Concorde

01 42 61 30 82

Closed until 2004

24-42-52-72-73-84-94

Rue de Rivoli

Road works to build an east-west axe started in 1802. It is lined by many luxury houses and a long arcade with many souvenir shops.

Notre-Dame de l'Assomption

The 17th century church has a large disproportionate dome. Since 1850, it has welcomed the Catholic Polish community in Paris.

263 bis rue saint Honoré *01 55 35 32 25*

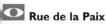

Rue de la Paix

It goes from the place Vendôme to the place de l'Opéra. It is the height of elegance and luxury with everything from jewellers to fashion designers.

Place Vendôme

Dedicated to Louis XIV, it was first called Place Royale. His statue was put up in 1609. The layout was decided by Jules Hardouin-Mansart. The square was destroyed during the Revolution and Napoleon I replaced the statue with a column covered in bas-relief, paying tribute to his campaign in 1805. A Cesar like statue of Napoleon I stands at the top of the column.

Place du marché Saint-Honoré

A Jacobin convent once stood on this square. It was replaced by the 'Club Revolutionnaire'. The market has disappeared and glass office building, designed by Ricardo Bofill, stands in its place. There is a pedestrian alleyway beneath.

Jardin des Tuileries

Catherine de Medici had an Italian style garden laid out with a fountain, a maze and a grotto. It was Le Nôtre who transformed into a French garden in 1664 to go with the Louvre. In the 18th century, it became one of the first public parks, offering relaxation and culture to the public at large. There are many statues, ponds and amenities for children and it is still a popular recreation park.

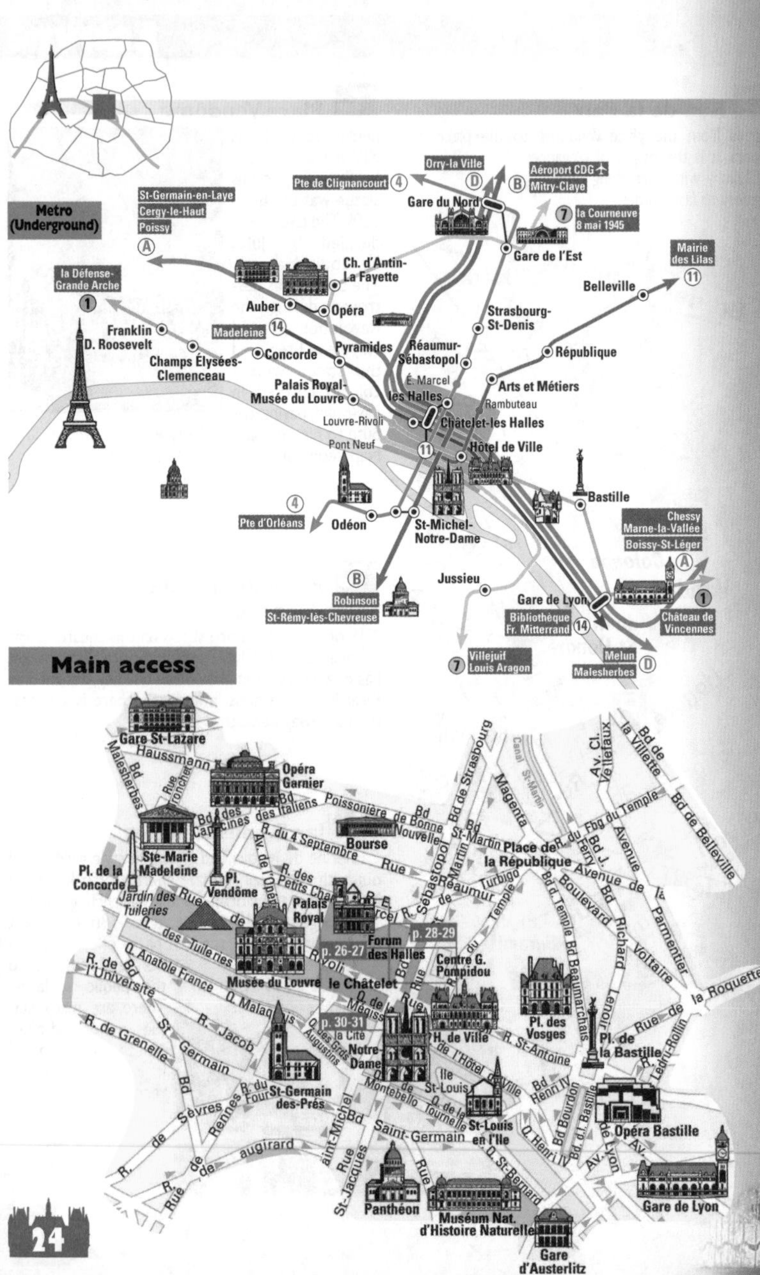
Metro (Underground)
Orry-la Ville
Pte de Clignancourt
Aéroport CDG
Mitry-Claye
Gare du Nord
la Courneuve 8 mai 1945
St-Germain-en-Laye
Cergy-le-Haut
Poissy
Gare de l'Est
Ch. d'Antin-La Fayette
Mairie des Lilas
la Défense-Grande Arche
Belleville
Auber
Opéra
Strasbourg-St-Denis
Franklin D. Roosevelt
Madeleine
Pyramides
Réaumur-Sébastopol
République
Champs Élysées-Clemenceau
Concorde
É. Marcel
Arts et Métiers
Palais Royal-Musée du Louvre
les Halles
Rambuteau
Louvre-Rivoli
Châtelet-les Halles
Pont Neuf
Hôtel de Ville
Bastille
Pte d'Orléans
Odéon
St-Michel-Notre-Dame
Chessy Marne-la-Vallée
Boissy-St-Léger
Jussieu
Robinson
St-Rémy-lès-Chevreuse
Gare de Lyon
Bibliothèque Fr. Mitterrand
Château de Vincennes
Villejuif Louis Aragon
Melun
Malesherbes
Main access
Gare St-Lazare
Opéra Garnier
Bourse
Ste-Marie Madeleine
Pl. de la Concorde
Pl. Vendôme
Jardin des Tuileries
Palais Royal
Place de la République
Forum des Halles
p. 26-27
p. 28-29
p. 30-31
Musée du Louvre
le Châtelet
Centre G. Pompidou
H. de Ville
Pl. des Vosges
Pl. de la Bastille
Notre-Dame
la Cité
St-Germain des-Prés
Ile St-Louis
St-Louis en l'Ile
Opéra Bastille
Panthéon
Muséum Nat. d'Histoire Naturelle
Gare d'Austerlitz
Gare de Lyon

Les Halles
Hôtel de Ville

Bourse de Commerce

The Commodities Exchange is housed in the old Corn Exchange with its metal and glass dome. It was built in the 18th century on the site of the Hôtel de Soisson, a convent commissioned by Catherine de Medici. Only one column is left from the original house which is thought to have been used as an observatory by an astrologer.

2 rue de Viarmes -

01 42 33 06 67

Mondays to Fridays from 9 am to 6 pm

67-74-85

Église Saint-Eustache

It was started in 1532 and it took over a century to finish. It is a mix of styles: Gothic, Renaissance and classic. It was restored by Balard in 1844 following a fire. It contains some wonderful 17th century stained glass windows by Philippe de Champaigne, old paintings and the tomb of Colbert.

2 impasse Saint-Eustache - *01 42 36 31 05*

Everyday from 9 am to 7.30 pm (8 pm in the summer)

29-67-74-85 - Web *www.st-eustache.org*

Fontaine des Innocents

It was built by Jean Goujon and Pierre Lescot on the site of the old church of the Innocent Saints and of its graveyard. The bones were transfered to the Catacombs in the 18th century.

Place Joachim Du Bellay

70-75

Jardin des Halles

Planted above the Forum, it covers a surface of 5 hectares. Children playgrounds, fountains and flower beds, lead from the church of St-Eustache to the Bourse de Commerce and the Fontaine des Innocents.

0 — 250 m

0 — 5 mn

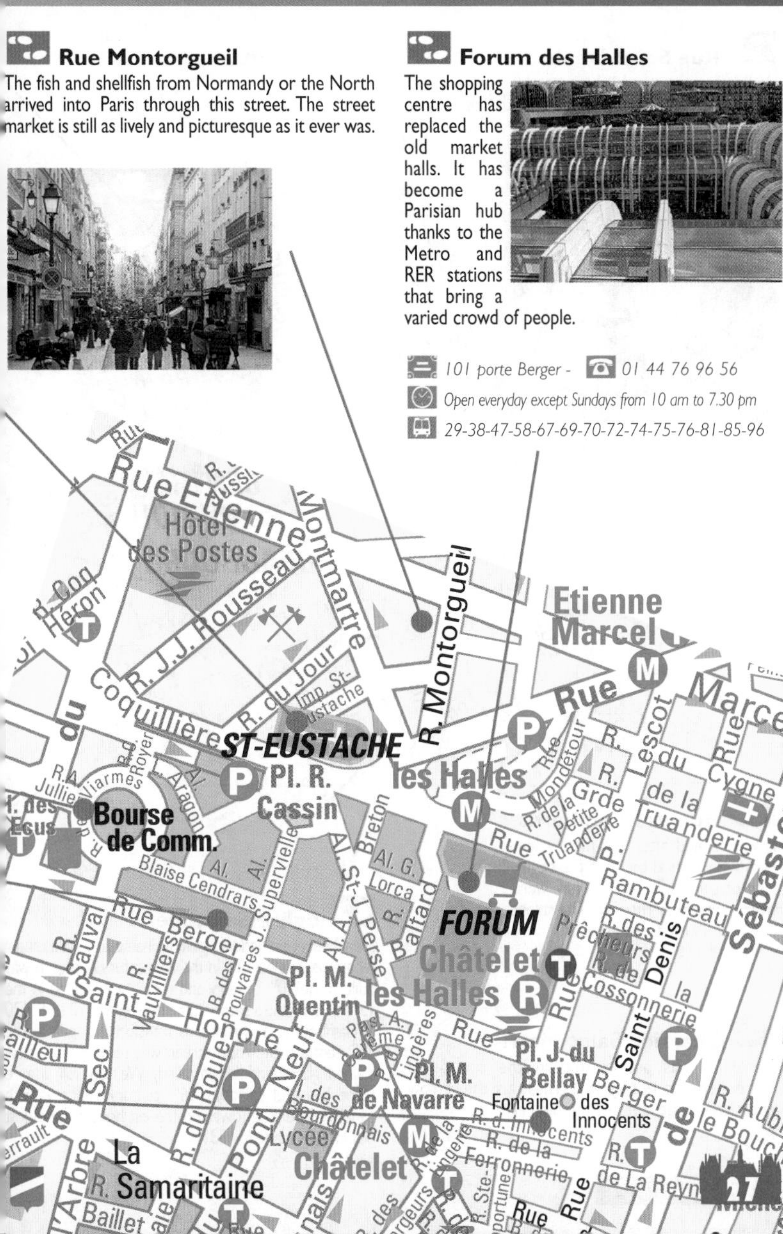

Rue Montorgueil

The fish and shellfish from Normandy or the North arrived into Paris through this street. The street market is still as lively and picturesque as it ever was.

Forum des Halles

The shopping centre has replaced the old market halls. It has become a Parisian hub thanks to the Metro and RER stations that bring a varied crowd of people.

101 porte Berger - 01 44 76 96 56

Open everyday except Sundays from 10 am to 7.30 pm

29-38-47-58-67-69-70-72-74-75-76-81-85-96

Rue Saint-Denis

Well known as a red light zone, this lively popular street used to lead from Paris to the Basilica at Saint-Denis.

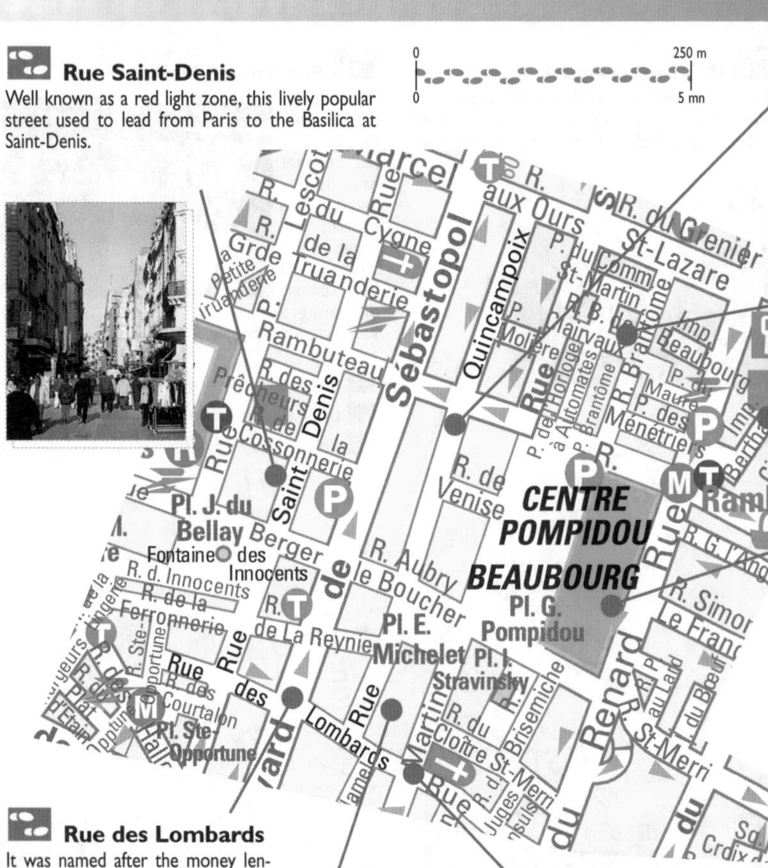

Rue des Lombards

It was named after the money lenders who settled there at the beginning of the 14th century. They were later replaced by the Jews. The street has kept its medieval aspect.

Église Saint-Merri

Saint Merri (or Mederic) gave his name to a little chapel where he was burried in the 7th century. A church was built in the 10th century and rebuilt a first time in the 13th century and a second time between 1520 and 1620 in Flamboyant Gothic. It was transformed again in the 18th century (the rood screen was removed and new stained glass windows installed). We can still admire some beautiful paintings, 16th century windows, rich panelling. The little tower on the left houses the oldest bell in Paris made in 1331.

38-47-76

Quartier Saint-Merri

Henri IV was assassinated in the rue de la Ferronnerie on 14 May 1610. These are the narrow and picturesque lanes of the old Paris.

Rue Quincampoix

\An old street with 17th and 18th century houses. It)ecame well known for its haberdashers and their guild from the 16th to the 18th centuries, Law's Bank with its speculative madness and resounding)ankruptcy and for the Epée de Bois Cabaret at N° 54.

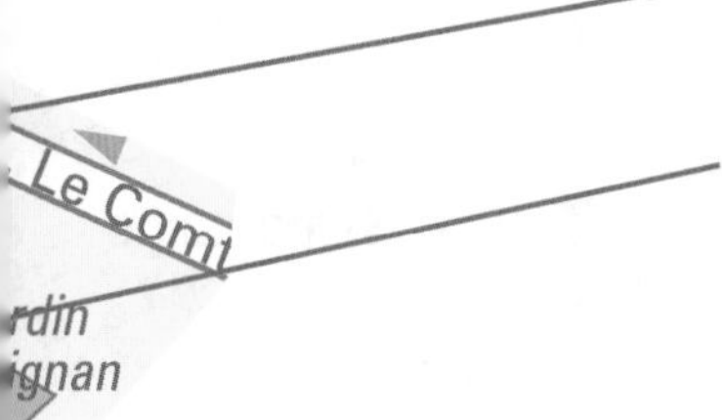

Centre Georges-Pompidou

Designed by Rogers and Piano and finished in 977, this huge set of pipes and beams boasts its

nodernity in this historic district. Its innovative and uzzling structure attracts millions of visitors every ear whether just curious or keen art and culture amateurs.

t houses several institutions:

The National Museum of Modern Art (MNAM): A ich collection of 20th century works of art (paintings, sculptures, architectural pieces and modern design).

The Research Institute for Acoustic Co-ordination and Music (IRCAM): It is a centre that specialises in experimenting on sounds and music, a creation studio, a training centre. It also organises concerts.

- The Public Information Library (BPI): A great number of books can be consulted as well as magazines, journals, maps, microfilms, videos, compact-disks, partitions, educational and language learning software, data documentations base, multi-media centre and world television.

There are also two cinemas in the centre and a temporary exhibition gallery.

Pl. Georges Pompidou - 01 44 78 12 33

Everyday except Tuesdays from 11 am to 10 pm, museum and exhibitions until 9 pm, the Atelier Brancusi from 2 pm to 6 pm.
The BPI (library) everyday from 12 noon to 10 pm except Tuesdays, Saturdays, Sundays and public holidays from 11 am to 10 pm.

Admission 10 euros, Reduced rate 8 euros.
Exhibitions: Admission 8.50 euros, Reduced rate 6.50 euros or 4.50 euros.
Museum/Brancusi's Studio/Exhibitions: Admission 5.50 euros, Reduced rate 3.50 euros.

38-47

www.centrepompidou.fr

Le Défenseur du Temps

The Guardian of Time, the animated clock where a man has to face a peril at every hour: a dragon, a bird or a crab or all three at once at 12 noon and at 6 pm. It has given its name to the district.

Musée de la poupée

A century of dolls is gathered here. They are displayed in show cases surrounded by the furniture and accessories of yesterday.

Impasse Berthaud - 01 42 72 73 11

Tuesdays to Sundays from 10 am to 6 pm

Admission rate 6 euros, Reduced rate 4 euros, 3 euros for under 18s.

29-38-47-75

La Samaritaine

It was named after a pump situated under the Pont-Neuf. The first store was opened in 1905 and the second in 1926. The latter with its Art Deco facade offers, from the top floor, a wonderful view over Paris.

 *19 rue de la Monnaie*

 *01 40 41 20 20*

Mondays to Saturdays from 9.30 am to 7 pm, late opening Thursdays until 10 pm

Balabus-21-24-27-58-67-69-70-72-74-75

Web *www.lasamaritaine.com*

Tour Saint-Jacques

The tower is what is left from the belfry of the old church of Saint-Jacques-de-la-Boucherie, destroyed in 1797. A statue of Blaise Pascal recalls the barometer experiments he carried out at the top of the tower in 1648.

47-75-96

Église Saint-Germain-l'Auxerrois

In the 7th century, there was a little chapel which was destroyed by the Norman in 886. Another church was built in the 12th century which was often altered in the following centuries (the porch and the nave in the 15th century, chapels and side doors in the 16th and 17th centuries).

It was almost destroyed in the 19th century before being completely restored in 1838 by Viollet-le-Duc, Lassus and Baltard.

It was the parish of the kings of France and its bells signalled the start of the Saint-Bartholomew riots, on the night of the 24-25 August 1572.

The church houses a bench by Le Brun, a Flemish altarpiece and 15th century stained glass windows in the transept.

2 place du louvre - *01 42 60 13 96*

From 8 am to 12.30 pm and from 3 pm to 7 pm

24-58-67-75-81

0 — 250 m
0 — 5 mn

BHV

›unded in 1856 by a peddler, it was first called the apoleon Bazar. The present building dates from the ›ginning of the 20th century. The DIY and household ›partments have always been its main attractions.

52 rue Rivoli - 01 42 74 90 00

Mondays to Saturdays from 9.30 am to 7 pm, te opening Wednesdays and Fridays until 8.30 pm

38-47-67-69-70-72-74-76-96 - Web www.bhv.fr

Hôtel de Ville

The first Hôtel de Ville (town hall) stood on the bank of the Seine. It was later transferred to the Place de Grève by Etienne Marcel in 1357. It was rebuilt by Bocador in 1533 but was only finished in 1628. Extended in 1837, it was totally destroyed by a fire during the Commune riots on 24 May 1871. It was rebuilt once more between 1874 and 1882, on the original plans.

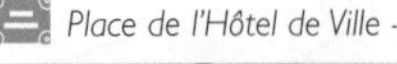

Place de l'Hôtel de Ville - 01 42 76 40 40

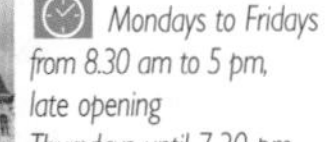

Mondays to Fridays from 8.30 am to 5 pm, late opening Thursdays until 7.30 pm

70-72-74

Web www.paris.fr

Place du Châtelet

'ntil 1802, a small castle stood on this ›te (hence the name). It was built in 1130 › defend the northern access to the Grand ›ont (the present Pont au Change bridge). It ›ays tribute to the victories of Napoleon I. 'he square was extended in 1858 when the ›oulevard Sebastopol was built. in 1862 two ›ymmetrical theatres by Davioud were ›dded.

21-67-81

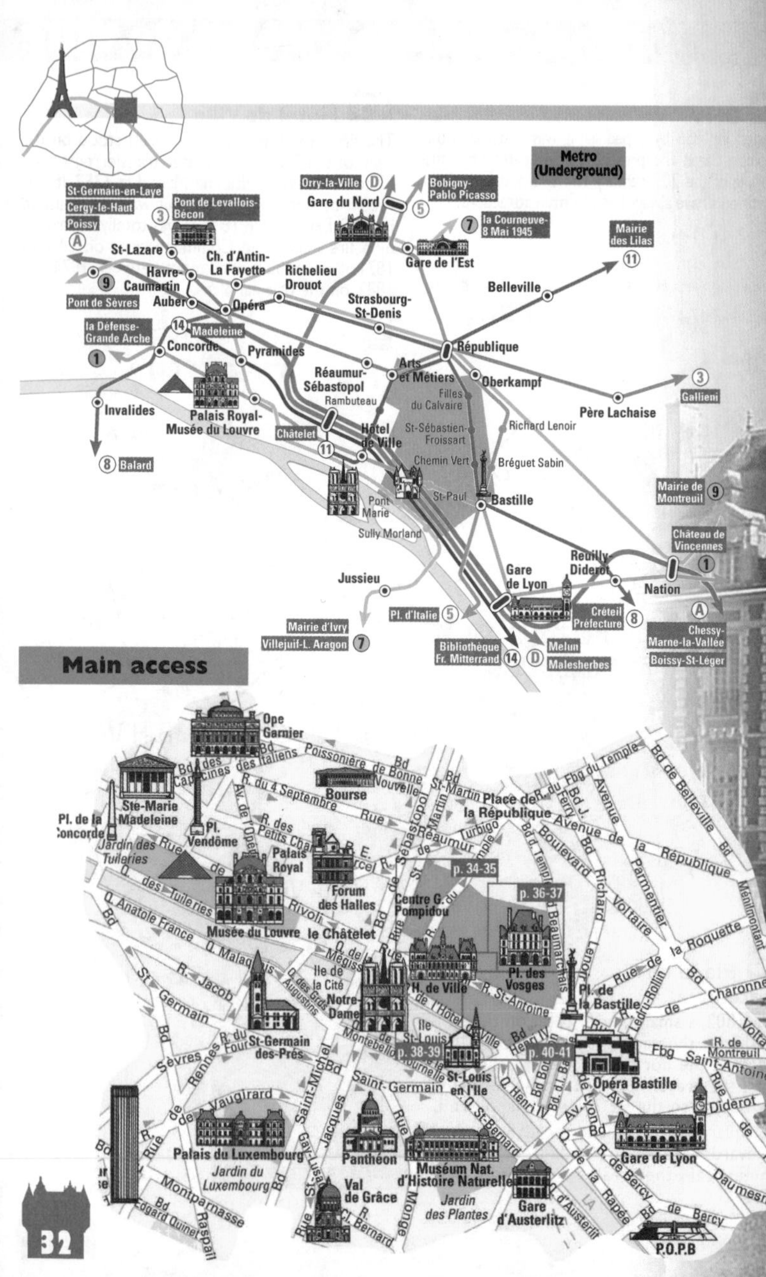
Metro (Underground)
St-Germain-en-Laye
Cergy-le-Haut
Poissy
Pont de Levallois-Bécon
Orry-la-Ville
Gare du Nord
Bobigny-Pablo Picasso
La Courneuve-8 Mai 1945
Gare de l'Est
Mairie des Lilas
St-Lazare
Ch. d'Antin-La Fayette
Richelieu Drouot
Havre-Caumartin
Auber
Opéra
Strasbourg-St-Denis
Belleville
Pont de Sèvres
la Défense-Grande Arche
Madeleine
Concorde
Pyramides
République
Réaumur-Sébastopol
Arts et Métiers
Oberkampf
Gallieni
Rambuteau
Filles du Calvaire
Père Lachaise
Invalides
Palais Royal-Musée du Louvre
Châtelet
Hôtel de Ville
St-Sébastien-Froissart
Richard Lenoir
Chemin Vert
Bréguet Sabin
Balard
St-Paul
Bastille
Mairie de Montreuil
Pont Marie
Sully Morland
Château de Vincennes
Reuilly-Diderot
Gare de Lyon
Nation
Jussieu
Pl. d'Italie
Créteil Préfecture
Mairie d'Ivry
Villejuif-L. Aragon
Bibliothèque Fr. Mitterrand
Melun
Malesherbes
Chessy-Marne-la-Vallée
Boissy-St-Léger
Main access
Ope Garnier
Ste-Marie Madeleine
Pl. de la Concorde
Pl. Vendôme
Bourse
Place de la République
Jardin des Tuileries
Palais Royal
Forum des Halles
p. 34-35
p. 36-37
Centre G. Pompidou
Musée du Louvre
le Châtelet
Ile de la Cité
Notre-Dame
H. de Ville
Pl. des Vosges
Pl. de la Bastille
St-Germain des-Prés
Ile St-Louis
p. 38-39
p. 40-41
St-Louis en l'Ile
Opéra Bastille
Palais du Luxembourg
Jardin du Luxembourg
Panthéon
Val de Grâce
Muséum Nat. d'Histoire Naturelle
Jardin des Plantes
Gare d'Austerlitz
Gare de Lyon
P.O.P.B

Le Marais

Musée d'Art et d'Histoire du Judaïsme

Housed in the Hôtel de Saint-Aignan (17th century), this museum has a collection of documents on Jewi culture (religion, people and art).

71 rue du Temple - *01 53 01 86 60*

Mondays to Fridays from 11 am to 6 pm, Sundays from 10 am to 6 pm.

29-38-47-57

Musée de l'Histoire de France - Archives nationales

There is very little left of the old Hôtel de Clisson, just the two towers that can be seen from the rue des Archives. On the site, Pierre-Alexis Delamair built the Hôtel de Soubise at the beginning of the 18th century. It has a large courtyard surrounded by an arched gallery, from where to admire the beautiful mansion.

Given to the Imperial Archives in 1808, it lat became the National Archives. The wonder apartment of the Prince and Princess, decorate by Germaine Boffrand, have remained intact.

60 rue des Francs-Bourgeois - *01 40 27 60 96*

Everyday except Tuesdays from 9.45 am to 5.30 pm, Saturdays and Sundays from 2 pm to 5.30 pm.

Admission: 3 euros – Reduced rate 2.50 euros - *29-75-96*

Eglise Notre-Dame des Blancs-Manteaux

It was built on the site of an old convent where the monks wore long white coats. The order was dissolved soon after and the church was occupied by the Hermit Brethren of Saint-Guillaume and then by the Benedictines, but the name survived. In the 17th century, the church was re-established and in the 19th century, Baltard extended the nave, added a chapel and re-assembled the facade of the Church of the Baranabites, destroyed by Haussmann. The chapel contains 17th century paintings and a marquetery chair from the same period.

1 rue Abbé Migne - *01 42 72 09 37* - *29-75*

Rue des Archives

It is a serie of short streets which were given that name because of the proximity of the National Archives. Several prestigious mansions line the lively street. There is also the Cloister of the Billettes.

Musée de la Chasse et e la Nature

e 17th century Hôtel Guénégaud was built by ançois Mansart. It escaped destruction and was ught by the City of Paris in 1960. François mmer and his wife put in their varied collections objects related to hunting: stuffed animals, intings, weapons, knives and trophies.

60 rue des archives

01 53 01 92 40

Tuesdays to Sundays from 11 am to 6 pm.

Admission 4.60 euros, Reduced rate 2.30 euros, nools 0.75 euros

29-75

Hôtel de Rohan

Built by P.A. Delamai for the Bishop of Strasbourg at the beginning of the 18th century. Its sober facade clearly indicates that several cardinals lived there. Napoleon I used it to house the Imperial Stationary. This later became the Royal and then the National Stationary. The building was poorly maintained until it was handed over to the National Archives in 1927.

87 rue Vieille du Temple - *01 40 27 60 09*

Everyday except Tuesdays from 12 noon to 6 pm.

Admission 5.50 euros, Reduced rates 4 euros

29-75-96

Rue Vieille du Temple

This street existed already in the 13th century. Old houses, and 17th century mansions line the street. Two are exceptional: the Hôtel Amelot de Bisseuil known as the Hôtel of the Dutch Ambassadors and the Hôtel Hérouet.

0 — 250 m
0 — 5 mn

Musée Carnavalet (Hôtel Carnavalet)

Built by Nicolas Dupuis in the 16th century. It was modified by François Mansart in the 17th century. There are many statues by Jean Goujon. In 1654, it was owned by Claude Boislevé who fell in disgrace with Fouquet. His assets were sold and the house was let to Madame de Sévigné. Bought by the City of Paris in 1886, it was transformed into a museum to house its historical collections. In 1889, the Hôtel Peletier de Saint-Fargeau (17th century) was annexed to welcome the Revolution Collections of the 19th and 20th centuries.

It is the whole history of Paris, from pre-historic times to our days, which is on display in these two buildings, with a collection of archaeological objects, scale models, paintings, sculptures and furniture.

Several rooms recreate the atmosphere and setting of the drawing rooms and apartments of the 17th and 18th centuries. There is a reconstruction of the Fouquet Jewellery shop (1900) and of the ballroom of the Hôtel de Wendel (1924).

23 rue de Sévigné - 01 44 59 58 58

Everyday except Mondays, from 10 am to 6 pm.

Temporary exhibitions, Admission 5.50 euros, Reduced rates 4 euros, Youth rate 2.50 euros Permanent collections: free

29-69-76-96

Musée Picasso (Hôtel Salé)

The house was built in the 17th century by Pierre Aubert de Fontenay. As he was in charge of collecting the salt tax, his house became known as the Hôtel Salé (the salt house). The Picasso Museum mov[ed] there in 1985, after major restoration work started [in] 1976. It has over 3500 pieces mostly donated [by] Jacqueline Picasso. They cover the different periods [of] the artist and the different techniques he used (pai[n]ting, drawing, collage, sculpture and ceramic).

5 rue de Thorigny - 01 42 71 25 21

Everyday except Tuesdays from 9.30 am to 6 pm in summe[r] and 9.30 to 6 pm in winter, late opening on Thursdays until 8 pm.

Admission 5.50 euros, Reduced rate 4 euros. A supplement of 1.22 euros for temporary exhibitions Under 18: free

PC-29-46-69-76-93

Musée Cognacq-Jay

Housed in the 18th century Hôtel Donon, its roo[ms] display collections of paintings, drawings, sculptu[res] and other works of art of the 18th century. It was t[he] collection of Ernest Cognacq and Marie-Louise J[ay] who founded the 'Samaritaine' department sto[re]. Paintings by Boucher and Fragonard, drawings [by] Watteau, oils by Mallet, Sax and Sèvres porcelains a[nd] the collection of Tobacco pots must be seen.

8 rue Elzévir - 01 40 27 07 21

Tuesdays to Sundays from 10 am to 6 pm

Free

29-69-76-96

Place du Marché Sainte-Catherine

The market settled on the ground of the priory of Sainte-Catherine du Val-des-Ecoliers, bought by Louis X[…] in the 17th century. The buildings surrounding the market square are the work of Caron. Several restaura[nts] have set their tables in the shade of the mulberry trees.

0 250
0 5 m

Place des Vosges

ıtands where the Hôtel Tournelles stood once, ıis XI and Louis XII died there and Henri II was rtally wounded by the lance of Captain ıntgomery during a joust. Henri IV decided to 'e the square built along very strict architectural ıs: identical stone and brick facades with arcades galleries. His wishes were respected and the ıare has survived with little alterations. ugurated in 1612, the Place Royale was very ɔular with the aristocracy, writers (Madame ˈigné, Victor Hugo, Théophile Gautier, Alphonse ıdet lived there) and other dignitaries. The squa- was renamed Place des Vosges in 1800 by poleon I as a tribute to the department which s the first to pay its taxes.

Maison de Victor Hugo

The Hôtel de Rohan-Guéménée was built at the beginning of the 17th century. Victor Hugo lived there from 1832 to 1848 and wrote Ruy Blas. It was turned into a museum in 1903 where manuscripts, drawings, photos, furniture and other objects from other houses retrace the life of the author.

6 place des Vosges

01 42 72 10 16

Tuesdays to Sundays from 10 am to 5.40 pm.

Free

Temporary exhibitions: 5 euros

20-29-65-69-96

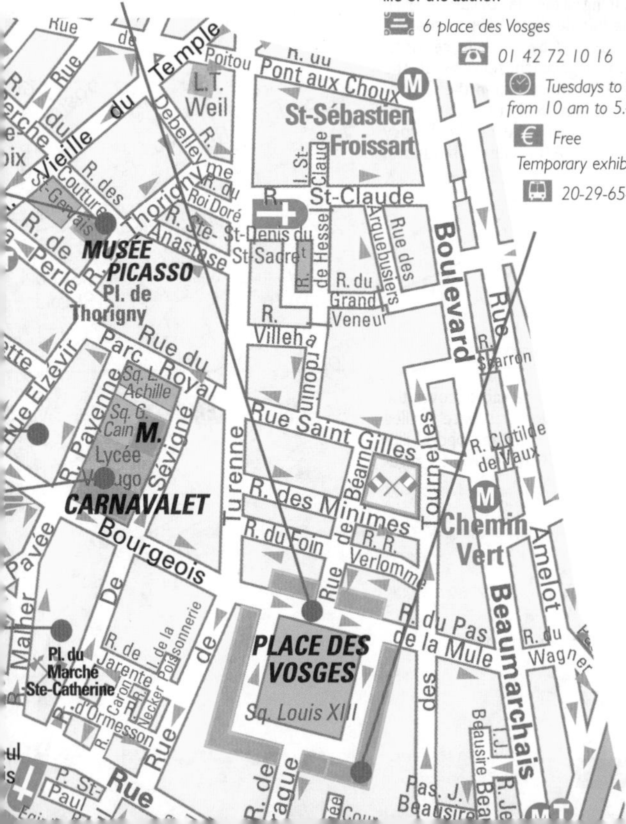

Hôtel de Sens

This late 15th early 16th century building is one of the last remaining example of the civilian architecture of the Middle-Ages. Built by the bishops of Sens, it was used by different services, including the Lyon stagecoach services at the beginning of the 18th century. When the City of Paris bought the house in 1911, it was in a terrible state. Restored, it now houses the Forney Library (Decorative Arts and Industrial Techniques).

1 rue Figuier

01 42 78 14 60

Village Saint-Pa

Bric-a-bra salesmen a antique de lers have se led in t square su rounded narrow med val lanes. Fro the rue d Jardins Sair Paul we c see wh remains of the wall of Philippe-Auguste built at the end the 17th century.

Musée de la Curiosité et de la Magie

Thanks to many accessories, we can discover the different sides of magic, which was once called 'funny physics' until 1815. Mirrors and optical illusions complete the museum. Magic shows are regularly given in the small theatre.

11 rue Saint-Paul

01 42 72 13 26

Wednesdays, Saturdays and Sundays from 2 pm to 7 pm. Closed in July and August

Admission 7 euros, Reduced rate 5 euros

67-69-76-86-87

www.museedelamagie.com

Église Saint-Paul - Saint Louis

Built in a Jesuit style copied on the church of Gesu In Rome. Originally, it was part of the Jesuit's house which became the Lycée Charlemagne (a school). Its impressive facade hides a dome that really lights up the nave.

The clock comes from the church of Saint-Paul destroyed in 1797. The major rt of the furniture and the decorations have been t. A few paintings are left, including a painting by gène Delacroix (Christ in the Olive Tree Gardens – 27) and statues of the Vierge de Douleur (the Virgin Pain) by Germain Pilon, 1586.

7 passage Saint-Paul - *01 42 72 30 32*

Balabus-96

Hôtel de Sully

The house was built at the end of the 17th century and bought by Sully. It is now occupied by the Historical Monuments Treasury. It is typical of aristocratic houses of the time with the main wing of the building between the courtyard and the garden. Several bas-reliefs can be seen from the garden. A second building is situated at the back of the garden, it is an 'orangerie' also called the Little Hôtel Sully.

48 rue Saint-Antoine - *01 42 78 49 32*

Balabus-96

Sq. Louis XIII
R. Necker
Rue
Rue Saint Antoine
R. de l'Hôtel St-Paul
R. de Birague
Imp. Guéménée
Cour Bérard
Pas. J. Beausire
R. Jean Beausire
R. d. Bastille
Bastille
Pl. de la Bastille
R. Daval
C. Damoye
Beautreillis
Musc
Ste-Marie
R. Castex
R. de Lesdiguières
Cœur
COLONNE DE JUILLET
Bastille
Petit
R. de la Cerisaie
Henri IV
Boulevard
Cousin
Sully Morland
de Chardin

Rue François Miron

There are two interesting beamed houses in this street that date back to the Middle-Ages and the Hôtel de Beauvais from whose balcony the queen of England watched the triumphal entry of Louis XIV. Mozart stayed there in 1763.

Église Saint-Gervais-Saint-Protais

This is Paris's oldest church on the right bank, according to Fortunat (6th century). Destroyed by the Norman in the 9th century, it was rebuilt several times and was not finished until the middle of the 17th century. Its classical facade is by Solomon de Bross but the rest of the building is Flamboyant Gothic. The organ dates from 1601, and was played by the Couperin family from 1653 to 1830. It has remarkable 17th century stained glass windows, several statues including a Virgin. The keystone of the chapel is 2.5 m in diameter.

 *13 rue des Barres*

 *01 48 87 32 02*

Balabus-63-76-96

Rue des Rosiers – Rue du Roi de Sicile

From the 12th century but mainly in the 19th and early 20th centuries, the Jewish community settle in these small streets. Synagogues, Kosher food stores, restaurants and oriental cake shops line t streets giving them an unique charm.

Rue des Francs-Bourgeois

ɪrmerly called rue des Poulies (pulleys), because of e pulleys used by the weavers, its present names ɪmes from a 16th century charity house whose ɪsidents were exempt from taxes.

ɪany 16th century houses and hôtels line the street ɪat leads from the Beaubourg district to the place ɪs Vosges.

Bibliothèque Historique de la Ville de Paris

It is housed in what was first the Hôtel d'Angoulême then the Lamoignon. It was built by Diane de France at the beginning of the 17th century.

Boileau, Madame de Sévigné and Racine were regular visitors at the time of Guillaume Lamoignon. The house was sold by the family at the end of the 18th century. It was later bought by the City of Paris which restored it in the 1960s.

24 rue Pavée - 01 44 59 29 40

Everyday except Sundays and public holidays from 9.30 am to 6 pm

29-69-76-96

Maison européenne de la Photographie

Housed in the early 18th century Hôtel Henault de Cantobre. It offers permanent exhibitions, which are often updated and temporary exhibitions that use the rich collection. Over 12 000 pieces have been presented to the public, since 1958. There is also a workshop, a library and video-library.

5, 7 rue de Fourcy - 01 44 78 75 00

Everyday except Mondays and Tuesdays from 11 am to 8 pm

Admission: 5 euros, Reduced rate: 2.50 euros Free on Wednesdays from 5 pm to 8 pm for children under 8

Balabus-67-69-76-96

Web *www.mep-fr.org*

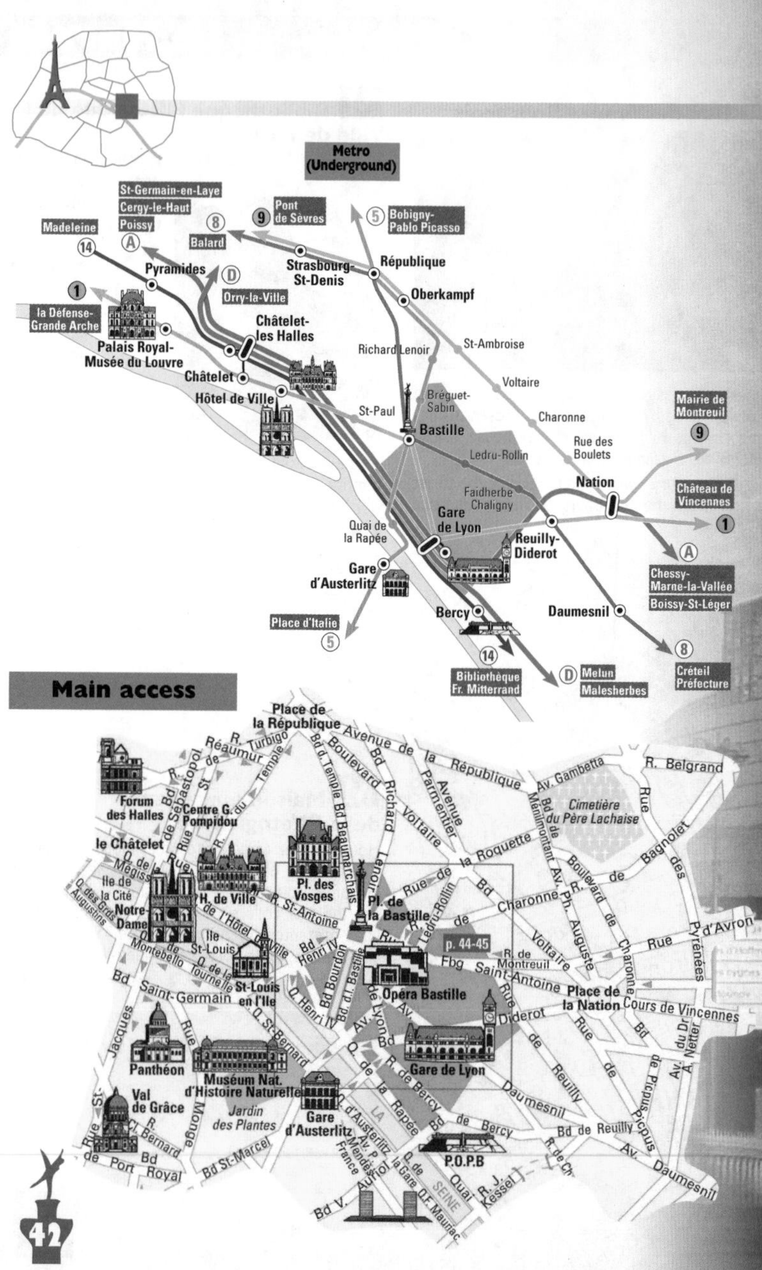
Metro
(Underground)
St-Germain-en-Laye
Cergy-le-Haut
Poissy
Madeleine
Pont
de Sèvres
Bobigny-
Pablo Picasso
Balard
Pyramides
Orry-la-Ville
Strasbourg-
St-Denis
République
Oberkampf
la Défense-
Grande Arche
Châtelet-
les Halles
Palais Royal-
Musée du Louvre
Richard Lenoir
St-Ambroise
Châtelet
Hôtel de Ville
Voltaire
Bréguet-
Sabin
St-Paul
Charonne
Bastille
Mairie de
Montreuil
Rue des
Boulets
Ledru-Rollin
Nation
Château de
Vincennes
Faidherbe
Chaligny
Gare
de Lyon
Quai de
la Rapée
Reuilly-
Diderot
Gare
d'Austerlitz
Chessy-
Marne-la-Vallée
Boissy-St-Léger
Bercy
Daumesnil
Place d'Italie
Bibliothèque
Fr. Mitterrand
Melun
Malesherbes
Créteil
Préfecture
Main access
Place de
la République
Forum
des Halles
Centre G.
Pompidou
le Châtelet
Cimetière
du Père Lachaise
Pl. des
Vosges
Pl. de
la Bastille
Ile de
la Cité
Notre-
Dame
H. de Ville
Ile
St-Louis
p. 44-45
Opéra Bastille
St-Louis
en l'Ile
Place de
la Nation
Panthéon
Gare de Lyon
Muséum Nat.
d'Histoire Naturelle
Val
de Grâce
Jardin
des Plantes
Gare
d'Austerlitz
P.O.P.B
R. Belgrand
Avenue de la République
Av. Gambetta
Bd Voltaire
R. de la Roquette
R. de Charonne
R. de Bagnolet
Rue d'Avron
Fbg Saint-Antoine
Cours de Vincennes
Bd Diderot
Rue de Reuilly
Bd de Reuilly
Av. Daumesnil
Bd de Bercy
Bd Saint-Germain
Bd St-Marcel
Bd de Port Royal
Rue Monge
Bd Beaumarchais
Bd Richard Lenoir
Bd Henri IV
Bd Bourdon
Av. Ledru-Rollin
Av. Parmentier
Rue de Picpus
Av. du Dr A. Netter
Q. de la Rapée
Q. d'Austerlitz
Q. St-Bernard
SEINE

Bastille

Place de la Bastille - Colonne de Juillet

It pays tribute to two revolutions: First the 1789 French Revolution, when on 14 July the Bastille fortress was stormed and destroyed and to the 'Trois Glorieuses' the three days of rioting in 1830 that led to the overthrow of King Charles X. The ashes of the 504 victims were first laid in a crypt below the column.

Rue de la Roquette - Rue de Lappe

Lively streets, the first is line with shops and cafés and th other with bars, restauran and nightclubs (Balaj Chapelle des Lombards) rem niscent of the popular balls the 19th century.

Pavillon de l'Arsenal

A permanent exhibition takes us through the main stages of the construction of Paris with plans, scale models and architect drawings.

 *21 Boulevard Morland*

 *01 42 76 33 97*

Open Tuesdays to Saturday from 10.30 am to 6.30 pm Sundays from 11.00 am to 7 pm

 *Free*

67-86-87

Opéra Bastille

Built on the site of the old Bastille Station, it wa inaugurated in 1989. This large modern building, a in glass and marble, is a popular and function opera house.

120 rue de Lyon - 01 40 01 17 89

Balabus-20-29-65-69-76-86-87-91

Bassin de l'Arsenal

The Paris marina lies at the confluence of the Seine River and the Saint-Martin Canal. A peaceful corner surrounded by greenery.

Gare de Lyon

Its clock dominated the world before the station welcomed the first TGVs (very fast trains). It also houses the well known and beautifully decorated 'Train Bleu' restaurant, the showcase of the Paris-Lyon-Mediterranée Trai Company.

Maison de la R.A.T.P.

It is both the headquarters of the Parisian Transpor Company and a museum. Its visit is essential to dis cover everything about the Paris metro.

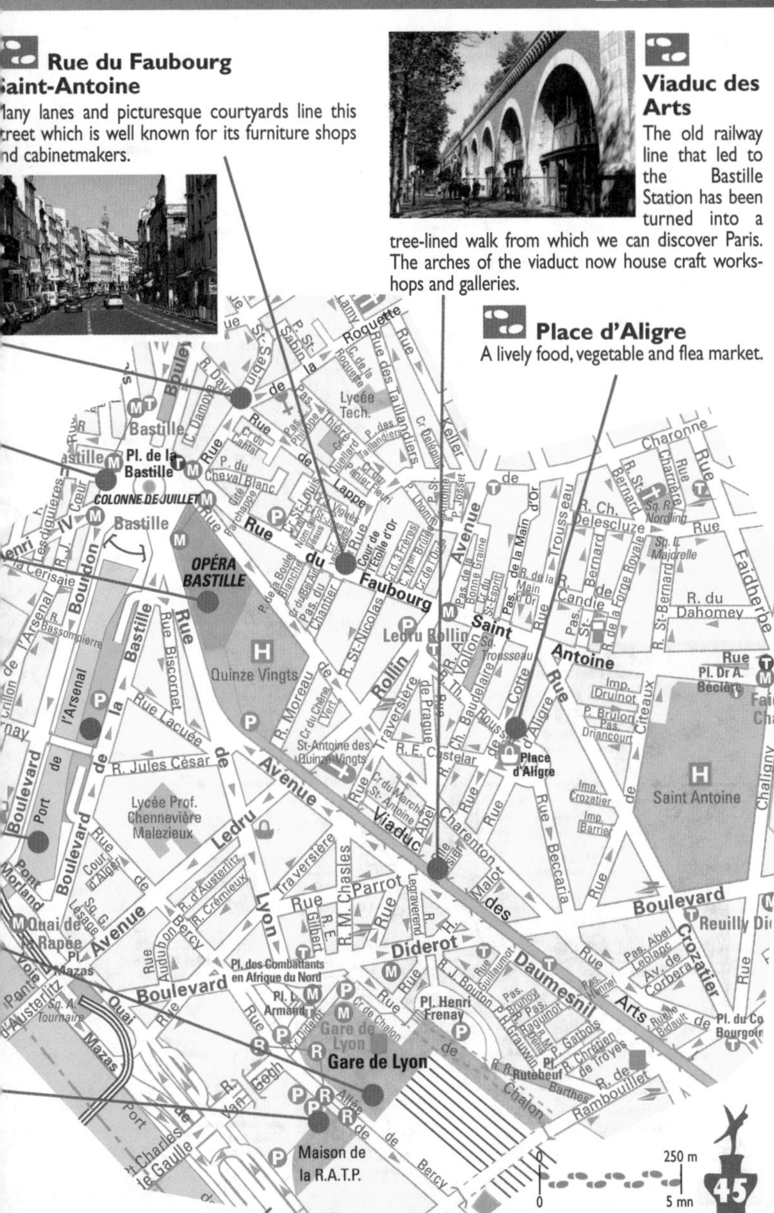

Rue du Faubourg aint-Antoine

lany lanes and picturesque courtyards line this treet which is well known for its furniture shops nd cabinetmakers.

Viaduc des Arts

The old railway line that led to the Bastille Station has been turned into a tree-lined walk from which we can discover Paris. The arches of the viaduct now house craft workshops and galleries.

Place d'Aligre

A lively food, vegetable and flea market.

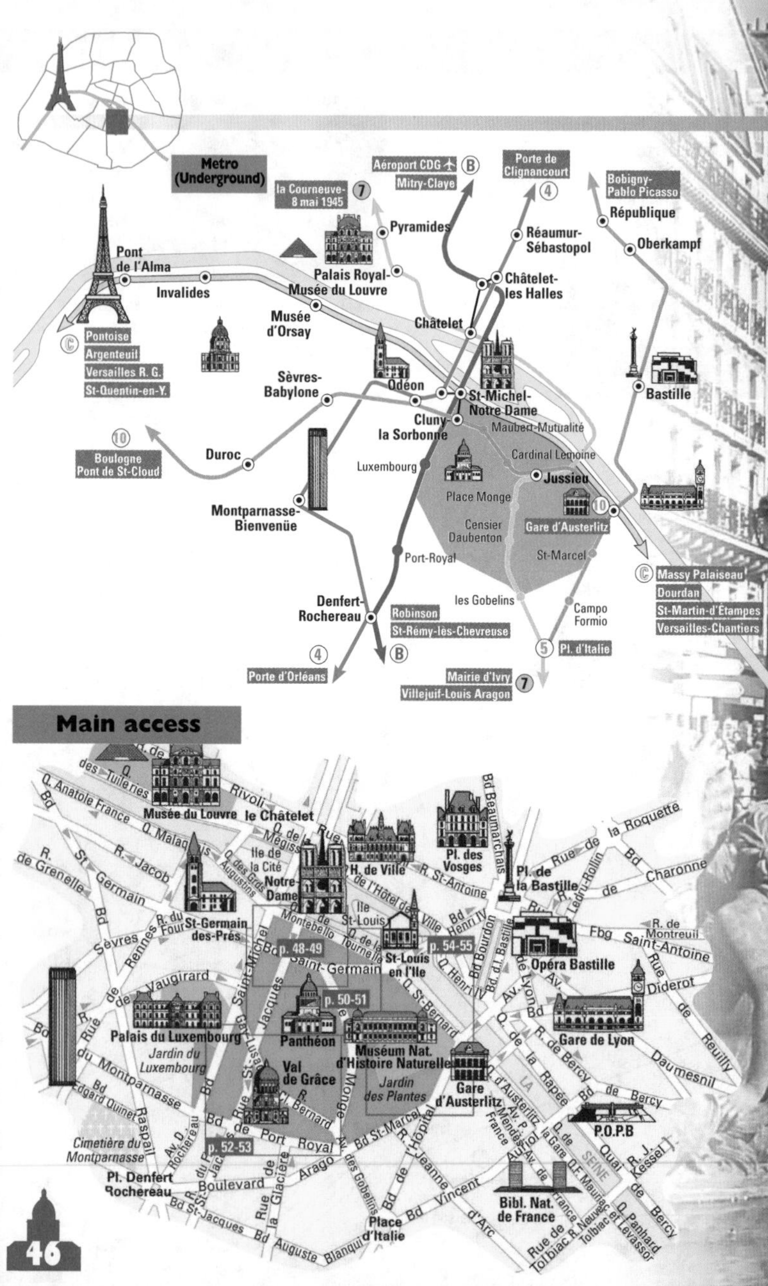
Metro (Underground)
Aéroport CDG
Mitry-Claye
Porte de Clignancourt
Bobigny-Pablo Picasso
la Courneuve-8 mai 1945
Pyramides
Réaumur-Sébastopol
République
Oberkampf
Pont de l'Alma
Invalides
Palais Royal-Musée du Louvre
Châtelet-les Halles
Musée d'Orsay
Châtelet
Pontoise
Argenteuil
Versailles R. G.
St-Quentin-en-Y.
Sèvres-Babylone
Odéon
St-Michel-Notre Dame
Bastille
Cluny-la Sorbonne
Maubert-Mutualité
Cardinal Lemoine
Boulogne Pont de St-Cloud
Duroc
Luxembourg
Jussieu
Place Monge
Montparnasse-Bienvenüe
Censier Daubenton
Gare d'Austerlitz
St-Marcel
Port-Royal
Massy Palaiseau
Dourdan
St-Martin-d'Étampes
Versailles-Chantiers
Denfert-Rochereau
les Gobelins
Campo Formio
Robinson
St-Rémy-lès-Chevreuse
Pl. d'Italie
Porte d'Orléans
Mairie d'Ivry
Villejuif-Louis Aragon
Main access
Musée du Louvre
le Châtelet
Pl. des Vosges
Ile de la Cité
Notre-Dame
H. de Ville
Pl. de la Bastille
St-Germain des-Prés
Ile St-Louis
St-Louis en l'Ile
Opéra Bastille
p. 48-49
p. 54-55
p. 50-51
p. 52-53
Palais du Luxembourg
Jardin du Luxembourg
Panthéon
Muséum Nat. d'Histoire Naturelle
Jardin des Plantes
Gare de Lyon
Val de Grâce
Gare d'Austerlitz
P.O.P.B
Cimetière du Montparnasse
Pl. Denfert Rochereau
Place d'Italie
Bibl. Nat. de France
Rivoli
Q. Anatole France
Q. Malaquais
R. Jacob
R. de Grenelle
St Germain
Bd Sèvres
R. du Four
Rennes
Vaugirard
Rue de la Roquette
Bd Beaumarchais
R. St-Antoine
Charonne
Ledru-Rollin
Fbg Saint-Antoine
R. de Montreuil
Diderot
Daumesnil
Reuilly
R. de Bercy
Bd de Bercy
Q. de la Rapée
Bd du Montparnasse
Bd Edgard Quinet
Raspail
Bd de Port Royal
Arago
Bd St-Marcel
Monge
Bd St-Jacques
Bd Auguste Blanqui
Bd Vincent Auriol
Rue de Tolbiac
Q. St-Bernard
Bd Bourdon
Bd Henri IV
Av. P. Mendès France
Q. F. Mauriac
Q. Panhard et Levassor
SEINE

Quartier Latin

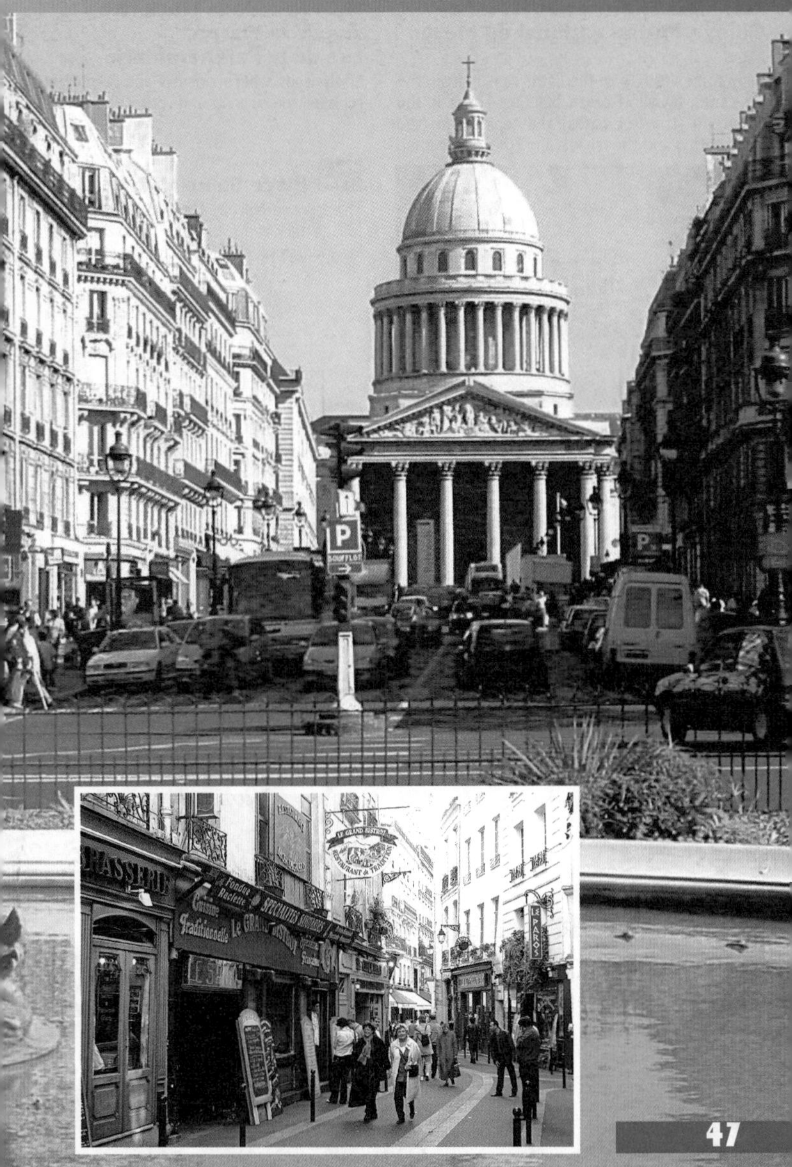

Thermes et Hôtel de Cluny - Musée national du Moyen Âge

Only some vestiges of the baths remain from the 3rd century Gallo-Roman building. There is the caldarium (the hot baths) the tepidarium (the tepid baths) and the frigidarium (the cold baths).

Cluny was built at the end of the 15th century to house visiting monks. Today, it is still one of the most beautiful examples of medieval architecture.

Until the revolution, it was owned by the monastery. It was later sold and in 1833, Alexander du Sommerard, a keen collector, rented the house for his collection. When he died, it was acquired by the state and turned into a museum. It now houses a rich collection of medieval objects and works of art like the famous 'La Dame à la Licorne' tapestry that shows us life in the Middle Ages.

6 place Paul Painlevé *01 53 73 78 16*

Mondays to Sundays, except Tuesdays from 9.15 am to 5.45 pm

Admission 5.50 euros, Reduced rate 4 euros

21-27-38-63-85-86-87

Boulevard Saint-Michel

Once the setting for youth protest, this large avenue has gradually sold its soul to hamburger stalls and boutiques of all sorts.

Rue de la Huchette, rue de la Harpe, rue de la Parcheminerie

Lively lanes where cinemas and restaurants have replaced the copyists and rotisseries of the past.

Place Saint-Michel

The fountain built by Davioud in the 19th century, is the ideal meeting place for youngsters from many countries.

Rue Galande, rue de la Bûcherie

Narrow lanes lined with many medieval houses.

Église Saint-Séverin-Saint-
'licolas

'he first chapel, built in ıemory of Séverin the olitaire, dates from the 13th entury (the first three rches of the nave, the sou-ıern aisle and the belfry). It /as extended several times ı the 14th and 15th centu-ies. It is Flamboyant Gothic /ith its double ambulatory nd its fanned vaulting falling ıto columns. In the 18th century, the facade was eplaced with that of the church of St-Pierre-aux-œufs. The stained glass windows date from the 4th, 15th and 16th centuries.

21-27

Église Saint-Julien-le-Pauvre

Next to each other we can find the oldest tree in Paris (a 400 years old locust tree in square Viviani) and its oldest church. Started in the 12th century, it was ransacked by the students in the 16th century and almost destroyed in the 17th century, before it was finally restored. It was transformed into a granary under the revolution. In 1881, it was given to the Greek catholic church. Now, it is the venue for many concerts.

79 rue Galande *01 43 54 52 16*

Balabus-24

La Sorbonne

The university still perpetuates the work of Robert de Sorbon who founded the first college in 1257 to teach theology to young monks. At the request of Cardinal Richelieu, the Sorbonne was rebuilt in the 17th century. It was later extended by Nenot at the end of the 19th century before becoming a world famous university.

21-27-38-63-85-86-87

Le Collège de France

The Collège de France was founded in 1530 by king François I to teach Latin and Greek. Over the centuries, a greater number of chairs were created, but the college remained independent. The lectures, always given by eminent scholars, are free and open to the public.

21-27-38-63-85-86-87

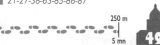

Le Panthéon

King Louis XV vowed to build the church of Saint-Geneviève when he was seriously ill in Metz. The task was trusted to Soufflot who opted for a style that mixed Greek and Gothic architectures. Completed in 1790, the Revolutionary Assembly decided to transform the church into a mausoleum to receive the ashes of the nation's great men. Engraved on the

front, we can read 'To its Great Men The Grateful Nation'. Although the church was restored as a place of worship by Napoleon I, it became a lay temple in 1885 when the ashes of Victor Hugo were laid to rest. Inside, the building is solemn and impressive by its size. Paintings tell the History of France.

Place du Panthéon

01 44 32 18 00

Everyday from 10 am to 6.30 pm in the summer and from 10 am to 6 pm in the winter.

84-89

Église St-Étienne-du-Mont

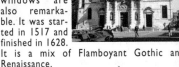

Famous for its rood screen and the cult of Sainte-Geneviève, its facade and stained glass windows are also remarkable. It was started in 1517 and finished in 1628. It is a mix of Flamboyant Gothic and Renaissance.

1 rue Saint-Étienne du Mont

01 43 25 38 49

84-89

Rue Soufflot

From the Luxembourg Garden, it offers a lovely perspective of the Pantheon.

Rue Maître Albert, rue de Bièvre

Old houses. The rue de Bièvre reminds us that the nearby river was diverted.

Musée de l'Assistance publique-Hôpitaux de Paris

Housed in a 17th century Hôtel, it tells us about the evolution of hospitals from the Hôtel-Dieu until now.

47 quai de la Tournelle - 01 46 33 01 43

Everyday except Mondays from 10 am to 6 pm

Admission 4 euros, Reduced rate 2 euros

24-47-63-86-87

Musée de la Préfecture de Police

It offers a large panorama of the history of public security and the Paris police through a wealth of documents and amazing legal archives.

The Police Station of the 5th arrondissement (2nd floor)
4 rue de la Montagne Ste-Geneviève

01 44 41 52 50

Mondays to Fridays from 9 am to 5 pm,
Saturdays from 10 am to 5 pm

Free - 24-47-63-86-87

Église Saint-Nicolas-du-Chardonnet

Built between the end of the 16th century and the middle of the 17th, its facade dates from 1934. Inside the style is Jesuit and there are paintings by Corot, Le Lorrain and Charles Le Brun. The latter is buried in the church next to his mother.

23 rue Bernardins - 01 44 27 07 90-

Arènes de Lutèce

Vestiges from the Gallo-Roman period, they were only rediscovered at the end of the 19th century when the rue Monge was built. Originally, the amphitheatre could seat between 10 and 15000 people but only part of the terraces were restored.

Rue de Navarre

47

Musée Curie

Housed inside the Radium Institute, it retraces the life and work of the Curies (4 Nobel Prizes), through authentic instruments, photographs and Marie Curie's desk and chemistry laboratory.

11 rue Pierre et Marie Curie

01 42 34 67 49

Mondays to Fridays from 1.30 pm to 5 pm, closed on public holidays and in August

free - 21-27

Rue de l'Estrapade, rue Lhomond, rue Vauquelin, rue de l'Arbalète, place L. Herr

And many others, all these names remind us of the Paris of the Middle-

Ages that we can discover here and there, in the old stones, the signposts or the vaulted cellars.

Église du Val-de-Grâce

Anne of Austria vowed to build a church if she had a son. Her wish was granted when the future Louis XIV was born in 1638. He laid the foundation stone at the age of 7. François Mansart started the building, Jacques Le Mercier took over between 1646 and 1648. The church was finished by Pierre Le Muet and Gabriel Le Duc in 1666. The magnificent dome and altar with dais were inspired from the church of Saint-Pierre-de-Rome. The cupola was painted by Mignard. The convent buildings were transformed into a military hospital

during the Fren Revolution. Tod they also house museum relating t story of the arm health services.

Place de la Contrescarpe

The memory of the Pleiade lingers on in this shady square surrounded by cafés.

Rue Mouffetard

Nicknamed the 'Mouffe', this old Roman road, is lined with old houses, shops of all kind, exotic restaurants. It still throbs with the hustle and bustle of the market streets of yesterday.

Église Saint-Médard

Built over a number of periods, it is a hotchpotch of styles: Flamboyant Gothic for the nave, Renaissance choir. There is a Louis XVI portal.

33 rue Daubenton - *01 44 08 87 00*

27-47

227 rue Saint-Jacques

01 40 51 40 00

21-27-38-83-91

Institut du Monde arabe

The building combines the modernity of glass and metal with the traditional Islamic decorative feature of the moucharabiah. It was founded to draw together Arab and Western cultures. It houses a museum of the history of Arab civilisation, a library and an audiovisual centre.

1 rue des Fossés St-Bernard

01 40 51 38 38

Everyday, except Mondays, from 10 am to 6 pm.

Admission 4 euros, Reduced rate 3 euros, Admission and exhibition 7 euros, Reduced rate 5.5 euros

24-63-67-86-87-89

Collection de Minéraux

This remarkable collection contains 2 000 minerals from the four corners of the world, sparkling with every colour of the rainbow.

Université Pierre et Marie Curie, 34 rue Jussieu

01 44 27 52 88

Everyday, except Tuesdays, from 1 pm to 6 pm

Admission 4,50 euros, Reduced rate 2 euros

24-63-67-86-87-89

Mosquée de Paris

It was built to commemorate the North African Muslims who fell in the First World War. Its style is Moorish. The decoration, inside, was completed by artisans from Muslim countries. In addition to the prayer area, there is a hammam and a tea room.

2 place du Puits de l'Ermite - 01 45 35 97 33

From Saturdays to Thursdays from 9 am to 12 noon and from 2 pm to 6 pm

Admission 3 euros, Reduced rate 2 euros

47-67-89

Jardin des Plantes

The garden of medicinal plants was create by Louis XIII in the 17th century. Ove the centuries it was extende by naturalists (Jussieu Buffon Daubenton)

zoo, green-
ouses, alpine,
se, iris and
nuals gardens
d many exo-
c trees from
e four cor-
ers of the
orld make it a
ant natural
useum.

5 rue Cuvier

24-57-61-63-67-89-91

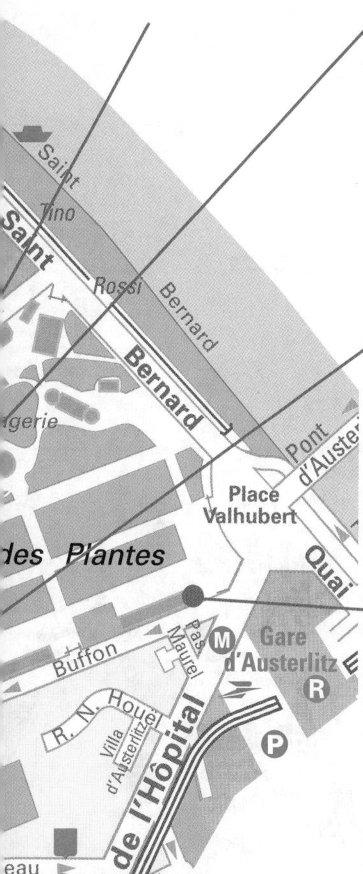

Muséum national d'Histoire naturelle

- Grande Galerie de l'Évolution

It lets us discover the great variety of animal species and understand the history of the living world and micro-organisms. It raises our awareness of the threats represented by men to the world's delicate balance.

36 rue Geoffroy Saint-Hilaire

01 40 79 36 00

Everyday except Tuesdays from 10 am to 6 pm, late night opening Thursdays until 10 pm

Admission 7 euros, Reduced rate 5 euros, inclusive of temporary exhibition 9 euros, reduced rate 5 euros

24-61-63-67-89-91

- Galerie de Minéralogie et de Géologie

It houses several collections: minerals, giant crystals, France's crown jewels, fossils and meteorites.

36 rue Geoffroy Saint-Hilaire

Everyday, except Tuesdays, from 10 am to 5 pm

Admission 5 euros, Reduced rate 3 euros

24-57-61-63-65-67-89-91

- Galerie d'Anatomie comparée et de Paléontologie

Reconstruction of thousands of skeletons of vertebrates, including dinosaurs. There are also fossils and a geology gallery.

2 rue Buffon

Everyday, except Tuesdays, from 10 am to 5 pm

Admission 5 euros, Reduced rate 3 euros

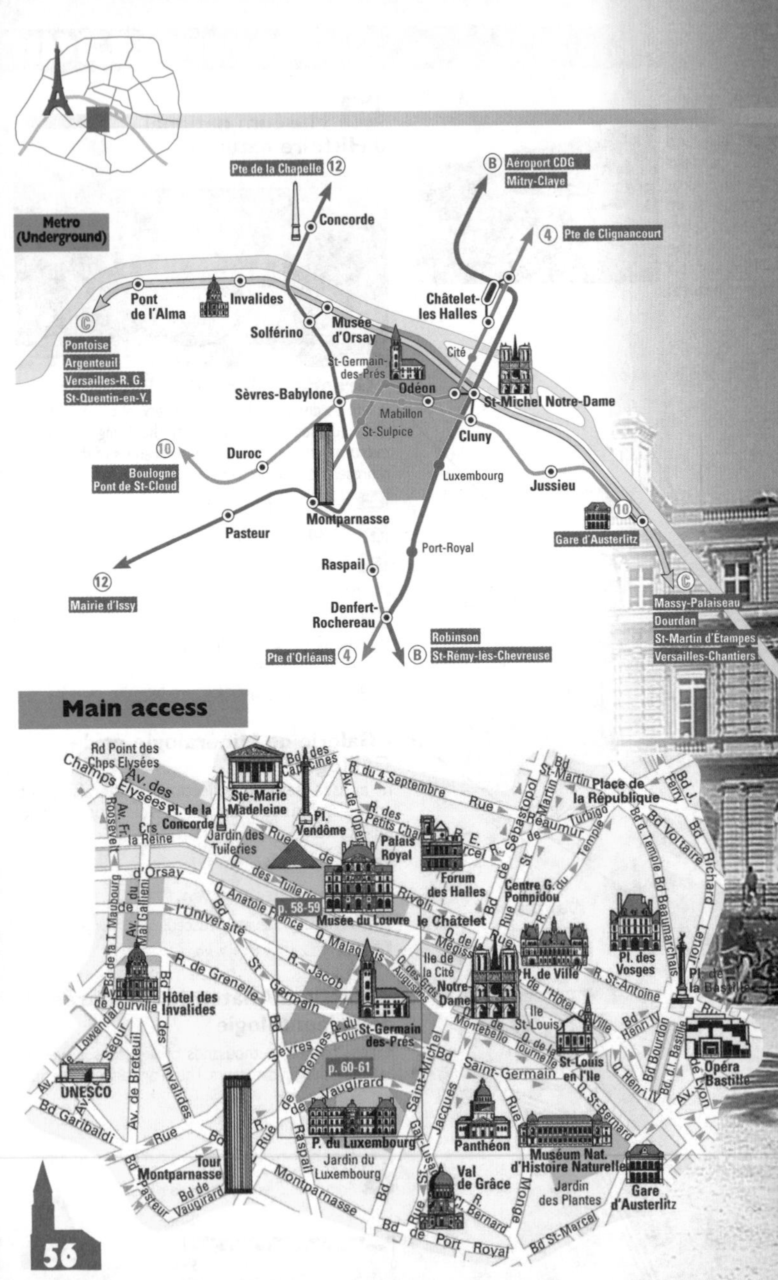

Metro (Underground)
Pte de la Chapelle
12
Concorde
Aéroport CDG
Mitry-Claye
B
4
Pte de Clignancourt
Pont de l'Alma
Invalides
Solférino
Musée d'Orsay
Châtelet-les Halles
C
Pontoise
Argenteuil
Versailles-R. G.
St-Quentin-en-Y.
Cité
St-Germain-des-Prés
Odéon
Sèvres-Babylone
Mabillon
St-Michel Notre-Dame
St-Sulpice
Cluny
10
Duroc
Boulogne
Pont de St-Cloud
Luxembourg
Jussieu
Montparnasse
Pasteur
Gare d'Austerlitz
Port-Royal
Raspail
12
Mairie d'Issy
Massy-Palaiseau
Dourdan
St-Martin d'Étampes
Versailles-Chantiers
Denfert-Rochereau
Robinson
St-Rémy-lès-Chevreuse
Pte d'Orléans
Main access
Rd Point des Chps Elysées
Champs Elysées
Av. des
Bd des Capucines
R. du 4 Septembre
Av. de l'Opéra
Ste-Marie Madeleine
Pl. de la Concorde
Pl. Vendôme
Av. Fr. Roosevelt
Crs la Reine
Jardin des Tuileries
Rue de Rivoli
R. des Petits Champs
R. E. Marcel
Palais Royal
Forum des Halles
Bd de Sébastopol
R. St-Martin
Bd St-Martin
Place de la République
Rue Réaumur
Turbigo
Bd Temple
Bd J. Ferry
Bd Voltaire
Bd Richard Lenoir
Q. d'Orsay
Q. des Tuileries
Q. Anatole France
Bd de l'Université
Av. du Mal Gallieni
Bd de la T. Maubourg
p. 58-59
Musée du Louvre
le Châtelet
Centre G. Pompidou
Rue du Temple
Bd Beaumarchais
Q. Malaquais
Q. de Mégisserie
Ile de la Cité
Q. des Grds Augustins
R. Jacob
R. de Grenelle
St-Germain
Notre-Dame
H. de Ville
Pl. des Vosges
R. St-Antoine
Pl. de la Bastille
Hôtel des Invalides
Av. de Tourville
Q. de l'Hôtel de Ville
Ile St-Louis
Bd Henri IV
St-Germain des-Prés
R. du Four
R. de Rennes
Bd de Sèvres
Q. de Montebello
Q. de la Tournelle
Bd Saint-Germain
St-Louis en l'Ile
Q. Henri IV
Bd Bourdon
Bd d.l. Bastille
Opéra Bastille
Av. de Lowendal
Av. de Ségur
Av. de Breteuil
Bd des Invalides
UNESCO
Bd Garibaldi
p. 60-61
R. de Vaugirard
Bd Saint-Michel
Rue St-Jacques
Rue Monge
Q. St-Bernard
Av. de Lyon
P. du Luxembourg
Panthéon
Rue Gay-Lussac
Raspail
Tour Montparnasse
Bd de Vaugirard
Bd Pasteur
Jardin du Luxembourg
Bd Montparnasse
Val de Grâce
R. Cl. Bernard
Muséum Nat. d'Histoire Naturelle
Jardin des Plantes
Gare d'Austerlitz
Bd de Port Royal
Bd St-Marcel

Saint-Germain-des-Prés

Musée Delacroix

Paintings, temporary exhibitions and objects that belonged to the artist are on display in this house where Delacroix lived from 1857 to his death in 1863.

6 rue de Furstenberg - 01 44 41 86 50

Everyday except Tuesdays and Wednesdays from 9.30 am to 5 pm

Admission 4 euros, Reduced rate 2.6 euros

39-63-70-86-95-96

www.musee-delacroix.fr

École des Beaux-Arts

The School of Fine Arts has taken over several bu dings including the church of the convent of th Petits-Augustins (17th century) and the Hôtel c Chanay (18th century). During the Frenc Revolution, Alexandre Lenoir turned it into th French Monuments Museum. In 1816, it was refurbi hed by Felix Duban and became the School of Fir Arts.

It is a school with a long tradition and an internati nal reputation. Its rich collection of books and worl of art are at the disposal of its researchers.

14 rue Bonaparte - 01 47 03 50 00

24-27-39-63-70-86-87-95-96

www.ensba.fr

Café de Flore - Les deux Magots

Writers like Apollinaire, Sartre, Prévert and many others came regularly to these cafés. They became the symbols of this district of artists and writers.

Église Saint-Germain-des-Prés

The first church was built on this site in the 6th century by Childebert I to receive the relics of Saint Vincent. Several Merovingian kings were buried there before it was destroyed by the Norman in the middle of the 9th century. The construction of the new abbey was started at the beginning of the new millennium and the choir was consecrated in the middle of the 12th century. Only the church remains from the 18th century estate. It was damaged during the French Revolution and restored in the 19th century as well as the 16th century abbey house. The 11th century nave was vaulted in the 17th century and the wall paintings by Hyppolyte Flandrin date from the 19th century.

3 place Saint-Germain-des-Prés

01 55 42 81 18

Everyday from 8 am to 7.45 pm

39-63-95

www.eglise-sgp.org

Institut de France

It is the seat of five prestigious academies including the famous Académie Française founded by Richelieu in 635. Mazarin asked Le Vau to design the building hich was first called the Collège des Quatre lations. In 1795, the Convention founded the stitute and the domed chapel was transformed at e beginning of the 19th century to welcome the vered assembly.

23 quai Conti - 01 44 41 44 41

21-24-25-58-69-70-72

www.institut-de-france.fr

Hôtel des Monnaies

Several buildings stood on this site before Louis XV asked Jacques-Denis Antoine to build l'Hôtel des Monnaies in the 18th century. There are many buildings and workshops behind the monumental facade facing the river.

Although the minting workshops were moved to the Gironde region, the museum traces the history of money in France through 2000 coins, 450 medals and token and their minting history.

11 quai Conti - 01 40 46 55 35

Tuesdays to Fridays from 11 am to 5.30 pm, Saturdays and Sundays from 12 noon to 5.30 pm

Admission 3 euros, Reduced rate 2.2 euros

Balabus-24-27 - www.monnaiedeparis.com

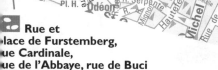

Rue Mazarine, passage Dauphine, rue de Nevers

Old and picturesque lanes which ran along the wall built by king Phillippe Auguste. Molière opened his first theatre in rue Mazarine.

Rue Saint-André-des-Arts

Opened in the 12th century, it led to the church of Saint-André-des-Arts (destroyed at the beginning of the 19th century). It is a very lively street lined with 18th century houses. Nearby, there are two very picturesque courtyards which are well worth a look: the Cour de Rohan and the Cour du Commerce Saint-André.

Rue et lace de Furstemberg, ue Cardinale, ue de l'Abbaye, rue de Buci

icturesque lanes with the hustle and bustle and charm of the 18th century.

Église Saint-Sulpice

The building of the church started in the middle of the 17th century with the architect Christophe Gaunard at the helm. The work was interrupted between 1678 and 1720. It was almost finished by Gilles-Marie Oppenord except for the facade which is the work of Jean-Nicolas Servandoni. The southern tower was never finished due to a shortage of funds. Inside the church is large and light and houses many works of art: two giant shell like fonts, frescos by Delacroix, the choir statues by Bouchardon and Pigalle, paintings by Van Loo and a great quality organ.

Carrefour de l'Odéon

It is the hub of a very lively district, throbbing wit history and culture. Danton lived in a house wher his statue now stands and philosophers, actor artists and scholars were often seen in the café theatres and nearby schools.

Rue de Rennes

Built in the middle of the 19th century by Haussmann, this thoroughfare led from Saint-Germain-des-Prés to the Montparnasse Station.

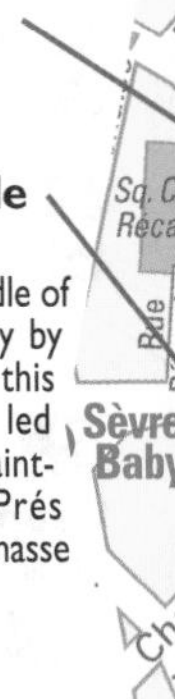

Rue de Vaugirard

It was an old Roman road. With its 4360 m, it is the longest street in Paris.

Jardin du Luxembourg

This large green space at the centre of Paris was created by Mary de Medici who missed the Italian gardens of her childhood. It is designed around a central octagonal pond bordered by two terraces. Its surface was increased under the French Revolution when the cloister of the Chartreux was annexed. But Haussmann's reduced it by half. It was open to the public as early as the 17th century. There are many statues and fountains in the park and a great variety of plants, an orchard and beehives. There are special amenities for children with rides, a puppet theatre and several play areas.

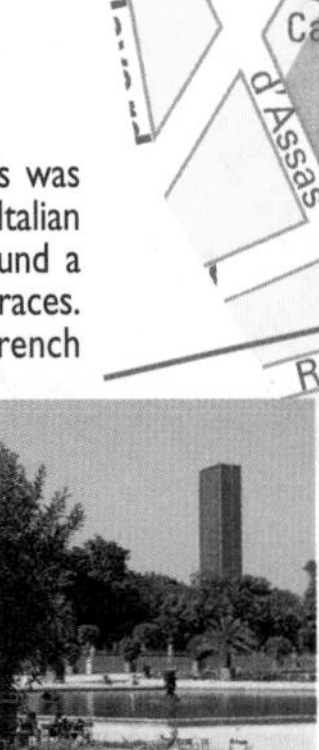

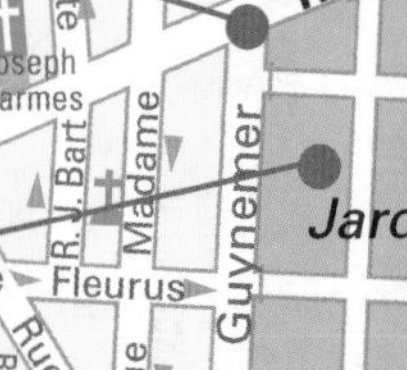

Sénat

The senators sit in the Palais du Luxembourg. With the Assemblée ationale, it forms the French Parliament.

t the beginning of the 17th century, Mary de edici bought the Petit Luxembourg, which is now e residence of the president of the senate. Then e asked Salomon de Brosse to build her a palace a style reminiscent of the Pitti Palace in Florence. When she died, it became the property of Gustave d'Orléans then that of the royal family before being transformed into a prison under the French Revolution. In 1799 it became the senate house and Chalgrin carried out the required transformation.

15 rue de Vaugirard - 01 42 34 20 60

Visits to the Palais du Luxembourg are organised on Mondays, Fridays and Saturdays, if the Senate is not in session. Debates can be attended on Tuesdays, Wednesdays and Thursdays.

58-84-89 - Web www.senat.fr

Musée d'histoire de la Médecine

It traces the history of medicine and surgery through illustrations, paintings, and special instruments from many different periods. The museum is housed in the René Descartes University.

12 rue de l'Ecole de Médecine

01 40 46 16 93

Everyday except Thursdays and Sundays from 2 pm to 5.30 pm

Admission 3.5 euros,
Reduced rate 2.5 euros

63-86-87

Fontaine de Médicis

Originally an artificial grotto(1620), the fountain was restored by Chalgrin in 1800. It was moved when the rue de Médicis was built. At the end of the 19th century, statues and a pond were added before the Regard Fountain was backed onto it.

Musée de Minéralogie

Housed in the Hôtel Vendôme (the Ecole des Mines), it offers lovers of beautiful stones, some of the richest collections of mineral in the world.

60 boulevard Saint-Michel

01 40 51 91 39

Tuesdays to Fridays from 1.30 pm to 6 pm and Saturdays from 10 am to 12.30 pm and from 2 pm to 5 pm.

Admission 5 euros, Reduced rate
2.5 euros,
Free for schools

38-82

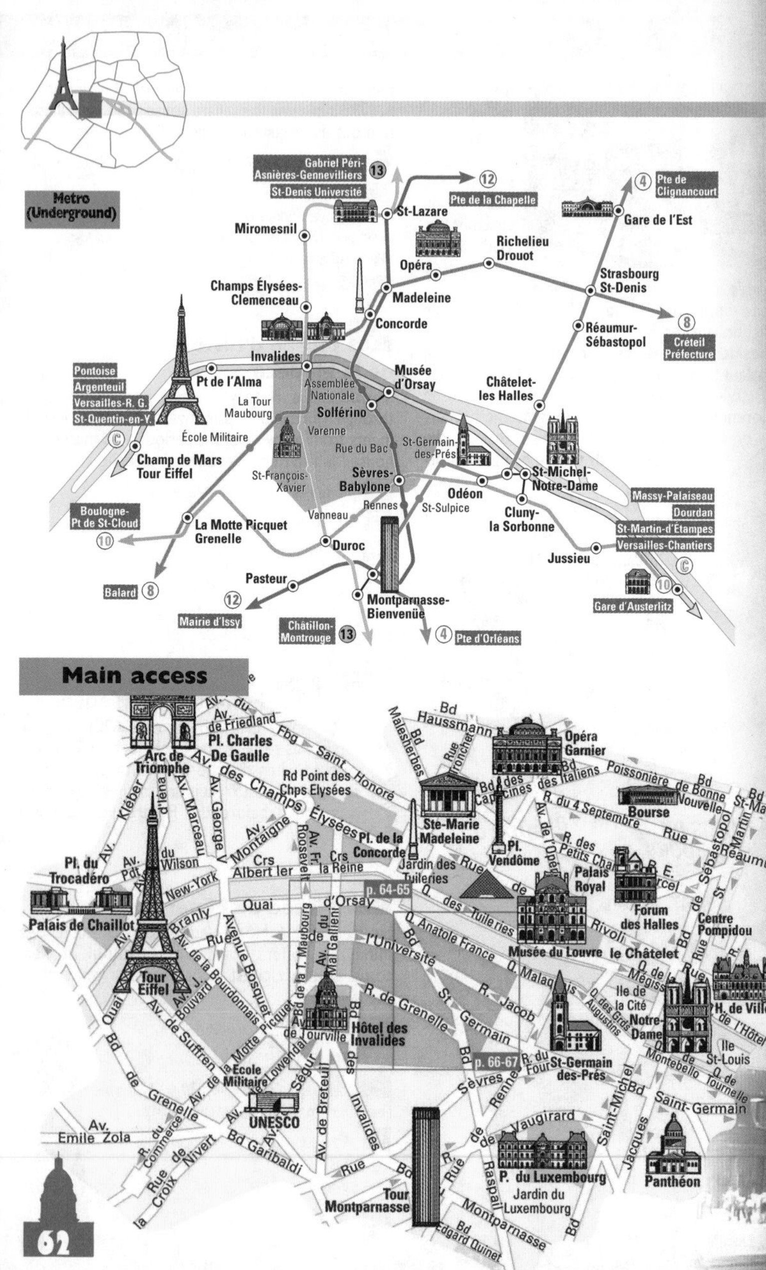
Metro (Underground)
Gabriel Péri-Asnières-Gennevilliers
St-Denis Université
13
12
Pte de la Chapelle
4
Pte de Clignancourt
St-Lazare
Gare de l'Est
Miromesnil
Richelieu Drouot
Opéra
Strasbourg St-Denis
Champs Élysées-Clemenceau
Madeleine
Concorde
8
Créteil Préfecture
Réaumur-Sébastopol
Invalides
Pontoise
Argenteuil
Versailles-R. G.
St-Quentin-en-Y.
Pt de l'Alma
Assemblée Nationale
Musée d'Orsay
Châtelet-les Halles
La Tour Maubourg
Solférino
C
École Militaire
Varenne
Rue du Bac
St-Germain-des-Prés
Champ de Mars Tour Eiffel
St-François-Xavier
Sèvres-Babylone
Odéon
St-Michel-Notre-Dame
Massy-Palaiseau
Dourdan
St-Martin-d'Étampes
Versailles-Chantiers
Boulogne-Pt de St-Cloud
10
Rennes
St-Sulpice
Cluny-la Sorbonne
Vanneau
La Motte Picquet Grenelle
Duroc
Jussieu
Balard
Pasteur
Gare d'Austerlitz
Mairie d'Issy
Montparnasse-Bienvenüe
Châtillon-Montrouge
Pte d'Orléans
Main access
Arc de Triomphe
Pl. Charles De Gaulle
Av. de Friedland
Fbg Saint Honoré
Bd Haussmann
Bd Malesherbes
Rue Tronchet
Opéra Garnier
Av. des Champs Élysées
Rd Point des Chps Elysées
Av. Kléber
Av. d'Iéna
Av. Marceau
Av. George V
Av. Montaigne
Av. Fr. Roosevelt
Ste-Marie Madeleine
Bd des Capucines
Bd des Italiens
Poissonière
Bd de Bonne Nouvelle
Bd St-Martin
Bourse
R. du 4 Septembre
Rue Réaumur
Bd de Sébastopol
Pl. de la Concorde
Pl. Vendôme
Av. de l'Opéra
R. des Petits Champs
Pl. du Trocadéro
Av. Pdt Wilson
Crs Albert Ier
Crs la Reine
Jardin des Tuileries
Rue de Rivoli
Palais Royal
R. E. Marcel
Palais de Chaillot
Av. de New-York
Quai d'Orsay
p. 64-65
Q. des Tuileries
Forum des Halles
Centre Pompidou
Rue Branly
Avenue Bosquet
Bd de la T. Maubourg
Av. du Mal Gallieni
Rue de l'Université
Q. Anatole France
Musée du Louvre
le Châtelet
Av. de la Bourdonnais
Tour Eiffel
Av. J. Bouvard
Hôtel des Invalides
R. de Grenelle
Bd St Germain
Q. Malaquais
R. Jacob
Q. de la Mégisserie
Ile de la Cité
Q. des Grds Augustins
Notre-Dame
H. de Ville
R. de l'Hôtel de Ville
Quai Bd de Grenelle
Av. de Suffren
Av. de la Motte Picquet
Av. de Tourville
Av. de Lowendal
Ecole Militaire
Ségur
Av. de Breteuil
Bd des Invalides
p. 66-67
R. du Four
St-Germain des-Prés
Bd Saint-Michel
Q. de Montebello
Ile St-Louis
Q. de la Tournelle
Bd Saint-Germain
Av. Emile Zola
UNESCO
R. du Commerce
Bd Garibaldi
Rue de Sèvres
Rue de Rennes
Rue de Vaugirard
Rue Saint-Jacques
Rue de la Croix Nivert
Tour Montparnasse
Bd Raspail
P. du Luxembourg
Jardin du Luxembourg
Panthéon
Bd Montparnasse
Bd Edgard Quinet

Invalides

Hôtel des Invalides

Although it was the project of Henri IV, it was Louis XV who, at the end of the 17th century, decided to give the go-ahead for the construction of a building devoted to poor or injured soldiers, hence 'invalides'. The construction was trusted to architect Libéral Bruant. Jules Hardouin-Mansart used his plans to build the church of the Dôme. Under the revolution, it became the Temple of Mars and has housed the ashes of Napoleon I since 1840. The Hôtel has returned to its initial vocation. It also houses 3 museums: the Army Museum, the Museum of Plans and Reliefs and the Museum of the Order of Liberation.

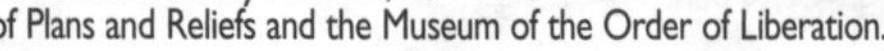

Esplanade des Invalides - *01 44 42 37 72*

Everyday from 10 am to 4.45 pm and until 5.45 pm from the 1st April to 30 September

Admission 6 euros, Reduced rate 4.5 euros, Free for children under 12

28-63-69-87-92

Musée de l'Armée

It houses the royal collections of weapons and armours and the Museum of the History of the Army.

129, rue de Grenelle - *01 44 42 37 72*

Musée de l'Ordre de la Libération

Opened in 1971, it re-traces the history of the occupation and the resistance during the Second World War, through a series of documents and souvenirs donated by the Companions of the Order of Liberation.

51 bis boulevard La Tour Maubourg - *01 47 05 04 10*

Musée des Plans et Reliefs

It contains about a hundred scale model of towns and fortresses. They were used to study military strategy.

6 boulevard des Invalides - *01 45 51 95 05*

Assemblée nationale

It consists in two palaces built at the same period: the Palais Bourbon, built by Girardin for Louise-Françoise de Bourbon, daughter of Louis XIV and the Hôtel de Lassay, which is now the residence of the President of the National Assembly.

It became national property under the revolution. In 1795, a semicircular assembly hall was built to receive the Council of the Five-Hundreds. Later, Napoleon I added the monumental facade with columns symmetrical to those of the church of the Madeleine on the other side of the place de la Concorde.

Major renovation work was carried out between 1828 and 1847 with a new assembly room and a gabled portico on the court side by Joly and new paintings by Delacroix that gave it its present appearance.

33 quai d'Orsay - 01 40 63 61 21

Saturdays at 10 am, 2 and 3 pm. You need proof of identity (national identity card, passport or driving licence)

Free admission - 24-63-73-83-84-93-94

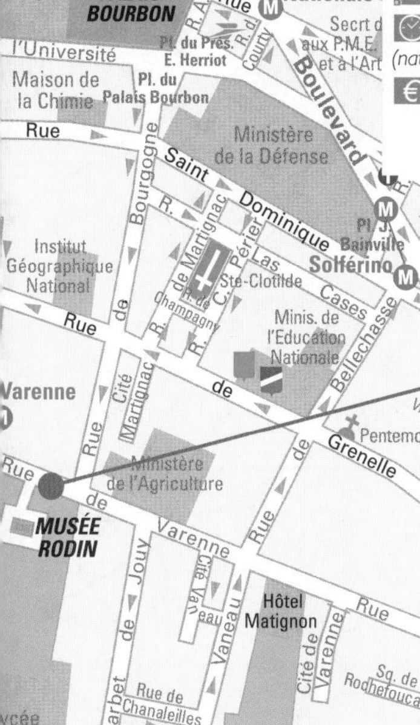

Musée Rodin

It is housed in the Hôtel Biron built at the beginning of the 18th century by Jean Aubert. It was acquired by the state and Rodin lived there a few years before he died. The house was restored and transformed into a museum in 1919. Many bronze and marble works by the artist are on display in the rooms and garden. Upstairs there are private collections. The museum also displays work by Camille Claudel and three paintings by Van Gogh.

77 rue de Varenne - 01 44 18 61 10

Everyday except Mondays, from 9.30 am to 5.45 pm (from 1st April to 30 September) and from 9.30 am to 4.45 pm (from 1st October to 31 March). The garden closed at 6.45 pm in summer and at 5 pm in winter.

Admission 5 euros, Reduced rate 3 euros

69-82-87-92

Palais de la Légion d'honneur (Hôtel de Salm)

In this palace built at the end of the 18th century, Bonaparte housed the order of the Legion d'Honneur 1802. A museum traces the history of the orders of chivalry and the creation of the legion of hono through a collection of objects and documents.

2 rue de la Légion d'honneur - 01 40 62 84 25

63-68-69-73-83-84-94

Rues de l'Université, de Lille, Saint-Dominique, de Grenelle

These streets are lined with many 18th century hôtels: Hôtel Pozzo di Borgo, Hôtel de Beauharnais, Hôtel de Seiguelay (the Trade Ministry), Hôtel de Sénectère, Hôtel de Fleury, Hôtel de Bienne, Hôtel de Noirmoutier, Hôtel du Châtelet and the Hôtel de Tavannes which dates from the 17th century. They are often occupied by adminsitrations or institutions.

Musée Maillol

Dina Vierny was Maillol's model. When she inherited his estate, she created this museum to present a great part of his paintings and sculptures. About twenty statues are displayed in the Tuileries gardens. There are also paintings by Gaugin, Bonnard, Le Douanier Rousseau and Kandinsky.

61 rue de Grenelle - 01 42 22 59 58

Everyday, except Tuesdays, from 11 am to 6 pm

Admission 7 euros, Reduced rate 5.50 euros

63-68-69-83-84

Hôtel Matignon

It has been the Prime Minister's residence since 1958. It was built by Jean-Baptiste Courtonne at the beginning of the 18th century for Prince Tinguy but was later bought by Jacques de Matignon and Talleyrand. For a time, it also became the Embassy of Austria-Hungary.
It boasts impressive interior decorations and a beautiful garden.

57 rue de Varenne - 01 42 75 80 00

69-82-87-92

M Musée d'Orsay

ıe Palais d'Orsay where the State Council and ɛ Account Court sat was destroyed during the ɔts of the Paris Commune. Instead, the Orléans ıil Company built a new station which was finisd in time for the 1900 Universal Exhibition. hen the station became too small, its hall was ed for auctions or as a theatre before narrowly caping destruction. The conversion into a late th and early 20th century art museum was decid in 1977. The museum opened in 1986.

The impressionists with their predecessors and successors are given pride of place. All the schools of painting, sculpture, archi-

tecture, cinema and graphic and decorative arts are represented.

The paintings that must be seen, amongst others, are: The Rouen Cathedral, harmony in blue by Claude Monet (1893), the Ball at the Moulin de la Galette, Montmartre, by Auguste Renoir (1876), the Circus by George Seurat (1890-1891), the Churchof Auvers-sur-Oise by Vincent Van Gogh (1890).

62 rue de Lille

01 40 49 48 14

Everyday, except Mondays, from 10 am to 6 pm, late opening Thursdays from 10 am to 9.45 pm, Sundays from 9 am to 6 pm

Permanent Collections
Admission 7 euros,
Reduced rate 5 euros, Free for children under 18
Temporary Exhibitions
Admission 8.50 euros, Reduced rate 6.50 euros

24-63-68-69-73-83-84-94

Web *www.musee-orsay.fr*

Église Saint Thomas-d'Aquin

In this palace built at the end of the 18th century, Bonaparte housed the order of the Legion d'Honneur in 1802. A museum traces the history of the orders of chivalry and the creation of the legion of honour through a collection of objects and documents.

1 rue Montalembert - *01 42 22 59 74*

39-68-69

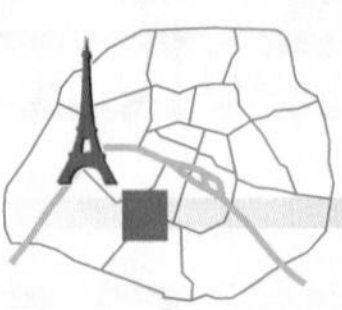

Metro (Underground)

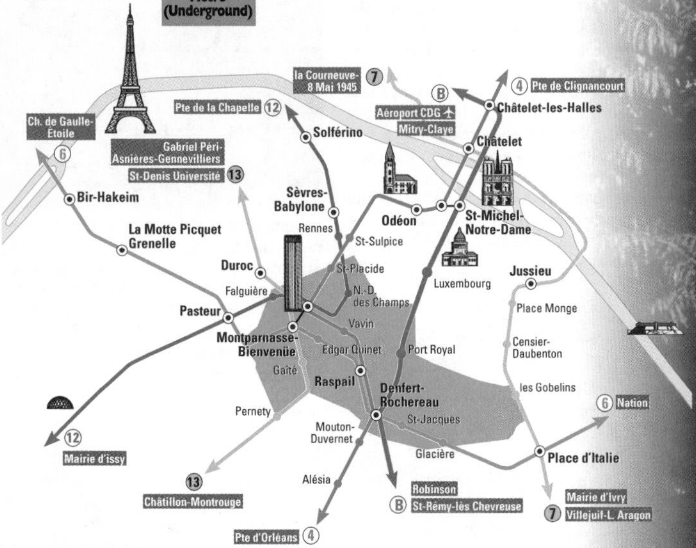

la Courneuve-8 Mai 1945
7
Pte de la Chapelle
12
Ch. de Gaulle-Étoile
6
Gabriel Péri-Asnières-Gennevilliers
St-Denis Université
13
Aéroport CDG
Mitry-Claye
B
4
Pte de Clignancourt
Châtelet-les-Halles
Châtelet
Solférino
Bir-Hakeim
Sèvres-Babylone
Rennes
St-Sulpice
Odéon
St-Michel-Notre-Dame
La Motte Picquet Grenelle
Duroc
St-Placide
Luxembourg
Jussieu
Falguière
N.-D. des Champs
Pasteur
Place Monge
Vavin
Montparnasse-Bienvenüe
Edgar Quinet
Port Royal
Censier-Daubenton
Gaîté
Raspail
Denfert-Rochereau
les Gobelins
6
Nation
Pernety
St-Jacques
12
Mairie d'issy
Mouton-Duvernet
Glacière
Place d'Italie
13
Châtillon-Montrouge
Alésia
Robinson
B
St-Rémy-lès Chevreuse
Mairie d'Ivry
7
Villejuif-L. Aragon
Pte d'Orléans
4

Main access

Hôtel des Invalides
Ecole Militaire
UNESCO
St-Germain des-Prés
Ile de la Cité
Notre-Dame
H. de Ville
Ile St-Louis
St-Louis en l'Ile
Palais du Luxembourg
Jardin du Luxembourg
Panthéon
Muséum Nat. d'Histoire Naturelle
Jardin des Plantes
Gare d'Austerlitz
Val de Grâce
Tour Montparnasse
Gare Montparnasse
Cimetière du Montparnasse
Pl. Denfert Rochereau
Place d'Italie
p. 70-71
p. 72-73
p. 74-75
Av. de Suffren
Av. de Tourville
Av. de Breteuil
Bd des Invalides
R. de Grenelle
Bd St-Germain
R. Jacob
Q. Malaquais
R. de Sèvres
R. de Rennes
R. du Four
Bd Saint-Michel
Bd Saint-Germain
R. de Vaugirard
Bd Garibaldi
Bd Pasteur
R. Lecourbe
Bd de Vaugirard
Bd Edgard Quinet
Bd Montparnasse
Bd Raspail
Bd de Port Royal
Bd Arago
Bd St-Marcel
Bd de l'Hôpital
R. Monge
Av. des Gobelins
Bd St-Jacques
Bd Auguste Blanqui
Av. d'Italie
Av. de Choisy
R. de Tolbiac
R. d'Alésia
Av. du Maine
R. Raymond Losserand
R. de la Convention
R. de Vouillé
R. Brancion
R. St-Antoine
Bd Henri IV
Q. St-Bernard

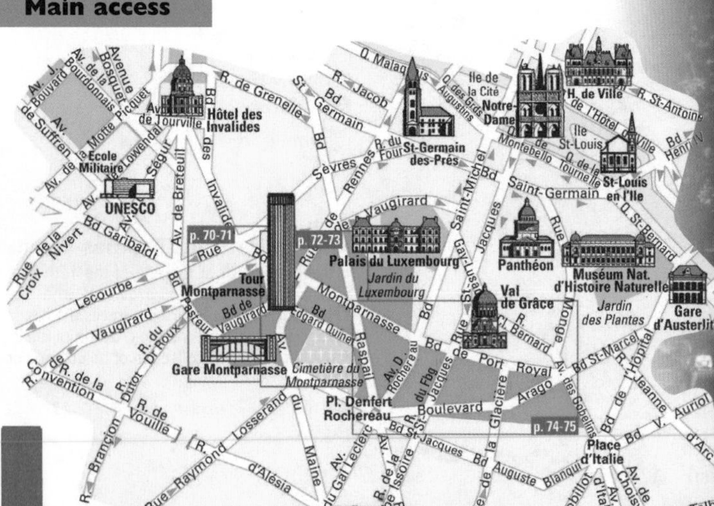

Montparnasse

Musée Bourdelle

The museum is housed in the studio and home that Antoine Bourdelle occupied from 1885 to his death in 1929. A wide range of his work (marble, plaster and bronze) is on display in the house(which has already been extended twice) and garden.

16 rue Antoine Bourdelle

01 49 54 73 73

Everyday, except Mondays, from 10 am to 6 pm

Free admission for permanent collections, Temporary exhibitions 4.5 euros, over 60s 3 euros, from 14 to 26 2 euros, free for the under 13

48-58-88-91-94-95-96

Musée de la Poste

It is the postal world through the ages that we find in this museum. How the mail was forwarded and the evolution of the different means used (horses, coaches, trains and planes) to carry messages faster and further. It traces the history of stamps and the way they were made. There are stamp collections, uniforms, calendars and post boxes.

31 boulevard de Vaugirard

01 42 33 06 67

Mondays to Fridays from 9 am to 6 pm

67-74-85

Musée du Montparnasse

This small museum offers 20th century paintings a exhibitions in a lovely green setting.

21 avenue du Maine

01 42 22 91 96

Wednesdays to Sundays from 1 pm to 7 pm

Admission 3.80 euros, Reduced rate 3.05 euros

28-58-92-94-96

Jardin Atlantique

Landscaped in 1944, it was designed to suggest the ocean, the destination of the trains, underneath. It includes theme gardens, play areas, sports grounds and 5 tennis courts.

Place de Catalogne, place de Séoul

The buildings that surround these squares were designed by Ricardo Boffil in his typical neo-classical style. The huge fountain, th 'Crucible of Time' is by Shamaï Haber.

Rue

R. Séguard

R. Brown

R. Mizon

Bd

Bd

Pas. Alexandre

Pasteur

Galerie

Tour Montparnasse

Opposite the station of the same name, stands the tower started in 1973. It is 200 m tall and has 59 floors. It takes 38 seconds to reach the top and the terrace with its wonderful panoramic views of Paris and its surroundings, on a good day.

33 avenue du Maine - *01 45 38 52 56*

Everyday from 9.30 am to 10.30 pm and 11.30 pm in summer

Ticket to the 59th floor 7.6 euros, Reduced rate 6.5 euros to the 56th floor 6.4 euros, Reduced rate 5.7 euros

28-82-89-92-94-95-96

Musée du Maréchal Leclerc de Hauteclocque et de la Libération de Paris - Musée Jean Moulin

Documents, photographs of the time, archives and mementoes retrace the life of these two men, heroes of the liberation of Paris (the Free French Forces) and of the Resistance during the Second World War.

23 allée de la 2e DB - *01 40 64 39 44*

Everyday, except Mondays, from 10 am to 5.40 pm

Admission free to Permanent Collections, Temporary Collections 4 euros, over 60s 3 euros, 14 to 26 years old 2 euros, Free for children under 13

28-48-58-91-92-94-95-96

La Coupole, le Dôme, la Rotonde, le Select

This is where artists met at the end of the 19th and beginning of the 20th centuries. They had their heydays in the 'Années Folles'. Blaise Cendrars, Modigliani, Matisse, Trotski, Sartre and Becket were regular patrons.

Rue de la Gaîté

This street is in some ways the symbol of this district, thriving, especially at night, with restaurants, cabarets and theatres.

Cimetière du Montparnasse

It is also called the South Side Cemetery. Opened in 1824 to replace the cemeteries that had been closed in the centre of Paris. Many artists are buried there including Baudelaire, Maupassant, Sartre, Simone de Beauvoir, Saint-Saëns and Bartholdi.

3 boulevard Edgar Quinet

01 44 10 86 50

Everyday from 8 am to 5.30 pm

68-88

0 — 250 m
0 — 5 mn

Musée Zadkine

This museum was founded in 1984 thanks to the donation made by the artist's wife to the city of Paris. Several rooms trace the evolution of Oship Zadkine's work through his sculptures in wood, stone, bronze and clay.

100 bis rue d'Assas

01 43 26 91 90

Everyday, except Mondays, from 10 am to 5.40 pm

Free Admission to Permanent Collections, Temporary collections 4 euros, over 60s 3 euros, 14 to 26 years old 2 euros, free for children under 13

68-88

Fondation Cartier

The glass and steel building was designed by architect Jean Nouvel. Since 1994, it has been Cartier's headquarters in France. It has exhibition rooms displaying work by contemporary artists from all the world.

261 boulevard Raspail - *01 42 18 56 51*

Everyday, except Mondays, from 12 noon to 8 pm, Nomad Night on Thursdays at 8.30 pm

Admission rate 5 euros, Reduced rate 3.5 euros, Free for children under 10

38-68

Web *www.fondation.cartier.fr*

Abbaye de Port-Royal

Only the chapel, the cloister and part of the convent are left of the abbey founded in the 17th century by the Cistercian sisters of Port-Royal des Champs in the Chevreuse Valley. They are now part of the Port-Royal Maternity Hospital.

Place Denfert-Rochereau

The copy of the Lion of Belfort pays tribute to the heroism of Colonel Denfert-Rochereau and his troops when they defended the town of Belfort during the 1870-1871 war.

Fontaine de l'Observatoire

ıated on the axe of the Paris Meridian, this magni-ınt fountain was inaugurated in 1874. It is the ırk of Jean-Baptiste Carpeaux (the Four Parts of World), Eugene Legrain (the Globe) and Emanuel ınet (the horses, dolphins and tortoises).

Observatoire de Paris

The idea for the observatory came from Louis XIV and Colbert, his minister. Its axe defined the Prime Meridian until 1911 when it was replaced by Greenwich. With its sides facing the four cardinal points, it is the oldest observatory in the world.

61 av. de l'Observatoire - 01 40 51 22 21

Open on the first Saturday of the month at 2.30 pm

Admission 4.6 euros, Reduced rate 2.3 euros

38-83-91 - Web www.obspm.fr

Manufacture des Gobelins

Founded by Colbert in the 17th century and housed in the property of the Gobelin family. It still produces tapestries and rugs using the traditional techniques of the time.

42 avenue des Gobelins 01 44 08 52 00

Guided visits on Tuesdays, Wednesdays and Thursdays at 2 pm and 2.45 pm

Admission 8 euros, free for children under 7

27-47-83-91

Catacombes

ıas at the end of the 18th century that the skeleıns from the disused cemeteries in the centre of is were moved to the old quarries.

1 place Denfert-Rochereau

01 43 22 47 63

Tuesdays to Fridays from 2 pm to 4 pm, Saturdays and Sundays from 9 am to 11 am and from 2 pm to 4 pm

Admission 4.10 euros, Reduced rate 2.90 euros

38-68

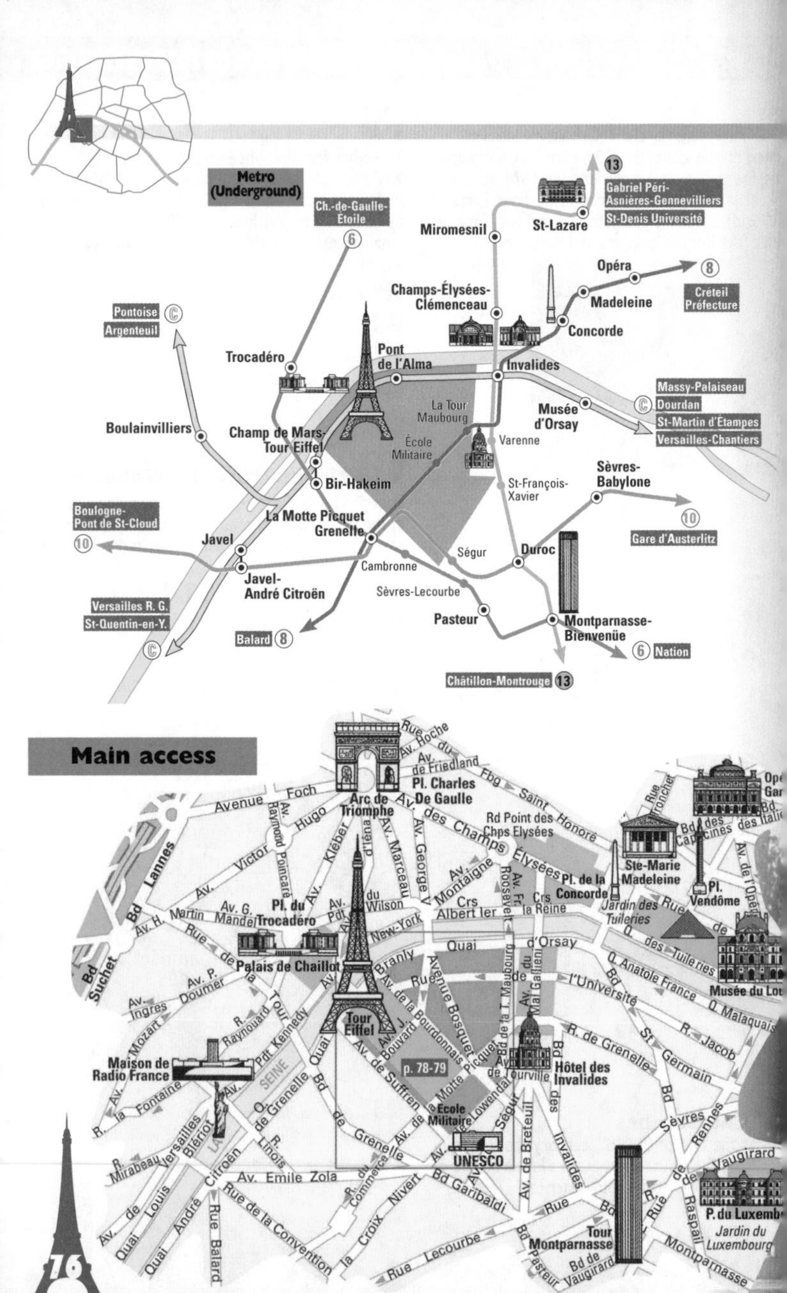
Metro (Underground)
Ch.-de-Gaulle-Etoile
6
13
Gabriel Péri-Asnières-Gennevilliers
St-Denis Université
Miromesnil
St-Lazare
Opéra
8
Créteil Préfecture
Champs-Élysées-Clémenceau
Madeleine
Concorde
Pontoise
Argenteuil
C
Trocadéro
Pont de l'Alma
Invalides
La Tour Maubourg
Musée d'Orsay
Massy-Palaiseau
Dourdan
St-Martin d'Étampes
Versailles-Chantiers
Boulainvilliers
Champ de Mars-Tour Eiffel
École Militaire
Varenne
Bir-Hakeim
St-François-Xavier
Sèvres-Babylone
Boulogne-Pont de St-Cloud
10
La Motte Picquet Grenelle
Gare d'Austerlitz
Javel
Ségur
Duroc
Cambronne
Javel-André Citroën
Sèvres-Lecourbe
Versailles R. G.
St-Quentin-en-Y.
Pasteur
Montparnasse-Bienvenüe
Balard
Nation
Châtillon-Montrouge
Main access
Arc de Triomphe
Pl. Charles De Gaulle
Rue Hoche
Av. de Friedland
Rue du Fbg Saint Honoré
Avenue Foch
Av. Raymond Poincaré
Hugo
Av. Kléber
Av. d'Iéna
Av. Marceau
Av. George V
Av. des Champs Élysées
Rd Point des Chps Elysées
Rue Tronchet
Bd des Capucines
Bd. des Italiens
Opéra Garnier
Bd Lannes
Av. Victor
Av. Montaigne
Av. Fr. Roosevelt
Pl. de la Concorde
Ste-Marie Madeleine
Pl. Vendôme
Av. de l'Opéra
Av. H. Martin
Av. G. Mandel
Pl. du Trocadéro
Av. Pdt Wilson
Av. du
Crs Albert Ier
Crs la Reine
Jardin des Tuileries
Rue de
New-York
Quai d'Orsay
Q. des Tuileries
Bd Suchet
Rue de la Tour
Palais de Chaillot
Av. Branly
Rue de
Avenue Bosquet
Bd de la T. Maubourg
Av. du Mal Gallieni
Rue de l'Université
Q. Anatole France
Musée du Louvre
Av. P. Doumer
Av. Ingres
Av. de la Bourdonnais
Bd St Germain
R. Jacob
Q. Malaquais
Av. Mozart
R. Raynouard
Pdt Kennedy
Quai
Tour Eiffel
Av. J. Bouvard
R. de Grenelle
Maison de Radio France
SEINE
Av. de Suffren
p. 78-79
Av. Motte Picquet
Av. de Tourville
Hôtel des Invalides
Bd des Invalides
Av. R. la Fontaine
Q. de Grenelle
Bd de Grenelle
Av. de Lowendal
École Militaire
Av. de Ségur
Av. de Breteuil
Bd Raspail
Rue de Sèvres
Bd de Rennes
R. Mirabeau
Versailles
Blériot
R. Linois
Av. de Saxe
UNESCO
Rue de Vaugirard
Av. Emile Zola
R. du Commerce
Av. Citroën
Rue de la Convention
Rue Balard
Av. de Quai Louis
Quai André
Rue de la Croix Nivert
Bd Garibaldi
Rue Lecourbe
Bd Pasteur
Bd de Vaugirard
Tour Montparnasse
P. du Luxembourg
Jardin du Luxembourg
Bd Montparnasse
76

Tour Eiffel

Tour Eiffel

It stands proud as the symbol of Paris. Although, its construction was a technical feat, it was heavily criticised when first built until its dimension made it an excellent radio transmitter. 300 m high, it took Gustave Eiffel, his teams of engineers and workers two years to assemble the 1800 beams and metal parts using 2.5 million rivets. It was completed on time for the 1889 Universal Exhibition where it was a great success. It has become one of the most visited monuments in the world, each floor offering a unique and unforgettable view of Paris.

Champ de Mars

01 44 11 23 23

9.30 am to 11 pm in (winter) and 9 am to 12 midnight (summer)

Elevator to 1st floor 3.70 euros, 2.30 euros – 2nd floor 7 euros, 3.90 euros Top floor 10.20 euros, 5.50 euros. Stairs to the 2nd floor, single rate 3.30 euros. Free for children under 3

42-69-72-82-87 - Web *www.tour-eiffel.fr*

Champ de Mars

It was intended as a practice field for the Military School. In 1794, it became the venue for the Feast of the Federation and it was turned into a racing course in 1833. Several Universal Exhibitions were held there before it was transformed into a public garden at the beginning of the 20th century. It is a popular area for a stroll. It is also the venue for mass gatherings and events. Since the year 2000, the Wall of Peace welcomes the peace messages of many visitors.

École Militaire

It was Louis XIV, who encouraged by his mistress Madame de Pompadour, decided t open a military school to train penniless young o cers. The classical building was designed by Jacque Ange Gabriel. It is topped by a quadrangular dom Napoleon Bonaparte was probably its most famo students. It still houses a military training centre a barracks.

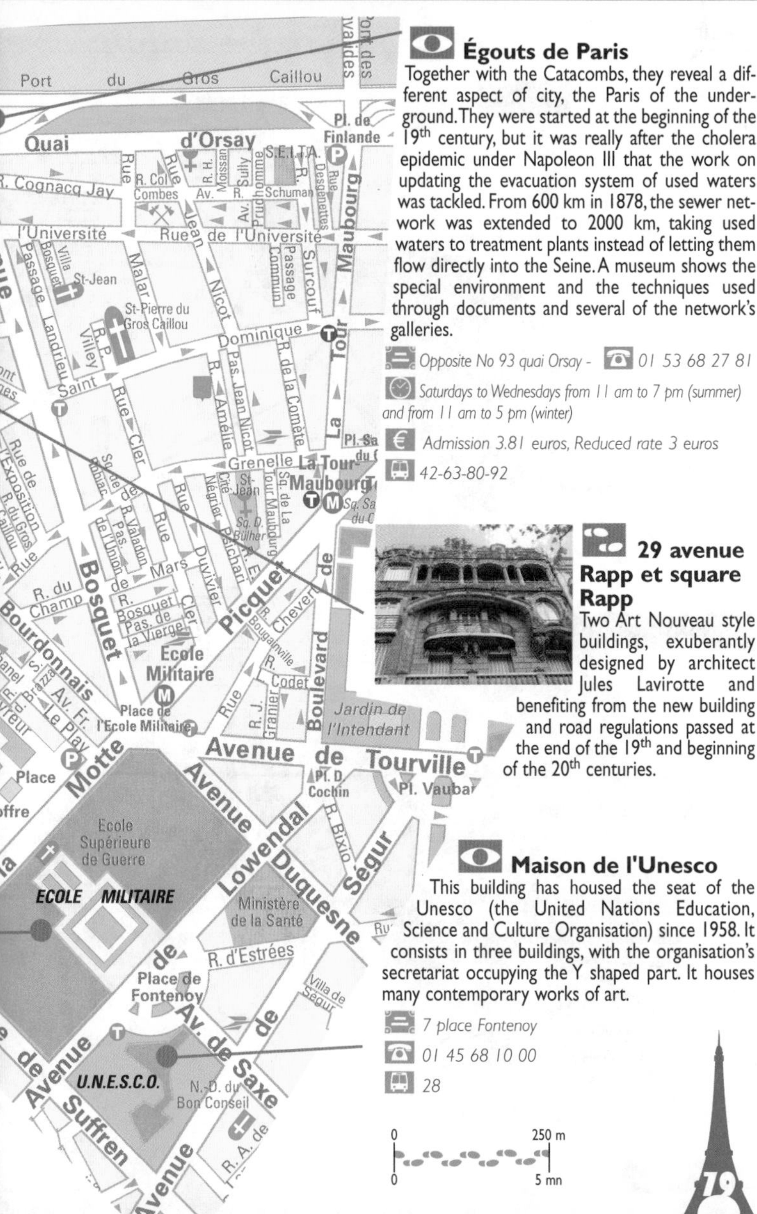

Égouts de Paris

Together with the Catacombs, they reveal a different aspect of city, the Paris of the underground. They were started at the beginning of the 19th century, but it was really after the cholera epidemic under Napoleon III that the work on updating the evacuation system of used waters was tackled. From 600 km in 1878, the sewer network was extended to 2000 km, taking used waters to treatment plants instead of letting them flow directly into the Seine. A museum shows the special environment and the techniques used through documents and several of the network's galleries.

Opposite No 93 quai Orsay - *01 53 68 27 81*

Saturdays to Wednesdays from 11 am to 7 pm (summer) and from 11 am to 5 pm (winter)

Admission 3.81 euros, Reduced rate 3 euros

42-63-80-92

29 avenue Rapp et square Rapp

Two Art Nouveau style buildings, exuberantly designed by architect Jules Lavirotte and benefiting from the new building and road regulations passed at the end of the 19th and beginning of the 20th centuries.

Maison de l'Unesco

This building has housed the seat of the Unesco (the United Nations Education, Science and Culture Organisation) since 1958. It consists in three buildings, with the organisation's secretariat occupying the Y shaped part. It houses many contemporary works of art.

7 place Fontenoy

01 45 68 10 00

28

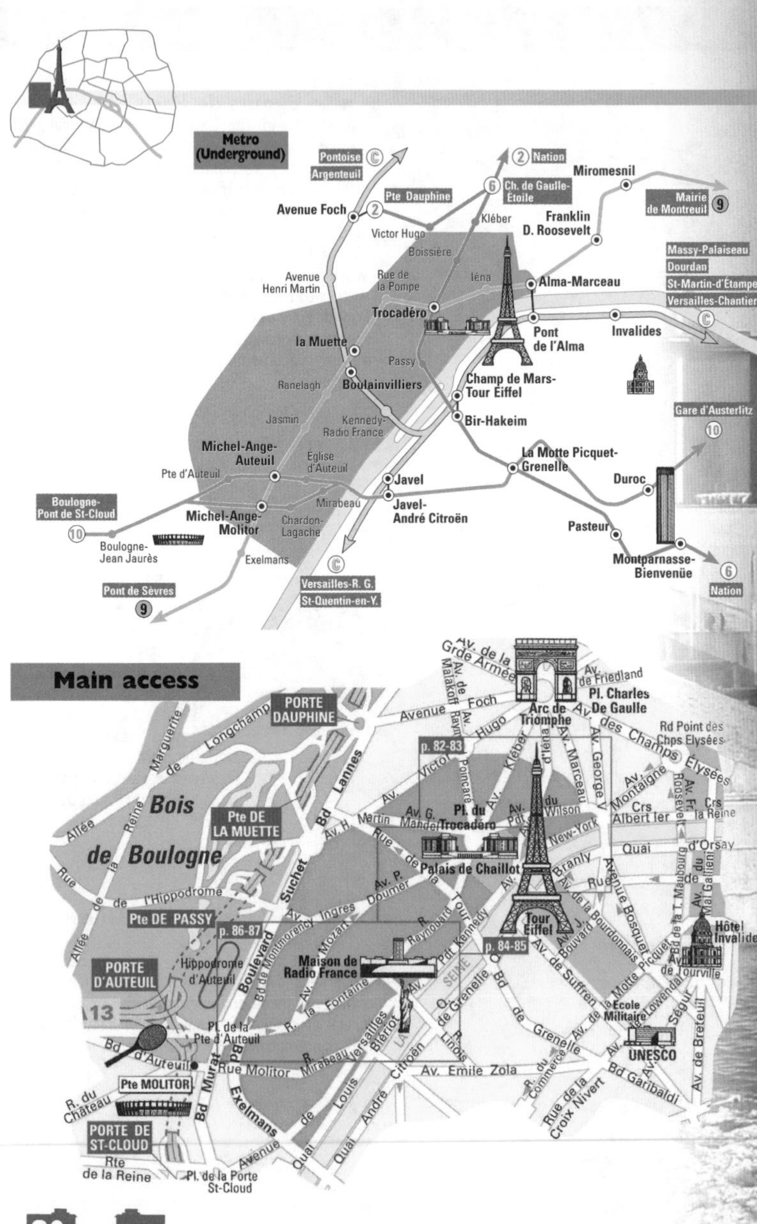

Metro (Underground)
Pontoise
Argenteuil
C
2 Nation
Miromesnil
6 Ch. de Gaulle-Étoile
Pte Dauphine
Avenue Foch
2
Victor Hugo
Kléber
Franklin D. Roosevelt
Mairie de Montreuil
9
Boissière
Massy-Palaiseau
Dourdan
St-Martin-d'Étampes
Versailles-Chantiers
Avenue Henri Martin
Rue de la Pompe
Iéna
Alma-Marceau
Trocadéro
Pont de l'Alma
Invalides
la Muette
Passy
Ranelagh
Boulainvilliers
Champ de Mars-Tour Eiffel
Bir-Hakeim
Gare d'Austerlitz
10
Jasmin
Kennedy-Radio France
Michel-Ange-Auteuil
Église d'Auteuil
La Motte Picquet-Grenelle
Pte d'Auteuil
Javel
Duroc
Boulogne-Pont de St-Cloud
Mirabeau
Javel-André Citroën
Michel-Ange-Molitor
Chardon-Lagache
Pasteur
10
Boulogne-Jean Jaurès
Exelmans
Montparnasse-Bienvenüe
6
Nation
Pont de Sèvres
9
Versailles-R. G.
St-Quentin-en-Y.
Main access
Av. de la Grde Armée
Av. de Malakoff
Av. de Friedland
Pl. Charles De Gaulle
Arc de Triomphe
PORTE DAUPHINE
Longchamp
Avenue Foch
Av. Raymond Poincaré
Av. Victor Hugo
Av. Kléber
Av. d'Iéna
Av. Marceau
Av. George V
Av. des Champs Élysées
Rd Point des Chps Elysées
p. 82-83
de Marguerite
Bd Lannes
Bois de Boulogne
Allée de la Reine
Pte DE LA MUETTE
Av. H. Martin
Av. G. Mandel
Pl. du Trocadéro
Av. du Pdt Wilson
Av. Montaigne
Av. Fr. Roosevelt
Crs Albert Ier
Crs la Reine
Av. New-York
Quai d'Orsay
Palais de Chaillot
Rue de la Pompe
Branly
Rue
Avenue Bosquet
Av. du Mal Gallieni
Bd Suchet
Rue de l'Hippodrome
Av. P. Doumer
Av. Ingres
R. Raynouard
Tour Eiffel
Av. de la Bourdonnais
Bd de la T. Maubourg
Hôtel Invalides
Pte DE PASSY
p. 86-87
Bd de Montmorency
Av. Mozart
Av. Pdt Kennedy
p. 84-85
Av. J. Bouvard
Av. de Suffren
Av. de la Motte Picquet
Av. de Tourville
PORTE D'AUTEUIL
Hippodrome d'Auteuil
Boulevard
Maison de Radio France
SEINE
Q. de Grenelle
Bd de Grenelle
Ecole Militaire
Av. de Lowendal
Av. de Ségur
A13
R. la Fontaine
Pl. de la Pte d'Auteuil
Av. de Versailles
R. Blériot
R. Linois
Av. du Commerce
UNESCO
Av. de Breteuil
Bd d'Auteuil
R. Mirabeau
Rue Molitor
Quai André Citroën
Av. Emile Zola
Bd Garibaldi
Pte MOLITOR
R. du Château
Bd Murat
Bd Exelmans
Rue de la Croix Nivert
PORTE DE ST-CLOUD
Avenue de Louis
Rte de la Reine
Pl. de la Porte St-Cloud

Trocadéro
Passy

Musée Guimet

It houses the National Museum of Asian Arts. It was set up for Emile Guimet's collections which he had gathered during his travels. He subsequently gave them to the state. Most of Asia is represented from Afghanistan to Japan and Indonesia with Khmer statues from Cambodia, Tibetan bronzes and paintings, silk paintings from Central Asia, Chinese ceramics, works of art and jewellery from India and a large collection of Japanese works of art.

6 place d'Iéna

01 56 52 53 00

Everyday except Tuesdays from 10 am to 6 pm

Admission to exhibition and museum 7 euros, Reduced rate 5 euros, Admission to temporary exhibition 5.5 euros, Reduced rate 4 euros, Reduced rate 18 – 25 and Sundays, Free for children under 18 and every first Sunday of the month

22-30-32-63-82 - Web *www.museeguimet.fr*

Panthéon Bouddhiste

This beautiful extension to the Guimet Museum surrounded by a Japanese garden. It houses a co lection of religious works of art (paintings an sculptures) from China and Japan.

19 avenue d'Iéna - *01 56 52 53 00*

Everyday except Tuesdays from 9.45 am to 5.45 pm

32-82

Cimetière de Passy

Created at the beginning of the 19th century, it is a very green cemetery where we can find the graves of Tristan Bernard, Claude Debussy, Edouard Manet and the actor Fernandel.

2 rue du Cdt Schlœsing - *01 47 27 51 42*

22-30-32

Palais Galliera

)uchess Galleria had this palace built at the end of ıe 19th century to house her art collections. lthough they were finally given to Genova, Paris ept the museum. It was turned over to the world f fashion and costumes in 1977. Three centuries of reativity are presented through a collection of ver 70 000 costumes, jewellery and accessories.

10 av. Pierre Ier de Serbie - 01 56 52 86 00

Everyday except Mondays from 10 am to 6 pm

Admission 7 euros, Reduced rate 5.50 euros

32

Église Saint-Pierre-de-Chaillot

Built in the 1930s by Emile Bois, it presents an imposing facade with a pediment carved by Henri Bouchard and inspired by the life of Saint Peter.

26 rue de Chaillot

01 47 20 12 33

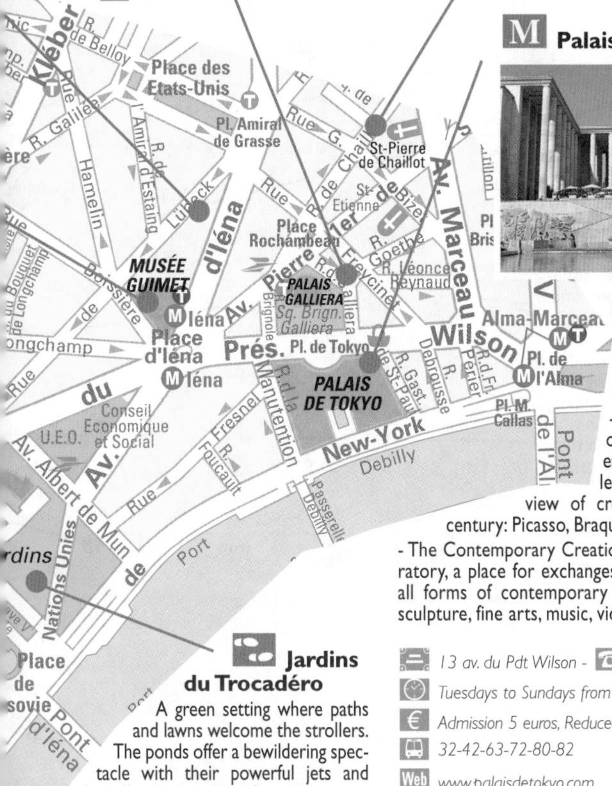

Palais de Tokyo

Built for the 1937 Universal Exhibition, it now houses two museums:

- The Paris Museum of Modern Art in the eastern wing. The collections offer a broad view of creativity in the 20th century: Picasso, Braque, Delaunay, Dufy…

- The Contemporary Creation Site is also a laboratory, a place for exchanges and a showcase for all forms of contemporary creativity (paintings, sculpture, fine arts, music, videos…).

13 av. du Pdt Wilson - 01 47 23 54 01

Tuesdays to Sundays from 12 noon to midnight

Admission 5 euros, Reduced rate 3 euros

32-42-63-72-80-82

www.palaisdetokyo.com

Jardins du Trocadéro

A green setting where paths and lawns welcome the strollers. The ponds offer a bewildering spectacle with their powerful jets and their illuminations at night.

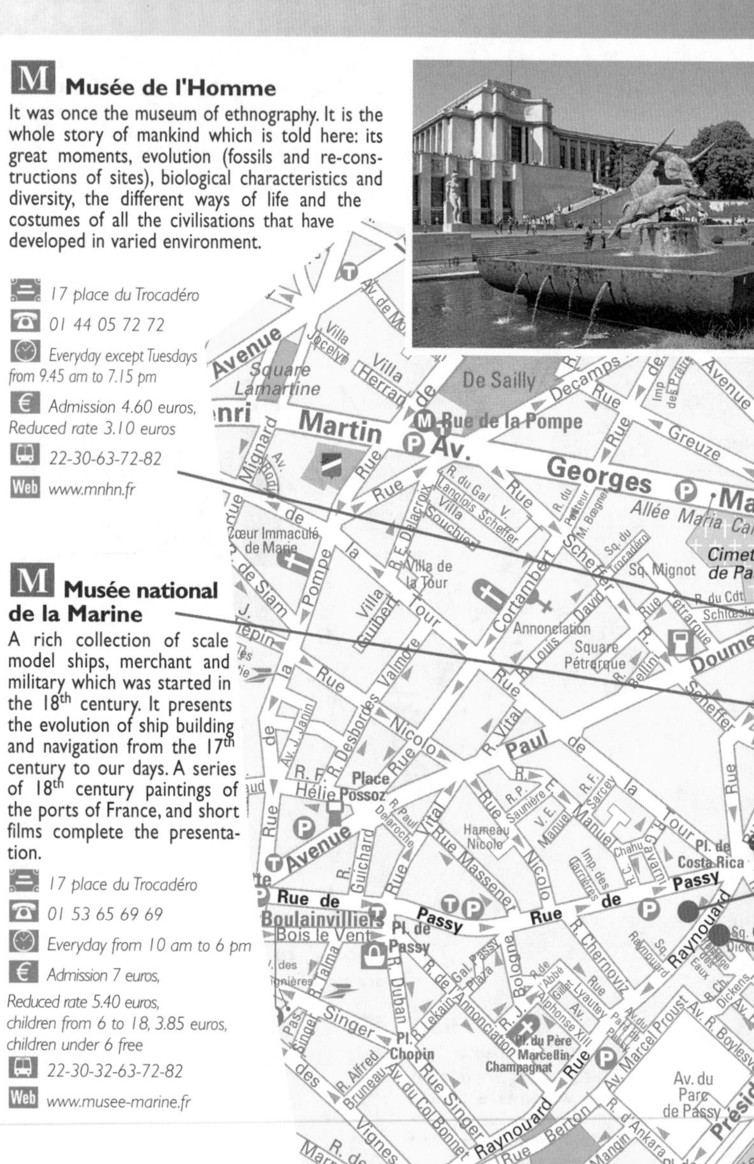

M Musée de l'Homme

It was once the museum of ethnography. It is the whole story of mankind which is told here: its great moments, evolution (fossils and re-constructions of sites), biological characteristics and diversity, the different ways of life and the costumes of all the civilisations that have developed in varied environment.

17 place du Trocadéro

01 44 05 72 72

Everyday except Tuesdays from 9.45 am to 7.15 pm

Admission 4.60 euros, Reduced rate 3.10 euros

22-30-63-72-82

www.mnhn.fr

M Musée national de la Marine

A rich collection of scale model ships, merchant and military which was started in the 18th century. It presents the evolution of ship building and navigation from the 17th century to our days. A series of 18th century paintings of the ports of France, and short films complete the presentation.

17 place du Trocadéro

01 53 65 69 69

Everyday from 10 am to 6 pm

Admission 7 euros, Reduced rate 5.40 euros, children from 6 to 18, 3.85 euros, children under 6 free

22-30-32-63-72-82

www.musee-marine.fr

Palais de Chaillot

The foundations are the only things left from the old Trocadéro Palace on which the Palais Chaillot was built for the 1937 Universal Exhibition. The Court of Human rights and Liberties stands between the two wings and offers a wonderful view over Paris and over the Trocadéro Garden and the Champ de Mars. The buildings house several museums, the Chaillot National Theatre and the French Film Archives, cinema's true memory.

Musée des Monuments français

It is closed for the time being and is due to reopen in 2005, as part of the Architecture and Heritage Museum. Through mouldings, scale models, photos and documents we can discover French monuments and different aspects of architectural creativity.

1 place du Trocadéro - *01 44 05 39 10*

Closed for renovation until 2005

Musée Clemenceau

In this apartment, where Clemenceau lived from 1895 to his death in 1929, documents and photos re-trace the life of the politician.

8 rue Benjamin Franklin

01 45 20 53 41 - *22-32*

Rue Raynouard, rue de Passy

They remind us of the what the village of Passy was like before it was attached to Paris in 1859. We can find the work of the Perret brothers at numbers 51 and 55 of the rue Raynouard.

Musée du Vin

Housed in the old quarries which were turned into cellars by the monks of the Passy monastery (15th century), the museum takes us through the world of vineyards and French wine thanks to farming and winemaking tools, wine tasting and vintage wines, conferences and seminars.

rue des Eaux, 5 square Charles Dickens - *01 45 25 63 26*

Everyday except Mondays from 10 am to 5.40 pm - *6 euros* - *72*

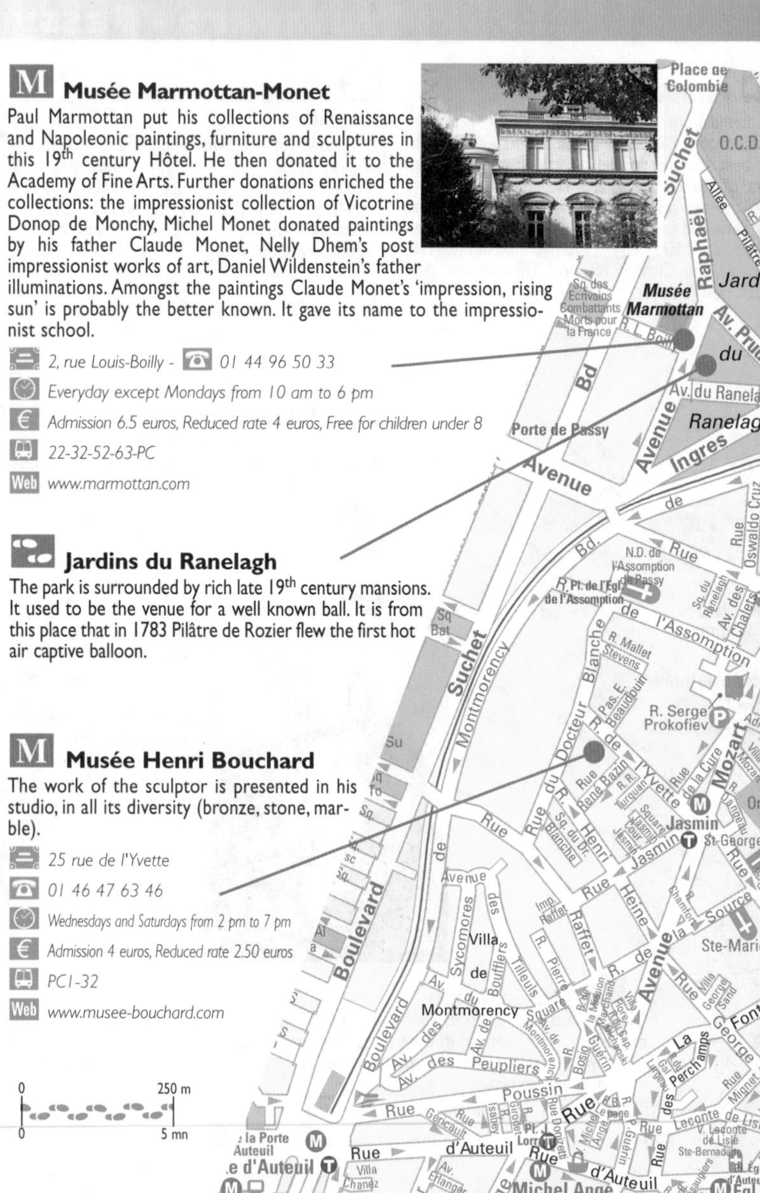

Musée Marmottan-Monet

Paul Marmottan put his collections of Renaissance and Napoleonic paintings, furniture and sculptures in this 19th century Hôtel. He then donated it to the Academy of Fine Arts. Further donations enriched the collections: the impressionist collection of Vicotrine Donop de Monchy, Michel Monet donated paintings by his father Claude Monet, Nelly Dhem's post impressionist works of art, Daniel Wildenstein's father illuminations. Amongst the paintings Claude Monet's 'impression, rising sun' is probably the better known. It gave its name to the impressionist school.

2, rue Louis-Boilly - 01 44 96 50 33

Everyday except Mondays from 10 am to 6 pm

Admission 6.5 euros, Reduced rate 4 euros, Free for children under 8

22-32-52-63-PC

Web *www.marmottan.com*

Jardins du Ranelagh

The park is surrounded by rich late 19th century mansions. It used to be the venue for a well known ball. It is from this place that in 1783 Pilâtre de Rozier flew the first hot air captive balloon.

Musée Henri Bouchard

The work of the sculptor is presented in his studio, in all its diversity (bronze, stone, marble).

25 rue de l'Yvette

01 46 47 63 46

Wednesdays and Saturdays from 2 pm to 7 pm

Admission 4 euros, Reduced rate 2.50 euros

PC1-32

Web *www.musee-bouchard.com*

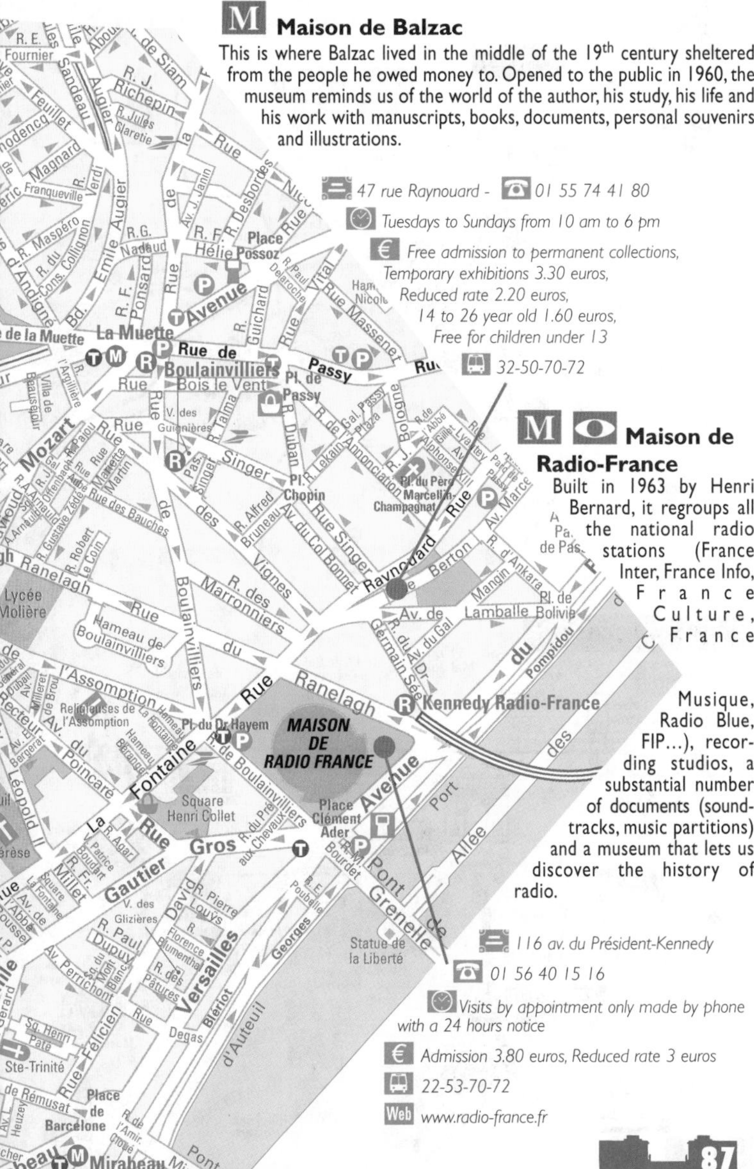

Maison de Balzac

This is where Balzac lived in the middle of the 19th century sheltered from the people he owed money to. Opened to the public in 1960, the museum reminds us of the world of the author, his study, his life and his work with manuscripts, books, documents, personal souvenirs and illustrations.

47 rue Raynouard - *01 55 74 41 80*

Tuesdays to Sundays from 10 am to 6 pm

Free admission to permanent collections,
Temporary exhibitions 3.30 euros,
Reduced rate 2.20 euros,
14 to 26 year old 1.60 euros,
Free for children under 13

32-50-70-72

Maison de Radio-France

Built in 1963 by Henri Bernard, it regroups all the national radio stations (France Inter, France Info, France Culture, France Musique, Radio Blue, FIP...), recording studios, a substantial number of documents (soundtracks, music partitions) and a museum that lets us discover the history of radio.

116 av. du Président-Kennedy

01 56 40 15 16

Visits by appointment only made by phone with a 24 hours notice

Admission 3.80 euros, Reduced rate 3 euros

22-53-70-72

www.radio-france.fr

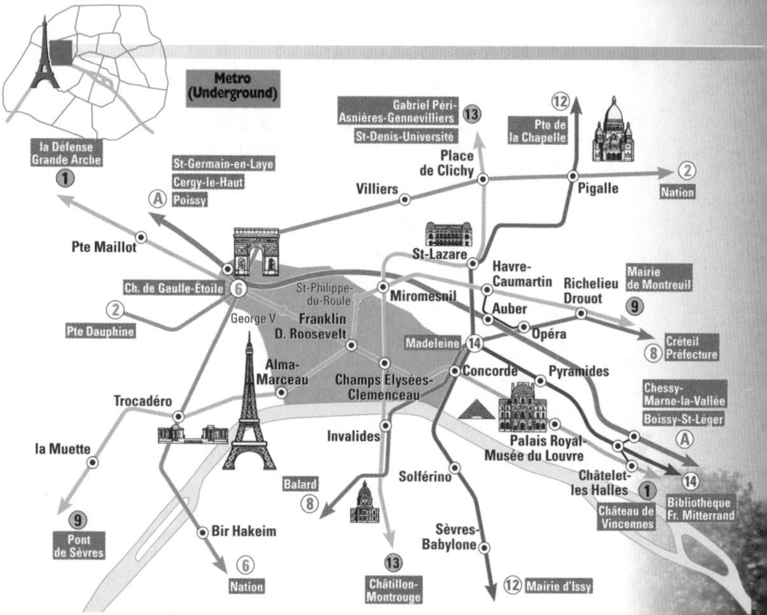

Metro (Underground)

la Défense Grande Arche
1
St-Germain-en-Laye
Cergy-le-Haut
A Poissy
Gabriel Péri-Asnières-Gennevilliers
St-Denis-Université
13
12
Pte de la Chapelle
Place de Clichy
Villiers
Pigalle
2 Nation
Pte Maillot
St-Lazare
Havre-Caumartin
Richelieu Drouot
Mairie de Montreuil
9
Ch. de Gaulle-Étoile
6
St-Philippe-du-Roule
Miromesnil
Auber
Opéra
2
Pte Dauphine
George V
Franklin D. Roosevelt
Madeleine
14
Créteil Préfecture
8
Alma-Marceau
Champs Élysées-Clemenceau
Concorde
Pyramides
Chessy-Marne-la-Vallée
Boissy-St-Léger
A
Trocadéro
Invalides
Palais Royal-Musée du Louvre
la Muette
Solférino
Châtelet-les Halles
1
14
Balard
8
Château de Vincennes
Bibliothèque Fr. Mitterrand
9
Pont de Sèvres
Bir Hakeim
Sèvres-Babylone
6
Nation
13
Châtillon-Montrouge
12 Mairie d'Issy

Main access

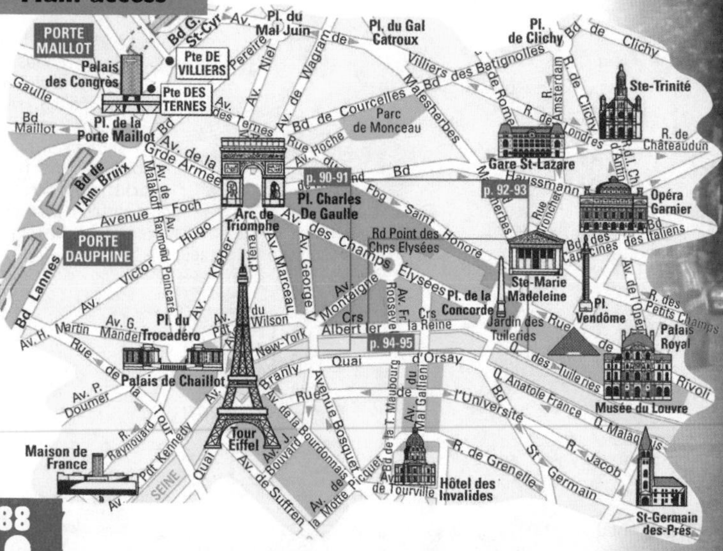

PORTE MAILLOT
Bd G. St-Cyr
Av. Pereire
Pl. du Mal Juin
Av. Niel
Av. de Wagram
Pl. du Gal Catroux
Pl. de Clichy
Bd de Clichy
Pte DE VILLIERS
Palais des Congrès
Pte DES TERNES
Gaulle
Bd Maillot
Pl. de la Porte Maillot
Av. des Ternes
Bd de Courcelles
Villiers
Bd des Batignolles
R. de Rome
R. Amsterdam
R. de Clichy
Ste-Trinité
Parc de Monceau
Malesherbes
R. de Londres
R. de Châteaudun
R. d'Antin
R. d. l. Ch.
Av. de la Grde Armée
Rue Hoche
Av. de Malakoff
Bd de l'Am. Bruix
Gare St-Lazare
p. 90-91
Bd Haussmann
p. 92-93
Opéra Garnier
Av. Foch
Pl. Charles De Gaulle
Fbg Saint Honoré
Rue Tronchet
Avenue
Av. Raymond Poincaré
Av. Hugo
Arc de Triomphe
Av. Kléber
Av. d'Iéna
Av. Marceau
Av. George V
Av. des Champs Élysées
Rd Point des Chps Élysées
Bd des Capucines
Bd des Italiens
PORTE DAUPHINE
Bd Lannes
Av. Victor
Av. Montaigne
Av. Fr. Roosevelt
Pl. de la Concorde
Ste-Marie Madeleine
Pl. Vendôme
Av. de l'Opéra
R. des Petits Champs
Av. H. Martin
Av. G. Mandel
Pl. du Trocadéro
Av. Pdt Wilson
Crs Albert Ier
Crs la Reine
Jardin des Tuileries
Rue de Rivoli
Palais Royal
Rue de Passy
Av. de New-York
p. 94-95
Quai d'Orsay
Q. des Tuileries
Palais de Chaillot
Branly
Avenue Bosquet
Av. du Mal Gallieni
Q. Anatole France
Av. P. Doumer
Av. de la Bourdonnais
Rue de l'Université
Musée du Louvre
R. Raynouard
Av. Pdt Kennedy
Tour Eiffel
Av. J. Bouvard
Bd de la T. Maubourg
Q. Malaquais
Maison de France
Quai
SEINE
Av. de Suffren
Av. de la Motte Picquet
Av. de Tourville
Hôtel des Invalides
R. de Grenelle
Bd St Germain
R. Jacob
St-Germain des-Prés
Av.

Champs-Élysées

Arc de Triomphe

It was Napoleon I who decided to build the arch to pay tribute to his Great Army's victories. The construction was trusted to architect Jean-François Chalgrin (until his death in 1811) then to one of his students. The construction was interrupted during the Restoration and the arch was not finished until 1836. Several bas-reliefs and hauts-reliefs decorate each side of the arch, illustrating the values of the Republic (the Marseillaise by François Rude, Triumph by Jean-Pierre Cortot, Resistance and Peace by Antoine Etex). Since 1921, it has been the resting place of the Unknown Soldier where the eternal flame is lit every night to the memory of all the soldiers who died in the First World War. From the top of the arch, there is a lovely view over the roofs of Paris and down the avenue des Champs-Elysées to the east and the avenue de la Grande Armée and the Defense to the west.

Place Charles de Gaulle

01 55 37 73 77

Everyday from 10 am to 10.30 pm (winter) and from 9.30 am to 11 pm (summer)

Admission 7 euros, Reduced rate 4.50 euros

22-30-31-52-73-92-Balabus

Place Charles de Gaulle

It was built under Louis XV, half-way between the Louvre and the Pont de Neuilly. It was also on the way to the General farms. Two tax pavilions were built on the roundabout at the end of the 18th century. The Arc de Triomphe was built at the beginning of the 19th century. It was only in the middle of the 19th century that the roundabout took on its present shape with its twelve converging avenues and the facades designed by Jacques-Ignace Hittorff. It was called the place de l'Etoile (the star) until 1970.

Le Fouquet's

Known th
world over, th
restaurant ha
become a myt
It has been a li
ted buildir
since 1990.
celebrated i
hundredth birt
day in 1999.

99 avenue des Champs-Elysées

01 47 23 50 00

42-73-Balabus

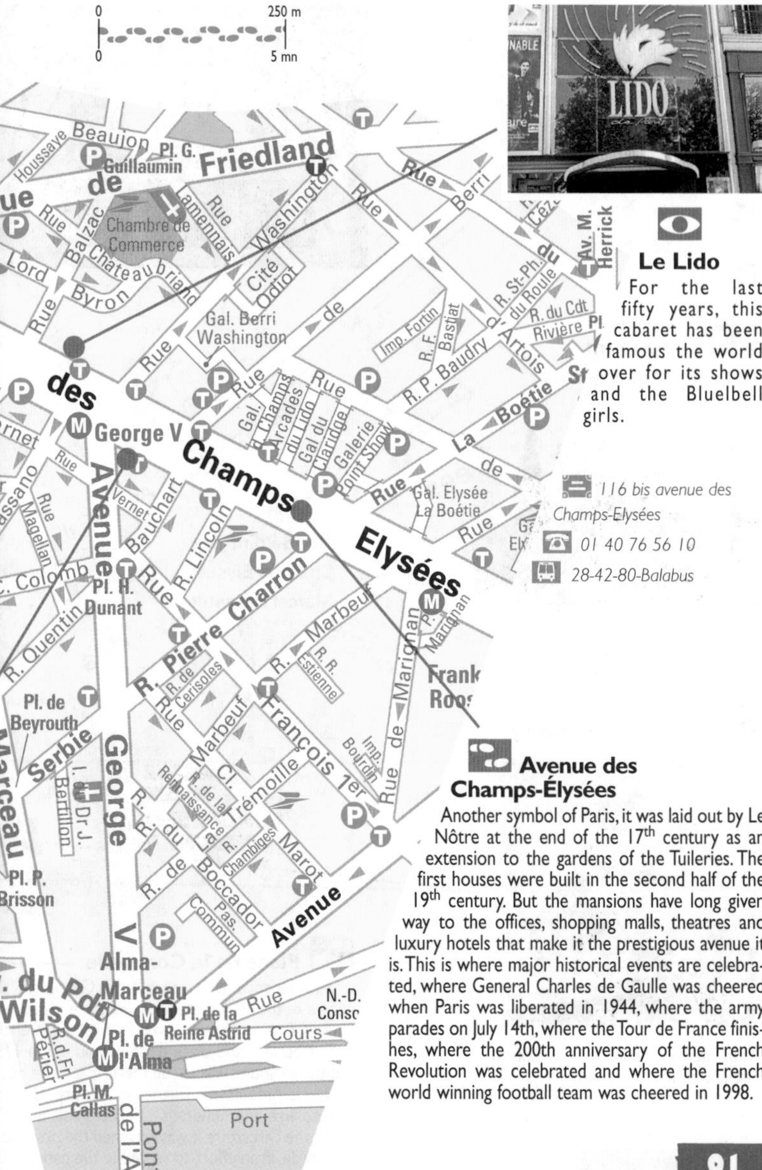

Le Lido

For the last fifty years, this cabaret has been famous the world over for its shows and the Bluelbell girls.

116 bis avenue des Champs-Elysées

01 40 76 56 10

28-42-80-Balabus

Avenue des Champs-Élysées

Another symbol of Paris, it was laid out by Le Nôtre at the end of the 17th century as an extension to the gardens of the Tuileries. The first houses were built in the second half of the 19th century. But the mansions have long given way to the offices, shopping malls, theatres and luxury hotels that make it the prestigious avenue it is. This is where major historical events are celebrated, where General Charles de Gaulle was cheered when Paris was liberated in 1944, where the army parades on July 14th, where the Tour de France finishes, where the 200th anniversary of the French Revolution was celebrated and where the French world winning football team was cheered in 1998.

Théâtre Marigny

It was called the 'Booffes-Parisien' when Offenbach played his operettas there. It was transformed into a panorama by Charles Garnier at the end of the 19th century and into a music-hall in 1893 (the Folies-Marigny) before it was renovated in 1925 and took its present name to welcome the most prestigious casts.

Avenue Marigny

01 53 96 70 00

28-52

Rond-Point des Champs-Élysées

This roundabout offers a lovely perspective towards the Arc de Triomphe.

Chevaux de Marly

They were sculpted by Couston at the end of the 18th century.

Place de la Concorde

It was designed by Jacques-Ange Gabriel in th middle of the 18th century to welcome a statue Louis XV riding a horse. It was first named after th king. It became the place de la Revolution in 179 and the guillotine was set up there. It saw the heac of Marie-Antoinette, Charlotte Corday, Danto Robespierre and hundreds of others roll. In 179 under the Directoire it was renamed the place de Concorde, in an effort to reconcile the nation afte

Palais de l'Élysée

ne Count of Evreux had this palace built by rmand-Claude Collet at the beginning of the 18th ntury. It later became the property of Madame de ompadour, of Madame de Beaujon and of the uchess de Bourbon before being bought by apoleon I in 1805 for his sister Caroline Murat. nis is where he abdicated after the '100 days', and here Louis-Napoleon organised the 1851 coup. It s been the official residence of the President of e Republic since 1871.

55 rue du Faubourg Saint-Honoré

01 42 92 81 00

52

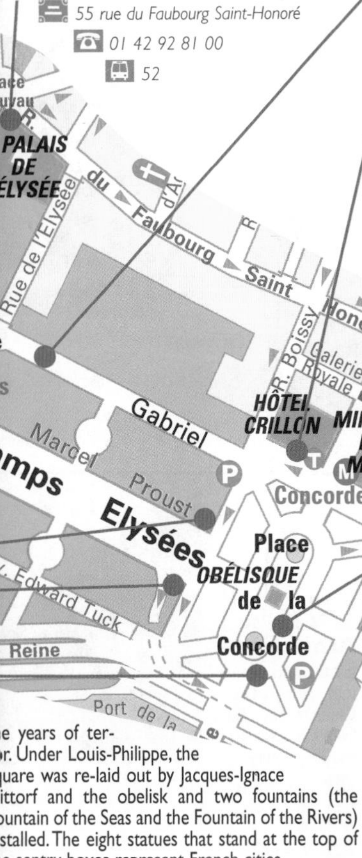

e years of ter-
or. Under Louis-Philippe, the
uare was re-laid out by Jacques-Ignace
ittorf and the obelisk and two fountains (the
ountain of the Seas and the Fountain of the Rivers)
stalled. The eight statues that stand at the top of
e sentry boxes represent French cities.

Avenue Gabriel

Bordered on the south side by the garden of the Champs-Elysées, its north side opens on the gardens of several 18th century mansions which now house the British Embassy and the Cercle de l'Union Interalliée. The street is named after the first architect of the place de la Concorde.

Hôtel de Crillon

Built on the corner of the rue Royale, in symmetry with the Hôtel de la Marine, it has been a luxury hotel since the beginning of the 20th century . It is also the headquarters of the Automobile Club de France.

10 place de la Concorde

Hôtel de la Marine

It was built at the same time as the Hôtel de Crillon, by Jacques-Ange Gabriel to close off the north side of the place de la Concorde. This richly decorated palace has been the Navy Ministry since 1789.

Place de la Concorde

Obélisque

Louis-Philippe decided to erect this monument, presented to him in 1831 by the Vice-Roy of Egypt, Mehmet-Ali. The obelisk comes from the temple of Ramses II in Luxor. Its installation met with many difficulties before it was finally stood up in front of a large crowd.

Place de la Concorde

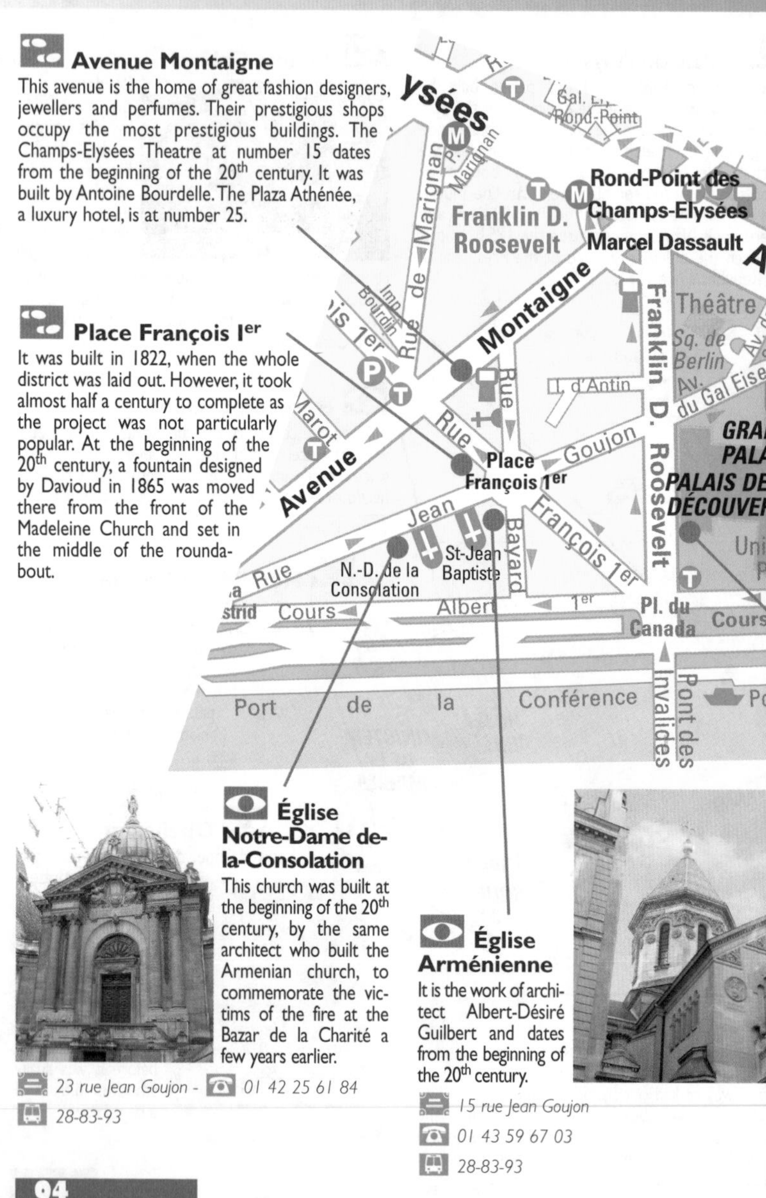

Avenue Montaigne

This avenue is the home of great fashion designers, jewellers and perfumes. Their prestigious shops occupy the most prestigious buildings. The Champs-Elysées Theatre at number 15 dates from the beginning of the 20th century. It was built by Antoine Bourdelle. The Plaza Athénée, a luxury hotel, is at number 25.

Place François Ier

It was built in 1822, when the whole district was laid out. However, it took almost half a century to complete as the project was not particularly popular. At the beginning of the 20th century, a fountain designed by Davioud in 1865 was moved there from the front of the Madeleine Church and set in the middle of the roundabout.

Église Notre-Dame de-la-Consolation

This church was built at the beginning of the 20th century, by the same architect who built the Armenian church, to commemorate the victims of the fire at the Bazar de la Charité a few years earlier.

23 rue Jean Goujon - 01 42 25 61 84

28-83-93

Église Arménienne

It is the work of architect Albert-Désiré Guilbert and dates from the beginning of the 20th century.

15 rue Jean Goujon

01 43 59 67 03

28-83-93

Grand Palais

ilt for the Universal Exhibition of 1900 by Henri eglane, Albert Louvet and Albert Thomas. It has onumental facades that mask a substantial metal ructure with a glass dome. It was intended for fine ts and welcomed several exhibitions, the 'Salon s Independants' or the 'Salon d'Automne' and ore recently the FIAC (the International Fair of Contemporary Arts). Major international exhibitions have been held regularly there since 1966.

3 avenue du Général-Eisenhower

01 44 13 17 30

Everyday, except Tuesdays, from 10 am to 8 pm, and Wednesdays from 10 am to 10 pm

Admission 8 to 10 euros, Reduced rate 5.50 to 8 euros

28-32-42-72-73-80-83-93

Web *www.rmn.fr*

Petit Palais

Built by Charles Girault for the 1900 International Exhibition, it now houses the Paris Fine Arts Museum. The rich collections come from donations (Dutuit: Egyptian Antiquity, Tuck: works of the 18th century), or from the collections of the City of Paris, like the work of impressionist painters.

Avenue Winston Churchill - 01 42 65 12 73

Closed until 2004

28-42-49-73-80

Palais de la Découverte

Housed in the west wing of the Grand Palais since 1937, it presents the many aspects of science, like astronomy, astrophysics, mathematics, physics and ology in a lively and amusing way. There is also a anetarium.

Avenue Franklin-D.-Roosevelt - 01 56 43 20 20

Tuesdays to Saturdays from 9.30 am to 6 pm, ndays and public holidays from 10 am to 7 pm

Admission 5.60 euros, Reduced rate 3.65 euros, anetarium supplement 3.05 euros

28-42-52-63-72-73-80-83-93

0 250 m
0 5 mn

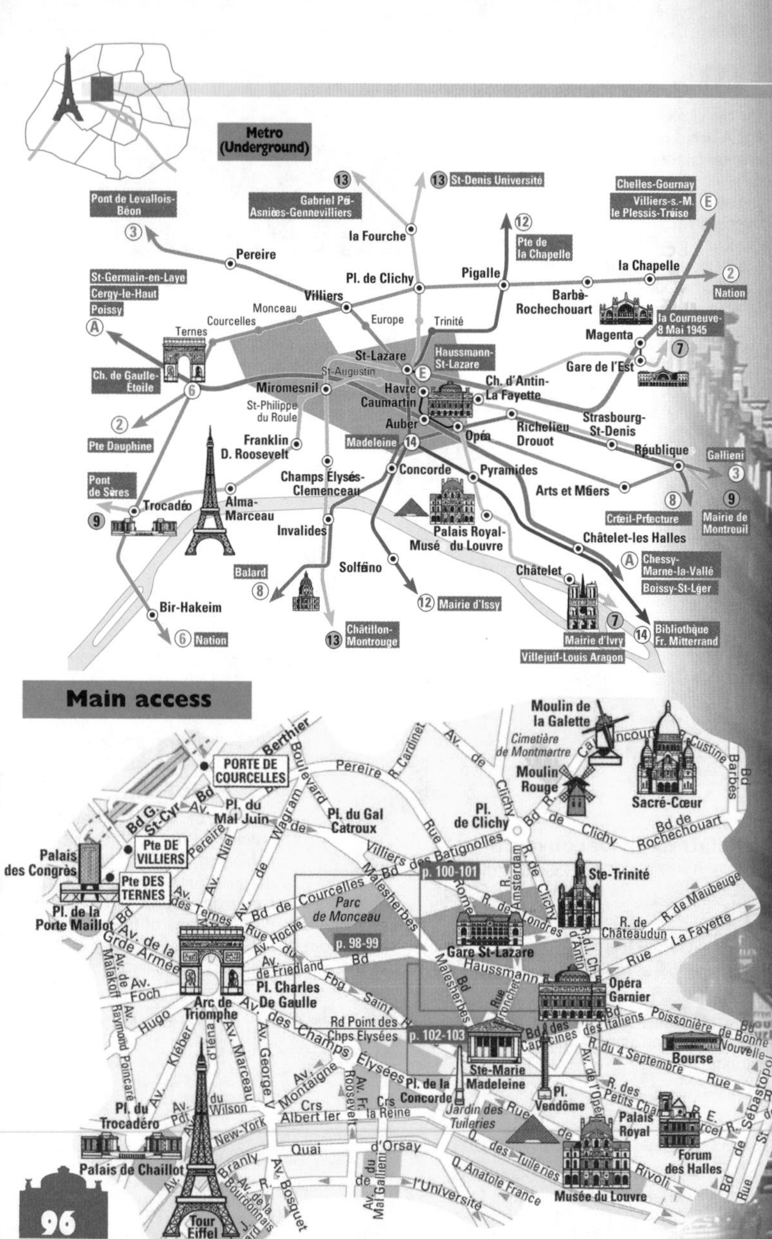
Metro (Underground)
Pont de Levallois-Béon
Gabriel Péi-Asnièes-Gennevilliers
13
13 St-Denis Université
Chelles-Gournay
Villiers-s.-M. le Plessis-Tréise
E
12
Pte de la Chapelle
3
Pereire
la Fourche
la Chapelle
2
Nation
St-Germain-en-Laye
Cergy-le-Haut
Poissy
A
Pl. de Clichy
Pigalle
Villiers
Monceau
Courcelles
Ternes
Europe
Trinité
Barbè-Rochechouart
la Courneuve-8 Mai 1945
Magenta
7
Gare de l'Est
St-Lazare
Haussmann-St-Lazare
Ch. de Gaulle-Etoile
St-Augustin
Miromesnil
Havre Caumartin
Ch. d'Antin-La Fayette
6
St-Philippe du Roule
Strasbourg-St-Denis
Auber
Richelieu Drouot
Opéa
Pte Dauphine
Franklin D. Roosevelt
Madeleine
14
République
Gallieni
Champs Élysés-Clemenceau
Concorde
Pyramides
Pont de Sèes
Arts et Mers
Trocadéo
Alma-Marceau
Crteil-Prfecture
Mairie de Montreuil
9
8
Invalides
Palais Royal-Musé du Louvre
Châtelet-les Halles
Chessy-Marne-la-Vallé
Boissy-St-Lger
Balard
Solféino
Châtelet
Bir-Hakeim
12 Mairie d'Issy
Bibliothque Fr. Mitterrand
Mairie d'Ivry
Châtillon-Montrouge
6 Nation
Villejuif-Louis Aragon
Main access
Moulin de la Galette
Cimetière de Montmartre
Moulin Rouge
Sacré-Cœur
Berthier
PORTE DE COURCELLES
Boulevard
Pereire
R. Cardinet
Av. de Clichy
Bd Barbès
Bd G. St-Cyr
Pl. du Mal Juin
Pl. du Gal Catroux
Pl. de Clichy
Bd de Clichy
Bd de Rochechouart
Palais des Congrès
Pte DE VILLIERS
Pte DES TERNES
Bd des Batignolles
Villiers
p. 100-101
Ste-Trinité
Pl. de la Porte Maillot
Av. des Ternes
Bd de Courcelles
Parc de Monceau
R. de Londres
R. d'Amsterdam
R. de Clichy
R. de Maubeuge
R. de Châteaudun
Rue La Fayette
Av. de la Grde Armée
Rue Hoche
p. 98-99
Gare St-Lazare
Av. de Friedland
Bd Haussmann
Opéra Garnier
Av. Foch
Arc de Triomphe
Pl. Charles De Gaulle
Fbg Saint H.
Rue Tronchet
Bd Malesherbes
Av. Hugo
Av. des Champs Élysées
Rd Point des Chps Elysées
p. 102-103
Bd des Capucines
Bd des Italiens
Poissonière
Bd de Bonne Nouvelle
R. du 4 Septembre
Bourse
Av. Kléber
Av. d'Iéna
Av. Marceau
Av. George V
Av. Montaigne
Av. Fr. Roosevelt
Pl. de la Concorde
Ste-Marie Madeleine
Pl. Vendôme
Av. de l'Opéra
R. des Petits Champs
Palais Royal
Pl. du Trocadéro
Av. du Pdt Wilson
Crs Albert Ier
Crs la Reine
Jardin des Tuileries
Rue de Rivoli
Av. de New-York
Quai d'Orsay
Q. des Tuileries
Palais de Chaillot
Q. Anatole France
Forum des Halles
Av. Bosquet
Av. du Mal Gallieni
Bd de l'Université
Musée du Louvre
Tour Eiffel
Bd de Sébastopol

Opéra

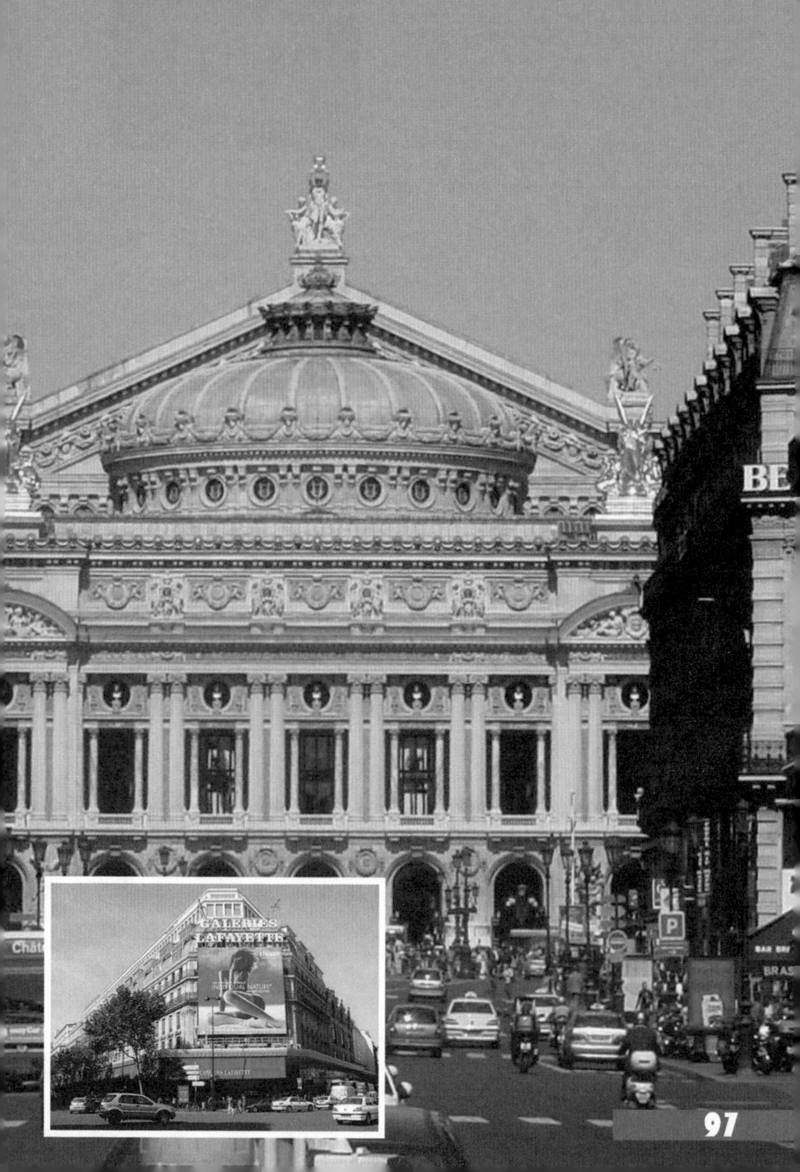

Parc de Monceau

It was at the end of the 18th century that the Duke of Chartres asked Carmontelle to build him a 'folly'. Later, the gardens were extended and landscaped by Thomas Blaikie. The park was acquired by the City of Paris in 1860. It was landscaped by Adolphe Alphand while Davioud designed the gates, the bridge and the artificial grotto. New plantations were also made (maples, planes, ginkgos, fig trees). The Chartres rotunda is what remains from the General Farm. It was built by Ledoux to house the tax office.

Musée Jacquemart-André

In 1869, Edouard André asked Henri Parent to build this mansion to house the art treasures he and his wife Nélie Jacquemart had collected. It opened to the public in 1913 when she donated it to the Institut de France. 18th century French and Italian Renaissance collections are presented in a richly decorated setting.

158 boulevard Haussmann

01 45 62 11 59

Every day from 10 am to 6 pm

Admission 8 euros, Reduced rate 6 euros, Free for children under 7

22-28-43-52-54-80-83-84-93

www.musee-jacquemart-andre.com

Église Saint-Philippe-du-Roule

It was built at the end of the 18th century by Jean-François Chalgrin on the plans of early Christian churches. An ambulatory by Hippolyte Godde and a catechism chapel by Victor Baltard were added in the middle of the 19th century. There is a fresco by Chassériau on the vault over the choir: Jesus Lowered from the cross (1855).

154 rue du Faubourg St-Honoré

01 43 59 24 56

Every day from 7.30 am to 7.30 pm from 15 July to 1st September, Saturdays and Sundays from 7.30 am to 12 noon and from 4 pm to 7.30 pm

52-83-93

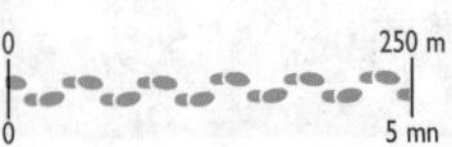

Musée Cernuschi

llowing a trip to the Far East, Henri Cernuschi, banker, had this mansion built to house the collections he brought back. Opened in 1898, the museum houses a vast collection of ancient Chinese bronzes, pottery and statuettes and many contemporary Chinese paintings.

77 avenue de Versailles

01 55 74 61 30

Closed until 2004

30-94

Musée Nissim de Camondo

Rebuilt at the beginning of the 20th century by René Sergent on the model of the 'Petit Trianon' to welcome 18th century objects (furniture, panelling, tapestries, porcelain) collected by Count Moise de Camondo. On his death, he donated the house and his collections to the Decorative Art Union. The museum is named after the count's son killed during the First World War.

63 rue de Monceau

01 53 89 06 40

Every day except Mondays and Tuesdays from 10 am to 5 pm

Admission 4.60 euros, Reduced Rate 3.10 euros

30-84-94

Web *www.ucad.fr*

Église Saint-Augustin

It was built by Victor Baltard at the end of the 19th century in a mix of styles (Roman, Renaissance and Byzantine) using for the first time, for a church of this size, a metal structure. A dome, four turrets and a triangular shape add to its originality.

46 boulevard Malesherbes

01 45 22 23 12

Everyday from 7 am to 7:30 pm

94

Rue du Faubourg Saint-Honoré

Several 18th century houses can still be seen along this street (the Cercle de l'Union Interalliée, the British Embassy, The residence of the United States' Ambassador, and the Home Office) as well as the premises of Hermés, the leather goods desi-

Gare Saint-Lazare

It was near the bridge of the place de l'Europe that the first railway platform was built. It was Paris's first railway station. The line ran from Paris to Saint-Germain. It was re-sited in 1851 and in 1885, Juste Lisch redesigned the station to give it its present appearance.

108 rue Saint-Lazare

01 53 42 00 00

20-21-24-26-29

Boulevard Haussmann

The street is mainly known for its department stores, the great centres of fashion that make the reputation of Paris. There is the Printemps which was founded in 1865 by Jules Jaluzot, a former employee of another store, the Bon Marché. Burnt down, it was rebuilt in 1885 by Paul Sédille. It was extended in 1905 by René Binet (the glass dome can still be seen on the 6th floor), and again in 1912 by George Wybo.

In 1895, Théophile Bader and Alphonse Kahn opened a shop in a haberdasher's. It became the Galeries Lafayette. The store was extended by Georges Chédanne in 1906 and by Ferdinand Chanut in 1910. The building between the rue Charras and the rue de Mogador was rebuilt in 1969. A wonderful glass dome dominates the store, also.

Église de la Trinité

The church was built in the second half of the 19th century by Theodore Ballu in a Renaissance style. Its steeple, two turrets, facade and arcades make it special. It is quite ornate outside and inside around the choir. There are also many paintings. Olivier Messiaen was one of its organists.

Place d'Estienne d'Orves

01 48 74 12 77

Everyday from 7 am to 8 pm

68-81

Paris Story

This is a mutlimedia audiovisual show that presents Paris through the great moments of its history. It takes 45 minutes and Victor Hugo is the virtual guide.

11bis rue Scribe - *01 42 66 62 06*

Everyday from 9 am to 7 pm (session every hour)

Admission 8 euros, Reduced rate 5 euros

42-68

ace de l'Opéra

igned by Haussmann at the heart of a prestis district. It is a very popular meeting place and arting point for a walk along the 'grands bouleds', a visit to the shops, to the theatres, the cine and the restaurants.

Olympia

A music hall and then a cinema, it was Bruno Coquatrix who in 1954 transformed it into the most popular concert hall in Paris. Performing at the Olympia is a must for singers and musicians.

28 boulevard des Capucines

01 47 42 25 49

22-52-66

Web *www.olympiahall.com*

La Madeleine

0 250 m
0 5 mn

Started in 1765 by Pierre Constant d'Ivry, it was not consecrated until a century later. In meantime people had thought of turning it in national library (during the revolution), int stock exchange or even a trade tribunal. It Napoleon I who decided to turn it into a ter dedicated to his Great Army. The project trusted to Vignon who sketched the Gr Temple. Louis XVIII handed the building to Catholic Church. There are many statues ins including the Baptism of Christ and the F Apostles by Rude and the Rapture of M Magdalene by Marochetti.

Place de la Madeleine

01 44 51 69 00

Everyday from 7 am to 7 pm, Sundays from 7 am to 1.30 pm and from 3.30 pm to 7 pm

24-42-52-84-94

Musée de la parfumerie ·agonard

·used in a 19th century mansion, it traces the tory of this art and its techniques from Egyptian antiquity to modern days through a rich collection of rare distillation objects, perfume burners, etchings, documents, presentation of extraction techniques and perfume composition.

9 rue Scribe - 01 47 42 93 40

Mondays to Saturdays from 9.30 am to 5.30 pm

Free

42-73-Balabus

www.fragonard.com

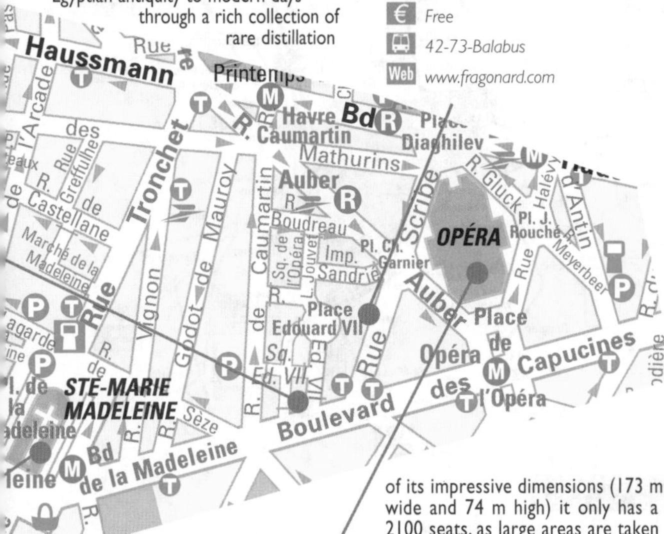

Opéra Garnier

ıpoleon III decided to build a new opera use and trusted its construction to Charles ırnier. It took thirteen years and the work of ıny artists and craftsmen to complete this ·ulous monument dedicated to opera. In spite of its impressive dimensions (173 m long, 125 m wide and 74 m high) it only has a capacity for 2100 seats, as large areas are taken by machinery, the lobby and rehearsal rooms.

On the outside the building is decorated with many statues including the Dance by Carpeaux. Inside the generous use of marble and rich decoration create an impression of luxury and majesty. A new ceiling was painted by Chagall in 1964, depicting several operas and ballets.

Since the new opera house at the Bastille was opened, the Opéra Garnier has concentrated on ballets with 154 dancers, including 10 Prima Ballerinas.

Place de l'Opéra

01 47 42 07 02

Everyday from 10 am to 4.30 pm

Admission 6 euros, Reduced rate 3 euros, Free for children under 10

21-22-27-29-42-53-66-68-81-95

www.opera-de-paris.fr

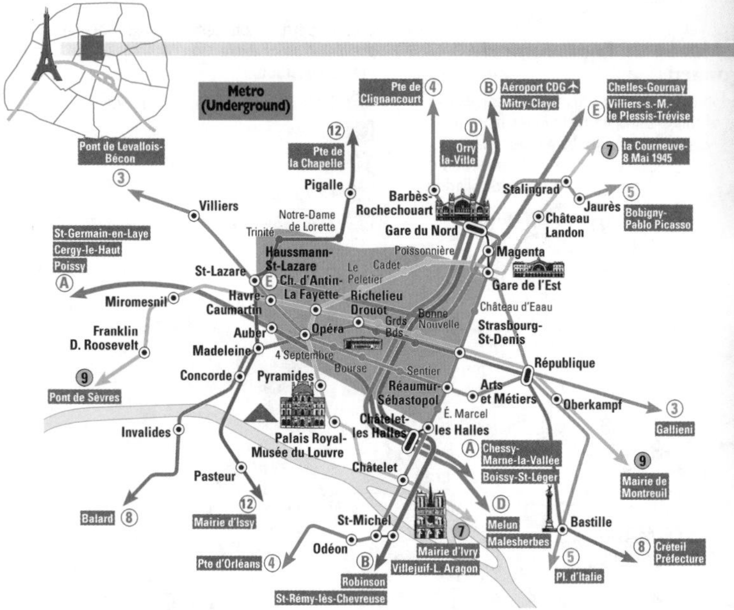

Metro (Underground)

Pont de Levallois-Bécon ③
Villiers
St-Lazare
St-Germain-en-Laye
Cergy-le-Haut
Poissy
Ⓐ
Miromesnil
Franklin D. Roosevelt
⑨ Pont de Sèvres
Havre-Caumartin
Auber
Madeleine
Concorde
Invalides
Balard ⑧
Pasteur
⑫ Mairie d'Issy
⑫ Pte de la Chapelle
Pigalle
Notre-Dame de Lorette
Trinité
Haussmann-St-Lazare
Ⓔ
Ch. d'Antin-La Fayette
Le Peletier
Cadet
Poissonnière
Richelieu Drouot
Opéra
Grds Bds
Bonne Nouvelle
4 Septembre
Bourse
Sentier
Pyramides
Palais Royal-Musée du Louvre
Réaumur-Sébastopol
Arts et Métiers
Châtelet-les Halles
É. Marcel
les Halles
Châtelet
St-Michel
Odéon
Pte d'Orléans ④
Ⓑ Robinson
St-Rémy-lès-Chevreuse
Villejuif-L. Aragon
⑦ Mairie d'Ivry
Melun
Malesherbes
Ⓓ
Ⓐ Chessy-Marne-la-Vallée
Boissy-St-Léger
Pte de Clignancourt ④
Ⓑ Aéroport CDG
Mitry-Claye
Ⓓ Orry la-Ville
Barbès-Rochechouart
Gare du Nord
Magenta
Gare de l'Est
Château d'Eaau
Strasbourg-St-Denis
République
Oberkampf
③ Gallieni
⑨ Mairie de Montreuil
Bastille
⑤ Pl. d'Italie
⑧ Créteil Préfecture
Stalingrad
Jaurès
Château Landon
⑤ Bobigny-Pablo Picasso
⑦ la Courneuve-8 Mai 1945
Ⓔ Chelles-Gournay
Villiers-s.-M.-le Plessis-Trévise

Main access

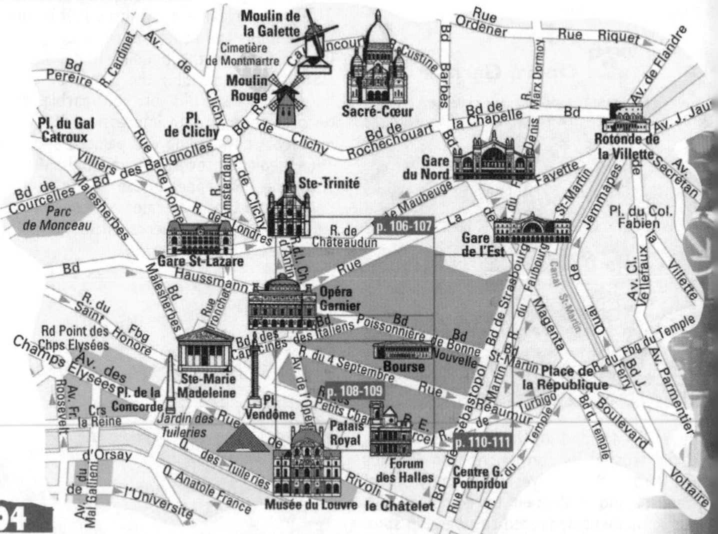

Moulin de la Galette
Cimetière de Montmartre
Moulin Rouge
Sacré-Cœur
Rue Ordener
Rue Riquet
Av. de Flandre
Bd Pereire
R. Cardinet
Av. de Clichy
R. Caulaincourt
R. Custine
Bd Barbès
R. Marx Dormoy
Pl. du Gal Catroux
Pl. de Clichy
Bd de Clichy
Bd de Rochechouart
Bd de la Chapelle
Rotonde de la Villette
Av. J. Jaurès
Rue des Batignolles
Bd de Courcelles
Villiers
Bd Malesherbes
Rue de Rome
R. Amsterdam
R. de Clichy
Ste-Trinité
Gare du Nord
R. La Fayette
R. de Maubeuge
Av. Secrétan
Parc de Monceau
R. de Londres
R. de Châteaudun
p. 106-107
Gare de l'Est
Pl. du Col. Fabien
Gare St-Lazare
R. d.l. Ch. d'Antin
Bd Haussmann
Rue
Opéra Garnier
Canal St-Martin
Quai de Jemmapes
Av. Cl. Vellefaux
la Villette
R. du Saint Honoré
Fbg
Bd Malesherbes
Rue Tronchet
Bd des Capucines
Bd des Italiens
Bd Poissonnière
Bd de Bonne Nouvelle
Bd de Strasbourg
R. du Faubourg St-Martin
Bd Magenta
Rd Point des Chps Elysées
Champs Elysées
Av. des
Ste-Marie Madeleine
R. du 4 Septembre
Av. de l'Opéra
Bourse
Bd St-Martin
Place de la République
R. du Fbg du Temple
Bd J. Ferry
Av. Parmentier
Av. Fr. Roosevelt
Pl. de la Concorde
Crs la Reine
Pl. Vendôme
p. 108-109
R. des Petits Champs
Rue Réaumur
Rue de Turbigo
Bd du Temple
Boulevard Voltaire
Jardin des Tuileries
Rue de Rivoli
Palais Royal
R. E. Marcel
Bd de Sébastopol
p. 110-111
Q. d'Orsay
Q. des Tuileries
Forum des Halles
Centre G. Pompidou
Rue du Temple
Av. du Mal Gallieni
Q. Anatole France
R. de l'Université
Musée du Louvre
le Châtelet

Grands Boulevards

Hôtel Drouot

The auction room was recently renovated. It represents a long tradition of auctions where amateurs bid against professionals.

9 rue Drouot - 01 48 00 20 20

Mondays to Saturdays from 11 am to 6 pm

20-39-42-48-67-74-85

Musée Grévin

In 1885, a journalist, Arthur Meyer thought of making wax puppets to the effigy of some famous personalities. With the help of cartoonist Alfred Grévin, the museum opened the following year. It was an immediate success. Historical and current settings display life-size models of politicians, artists, sportsmen and women. The Palais des Mirages which was opened for the 1900 Universal Exhibition recreates the magic of mirrors and light.

10 boulevard Montmartre

01 47 70 85 05

Everyday from 10 am to 7 pm

Admission 15 euros,
Reduced rate (6 to 14 year-old) 9 euros

20-39-48-67-74-85

www.musee-grevin.com

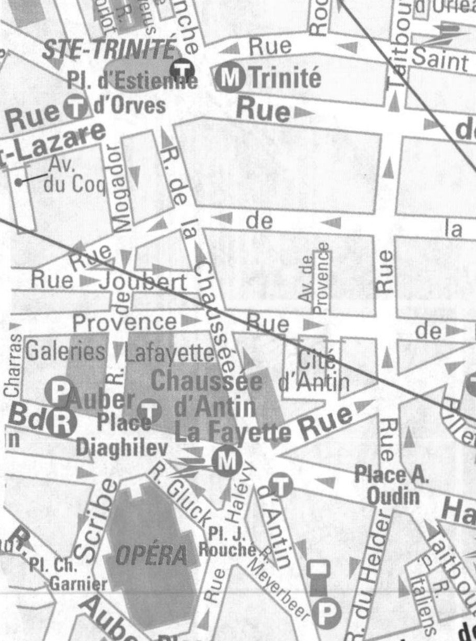

Musée Gustave Moreau

ɔrtly before his death at the end of the 19th cen-
y, the painter Gustave Moreau turned his studio
ɔ a museum. It has remained as he left it.
ɔusands of works of art (lots of paintings, sketches
l watercolours) reveal all the talent of the artist.

14 r. de la Rochefoucauld - *01 48 74 38 50*

Everyday except Tuesdays from 10 am
12.45 pm and from 2 pm to 5.15 pm

Admission 3.50 euros, Reduced rate 2.30 euros

67-74

Musée du Grand Orient de France

is is the museum of the Grand Lodge of France, it
ls us the history of the French Free-Masons with
: help of documents and other objects.

16 rue Cadet - *01 45 23 20 92*

Tuesdays to Saturdays from 2 pm to 6 pm

2 euros - *26-42-43-48*

Web *www.godf.org*

Les Folies-Bergère

Another mythical venue, this cabaret was opened at the end of the 19th century. It presented the first music-hall shows. Some of the greatest artists have performed there: Mistinguett, Maurice Chevalier, Joséphine Baker, Zizi Jeanmaire…

32 rue Richer - *01 44 79 98 98*

26-32-42-43-49 - Web *www.foliesbergere.com*

Passage Jouffroy

Opened in the middle of the 19th century, under its glass ceiling we can find many little shops each more charming than the other.

La Bourse

The Stock Exchange was built at the beginning of the 19th century by Alexandre-Theodore Brongniart at the request of Napoleon I. Although the Trade Exchange moved out into the Corn Exchange, it still had to be extended at the beginning of the 20th century. Although the trading room, replaced by computers in 1987, is just a fading memory, quotations remain as real as ever.

 *rue Notre-Dame des Victoires -*  *29*

Bibliothèque nationale (site Richelieu)

It was Colbert who in the middle of the 17th century, paved the way for the installation of the Royal Library (created by Charles V) in two Hôtels in rue Vivienne. It was extended several times by taking over part of the Palais Mazarin and of the Hôtel Tubeuf (17th century), with the addition of two galleries (Robert de Cotte in the 18th century) and new buildings in the 19th century. It was then that architect Henri Labrouste built the Prints Reading Room. Since the prints and journals were moved to the Tolbiac site, the Richelieu site has concentrated on manuscripts, maps, coins and notes, medals and music sheets.

 *58 rue de Richelieu*

 *01 53 79 59 59*

Everyday except Sundays from 9 am to 7 pm

 *20-29-39-67-74-85*

Web *www.bnf.fr*

Boulevard des Italiens, boulevard Montmartre

These lively avenues are lined with banks, theat cinemas and restaurants which are often open u very late at night.

Galerie Colbert, galerie Vivienne

These two remar-kable galleries d from the beginning the 19th century. Th benefited from proximity of the Pa Royal before go into decline. They h recently been rest red. The Colbe Gallery now belor to the Natio Library and the sh in the Gallery Vivien are again as lively as they once were.

Passage des Princes, passage des Panoramas, alerie Montmartre

hey form a world of their own, different from their surrounding streets. Very ısy, their decoration and shops have a unique and quaint charm. The passage ınorama owes its name to the shows where pictures were projected in ompe-l'œil.

Place des Victoires

Designed by Jules Hardouin-Mansart at the end of the 17th century, it boasted a statue of Louis XIV donated by Marchal de la Feuillade. The original statue was destroyed during the French Revolution and a new equestrian statue of Louis XIV was designed by François-Joseph Bosio in the 19th century. The roundabout has kept its initial layout in spite of improvement work carried out in the 19th century. It is surrounded by luxury shops and fashion designers.

Église Notre-Dame des Victoires

he church is the only part that is left of the 'Barefoot Angustin' convent known as the 'petits pères', built 1629. The other buildings were destroyed in the 19th century. The convent was built by Louis XIII to thank ıe Virgin for his victories, especially the one at La Rochelle and took over a century to be ompleted. Inside we can find a 1740 buffet organ and several paintings by Carl Van Loo (18th entury). This is where Jean-Baptiste Lulli is burried.

6 rue Notre-Dame des Victoires - *01 42 60 90 47* - *48-85*

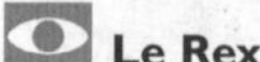

Le Rex

Built in the style of American cinemas, it was inaugurated in 1932. With its large hall, starry ceiling and water show, it perpetuates the art's legend and glamour. The 'Etoiles du Rex' take us backstage through the world of cinema.

Boulevard Poissonnière

08 36 68 05 96

Wednesdays to Sundays from 10 am to 7 pm

Admission 7 euros, Reduced rate (- 12) 6 euros, from 5 pm to 7 pm 4.50 euros

20-39-48

Web *www.legrandrex.com*

Rue de Cléry, rue des Petits Carreaux, passage du Caire, passage du Grand Cerf

These streets and lanes are typical of the popular 'Sentier' district. In the 17th century the district was full of very shady characters, beggars and robbers but now it has specialised in the rag trade. Some of its busy streets are reminiscent of Bonapare's Egyptian campaign.

Musée des Cristalleries de Baccarat

Housed in the middle of the rue du Paradis, it boasts all the great names of porcelain and the art of table setting. Through the objects on display, the museum traces the evolution of styles and techniques.

30 bis rue du Paradis. Please note that in July 2003, ***the museum will move to Place des Etats-Unis***

01 47 70 64 30

Open Monday to Saturdays from 10 am to 6 pm

3 euros

26-42-43-48 - Web *www.baccarat.fr*

Église Notre-Dame de Bonne Nouvelle

It was built by Etienne Hippolyte Godde at the beginning of the 19th century in a neo-classical style, although the 17th century belfry was kept. It boasts many paintings.

19 rue Beauregard - *01 42 33 65 74*

Porte Saint-Denis

This arch was built in the 17th century by François Blondel to celebrate the victories of Louis XIV on the Rhine. The sculptures and bas-reliefs depict the taking of Maastricht and the crossing of the Rhine.

Tour Jean-sans-Peur

It is the only thing left from the Hôtel Bourgogne, an early 15th century mansion built by Robert de Helbuterne for the Duke Jean. It is one of the rare example of medieval architecture in Paris. There we can see the room of Jean-sans-Peur and a magnificent spiral staircase.

20 rue Étienne Marcel - *01 40 26 20 28*

From 1.30 pm to 6 pm in term time: Wednesdays, Saturdays, Sundays. Everyday, except Mondays during school holidays

Admission 5 euros, Rduced rate 3 euros, Free for chidren under 7, Guided visits at 3 pm, 8 euros

29 - Web *perso.wanadoo.fr/tourjeansanspeur*

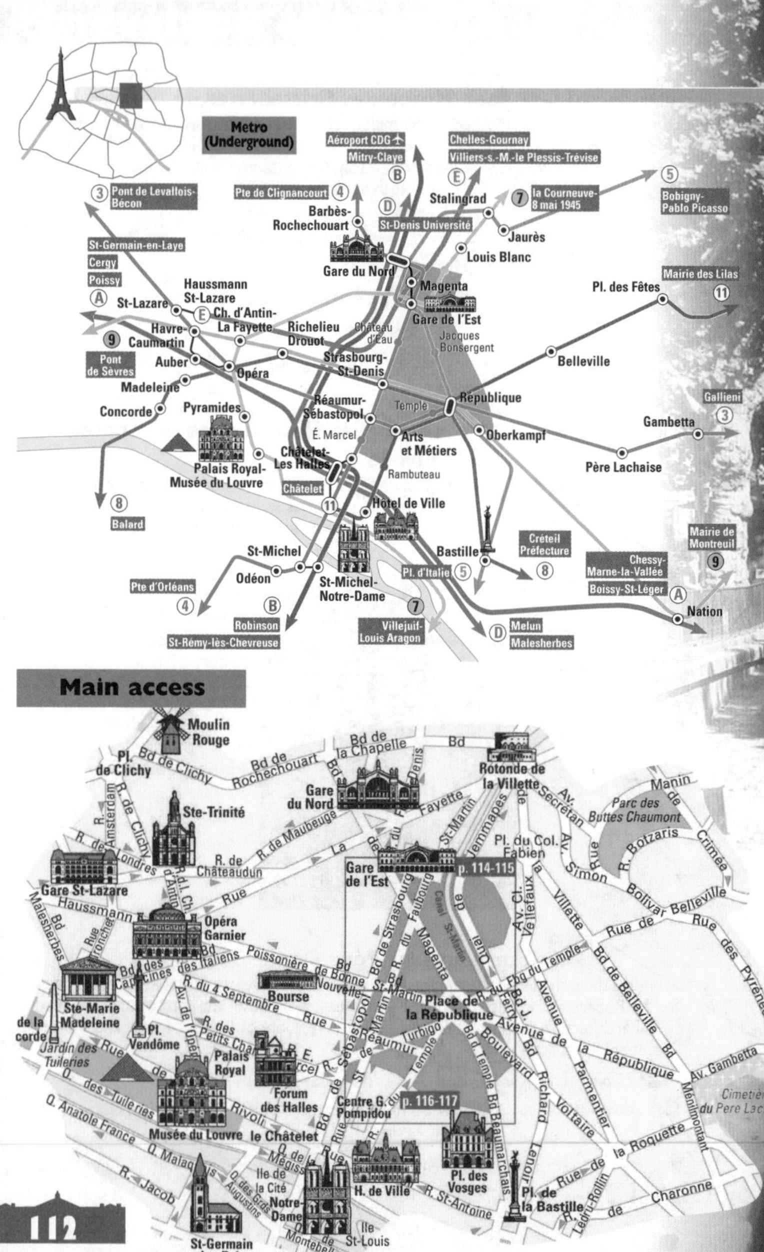
Metro (Underground)
Aéroport CDG
Mitry-Claye
Chelles-Gournay
Villiers-s.-M.-le Plessis-Trévise
Pont de Levallois-Bécon
Pte de Clignancourt
Barbès-Rochechouart
St-Denis Université
Stalingrad
la Courneuve-8 mai 1945
Bobigny-Pablo Picasso
Jaurès
Louis Blanc
St-Germain-en-Laye
Cergy
Poissy
Gare du Nord
Magenta
Gare de l'Est
Mairie des Lilas
Pl. des Fêtes
Haussmann St-Lazare
St-Lazare
Ch. d'Antin-La Fayette
Havre-Caumartin
Richelieu Drouot
Château d'Eau
Jacques Bonsergent
Pont de Sèvres
Auber
Opéra
Strasbourg-St-Denis
Belleville
Madeleine
République
Concorde
Pyramides
Réaumur-Sébastopol
Temple
Gallieni
Gambetta
É. Marcel
Arts et Métiers
Oberkampf
Palais Royal-Musée du Louvre
Châtelet-Les Halles
Père Lachaise
Châtelet
Rambuteau
Balard
Hôtel de Ville
Créteil Préfecture
Mairie de Montreuil
St-Michel
Bastille
Chessy-Marne-la-Vallée
Pl. d'Italie
Odéon
St-Michel-Notre-Dame
Boissy-St-Léger
Pte d'Orléans
Nation
Robinson
St-Rémy-lès-Chevreuse
Villejuif-Louis Aragon
Melun
Malesherbes
Main access
Moulin Rouge
Pl. de Clichy
Bd de Clichy
Bd de Rochechouart
Bd de la Chapelle
Rotonde de la Villette
Gare du Nord
Ste-Trinité
Parc des Buttes Chaumont
R. de Maubeuge
Pl. du Col. Fabien
Gare St-Lazare
R. de Châteaudun
Gare de l'Est
p. 114-115
Canal St-Martin
Opéra Garnier
Bd Haussmann
Bd des Capucines
Bd des Italiens
Poissonière
Bd de Bonne Nouvelle
Bourse
R. du 4 Septembre
Place de la République
Ste-Marie Madeleine
Pl. de la Concorde
Pl. Vendôme
Jardin des Tuileries
Palais Royal
Forum des Halles
Centre G. Pompidou
p. 116-117
Musée du Louvre
le Châtelet
Q. des Tuileries
Q. Anatole France
Rue de Rivoli
Ile de la Cité
Notre-Dame
H. de Ville
Pl. des Vosges
Pl. de la Bastille
R. St-Antoine
Ile St-Louis
St-Germain des-Prés
R. Jacob
Bd Voltaire
Avenue de la République
Av. Gambetta
Cimetière du Pere Lacha
Rue de la Roquette
Rue de Charonne
Rue des Pyrénées
Bd de Belleville
Rue de Belleville
Av. Parmentier
Bd Richard Lenoir
Bd Beaumarchais

République

Gare de l'Est

The left side of the station was built in the middle of the 19th century to house the Strasbourg line. It was extended a few years later and took on its present name (the East Station). It was extended further between 1924 to 1931. When the right side was built, it doubled the station's surface. The statues on the facade represent cities and rivers from the East of France.

Passage Brady

Built in 1828, this passage has become a world of its own where the smell of incense and spices fills the Indo-Pakistani food and craft shops and restaurants.

Conservatoire national des Arts et Métiers

It was in the 11th century that King Henri I built a priory on the ruins of a monastery ransacked by the Norman in the 9th century. Although intended for the canons of Saint-Martin-des-Champs it was administered by the Cluny Abbey. There is very little left of the priory, only the remains of the boundary wall (13th century), the refectory designed by Pierre de Montreuil in the 12th century (it is now a library) and the old church with its choir and its 12th century chapels, the 13th century nave and the 19th century facade. During the French Revolution, the buildings were confiscated and given to the National Conservatory of Arts and Crafts in 1794. Extended in the 19th century and renovated several times in the 19th and 20th centuries. The conservatory is now a further education teaching and research establishment concerned mainly with technology and the spreading of science.

292 rue Saint-Martin

01 40 27 20 00

20-38-47-75

Web *www.cnam.fr*

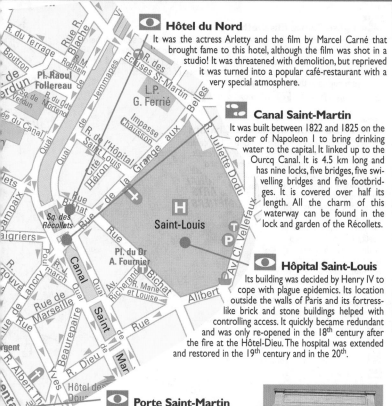

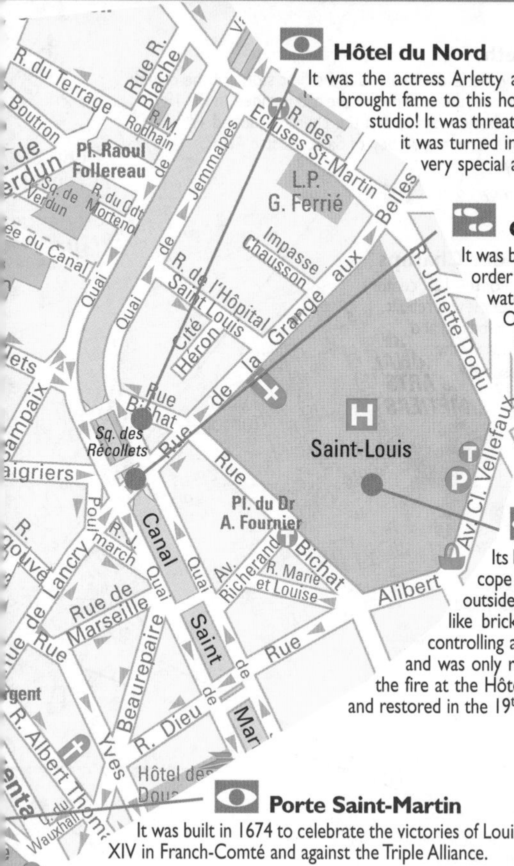

Hôtel du Nord

It was the actress Arletty and the film by Marcel Carné that brought fame to this hotel, although the film was shot in a studio! It was threatened with demolition, but reprieved it was turned into a popular café-restaurant with a very special atmosphere.

Canal Saint-Martin

It was built between 1822 and 1825 on the order of Napoleon I to bring drinking water to the capital. It linked up to the Ourcq Canal. It is 4.5 km long and has nine locks, five bridges, five swivelling bridges and five footbridges. It is covered over half its length. All the charm of this waterway can be found in the lock and garden of the Récollets.

Hôpital Saint-Louis

Its building was decided by Henry IV to cope with plague epidemics. Its location outside the walls of Paris and its fortress-like brick and stone buildings helped with controlling access. It quickly became redundant and was only re-opened in the 18th century after the fire at the Hôtel-Dieu. The hospital was extended and restored in the 19th century and in the 20th.

Porte Saint-Martin

It was built in 1674 to celebrate the victories of Louis XIV in Franch-Comté and against the Triple Alliance.

Musée des Arts et Métiers

is partly housed in the old church of Saint-lartin-des-Champs. It offers visitors a large pan-rama of techniques through thematic visits, emonstrations, workshops and the presentation f many machines (steam, gas or diesel engines, olar energy ovens, cars and aeroplanes) and cientific instruments in the fields of mechanics, onstruction, materials and transport. Amongst iose one must not miss Pascal's calculator, the ımière Brothers' cinematographer, Clement der's aeroplane, Foucault's pendulum which was sed to demonstrate the earth's rotation.

60 rue Réaumur - 01 53 01 82 00

Tuesdays to Sundays from 10 am to 6 pm, Late opening Thursdays until 9.30

Admission 5.50 euros, Reduced rate3.80 euros

20-38-39-47

www.arts-et-metiers.net

Église Sainte-Élisabeth

At the beginning of the 17th century, Marie de Medici laid the first stone of the church and of the convent of the Franciscan nuns, the community she had founded. In the 19th century, statues were added to the classical facade and the church acquired 17th century Flemish bas-reliefs that came from the Abbey of Saint-Vaast d'Arras. They were put up in the ambulatory.

195 rue du Temple - *01 49 96 49 10* - 75

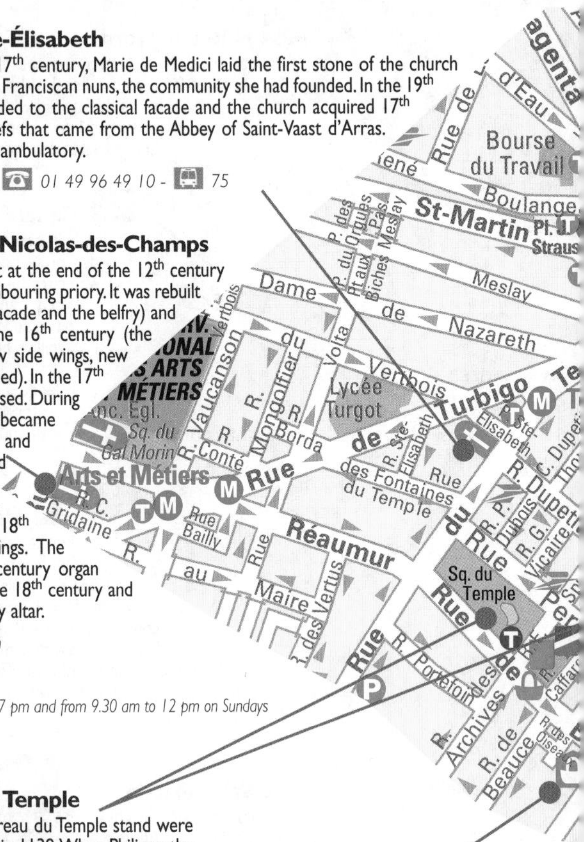

Église Saint-Nicolas-des-Champs

The first church was built at the end of the 12th century by the monks of the neighbouring priory. It was rebuilt in the 15th century (the facade and the belfry) and the layout changed in the 16th century (the chapels were moved, new side wings, new spans and a side door added). In the 17th century the belfry was raised. During the French Revolution it became the Temple of Hymen and Fidelity but was returned to the church in 1802. The chapels are decorated with beautiful 17th, 18th and 19th century paintings. The church also has a 17th century organ which was restored in the 18th century and a remarkable 18th century altar.

254 rue Saint-Martin

01 42 72 92 54

Everyday from 9 am to 7 pm and from 9.30 am to 12 pm on Sundays

20-38-47

Quartier du Temple

The garden and the Carreau du Temple stand were the Templars had settled in 1139. When Philippe the Beautiful suppressed the order at the beginning of the 14th century, they were replaced by the order of the Hospitaller of Saint-John-of-Jerusalem. The fortifications were destroyed in the 17th century, the church at the end of the 18th century, the dungeon at the beginning of the 19th century and the palace in the middle if the 19th. During the French Revolution, the palace was used as a state prison and the royal family was jailed there. The garden was designed by Alphand in 1857. The market was built in 1863, but only two halls are left and they still specialise in garments.

Marché des Enfants Rouges

It is the venue for the oldest covered market in Pa (created at the beginning of the 17th century). Withc the support of the people of the district it would ha disappeared long ago to make way for property dev lopers. It was renovated a few years ago.

rue de Bretagne

Place de la République

It was built by Haussmann at the same time as the Vérines barracks on the north-western side of the square. The Magasins Réunis were later built in the same style on the other side of the rue du Faubourg du Temple. The original fountain was no longer fit for such a grand square and was moved. The new fountain was also found lacking so it was not until 1883 that the present statue by Leopold and Charles Morice was erected in the middle.

Cirque d'Hiver

It was 150 years ago that this circus was built by Jacques-Ignace Hittorff. In 1934, the four brothers Bouglione bought it. It has since remained the magical space of the Bouglione family although it is the venue for other performers too. The Bougliones perpetuate with great passion the tradition of quality circus shows that dreams are made of for young and old alike.

110 rue Amelot

01 47 00 28 81

20-65-96

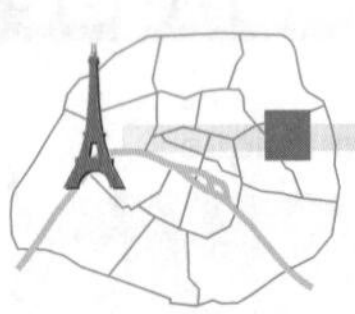

Metro (Underground)

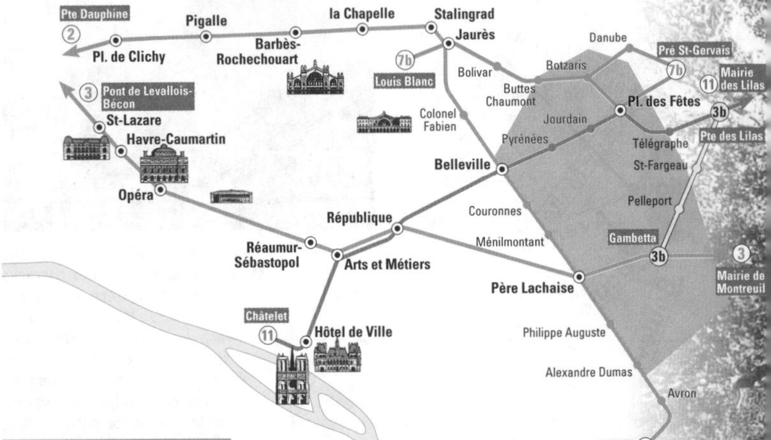

Pte Dauphine
2
Pl. de Clichy
Pigalle
Barbès-Rochechouart
la Chapelle
Stalingrad
Jaurès
7b
Louis Blanc
Bolivar
Colonel Fabien
Buttes Chaumont
Botzaris
Danube
Pré St-Gervais
7b
11
Mairie des Lilas
Pl. des Fêtes
3b
Jourdain
Pyrénées
Télégraphe
Pte des Lilas
St-Fargeau
Pelleport
Belleville
3
Pont de Levallois-Bécon
St-Lazare
Havre-Caumartin
Opéra
République
Couronnes
Ménilmontant
Gambetta
3b
3
Mairie de Montreuil
Réaumur-Sébastopol
Arts et Métiers
Père Lachaise
Châtelet
11
Hôtel de Ville
Philippe Auguste
Alexandre Dumas
Avron
Nation
2

Main access

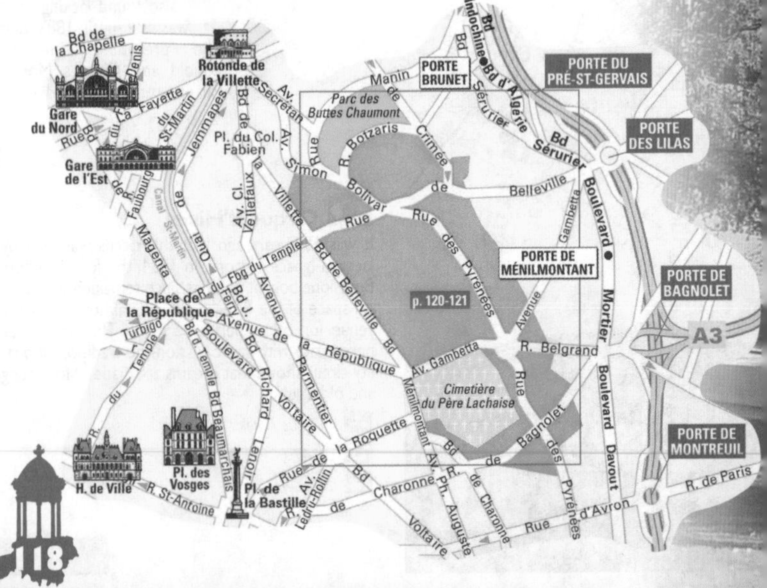

Bd de la Chapelle
Denis
Rotonde de la Villette
Gare du Nord
Rue du Fbg Denis
Bd de la Fayette
Gare de l'Est
Bd de Magenta
R. du Faubourg St-Martin
Canal St-Martin
Quai de Jemmapes
Bd de la Villette
Av. Secrétan
Pl. du Col. Fabien
Av. Cl. Vellefaux
Av. Simon Bolivar
Rue Manin
Parc des Buttes Chaumont
Rue Botzaris
R. de Crimée
PORTE BRUNET
Bd d'Indochine
Bd d'Algérie
Bd Sérurier
PORTE DU PRÉ-ST-GERVAIS
PORTE DES LILAS
Rue de Belleville
Rue des Pyrénées
Avenue Gambetta
PORTE DE MÉNILMONTANT
Boulevard Mortier
R. du Fbg du Temple
Bd de Belleville
p. 120-121
Place de la République
Turbigo
Bd J. Ferry
Avenue Parmentier
Avenue de la République
Av. Gambetta
R. Belgrand
PORTE DE BAGNOLET
A3
Rue du Temple
Bd du Temple
Bd Beaumarchais
Boulevard Voltaire
Bd Richard Lenoir
Bd de Ménilmontant
Cimetière du Père Lachaise
Rue de Bagnolet
Boulevard Davout
PORTE DE MONTREUIL
R. de Paris
Rue de la Roquette
H. de Ville
Pl. des Vosges
Pl. de la Bastille
R. St-Antoine
Av. Ledru-Rollin
R. de Charonne
Bd Voltaire
Av. Ph. Auguste
Rue d'Avron
Rue des Pyrénées

Ménilmontant
Père-Lachaise

Parc des Buttes Chaumont

It was at the end of the 19th century, that Alphand transformed this 'Mont Chauve' (the 'bald hill', an old gypsum quarry), into a romantic space where people could have a stroll and relax. In the middle of the park there is an island accessible across two bridges that dominate the park. At the top of the hill, a temple was built on a belvedere from which one can admire the wonderful views.

Place Armand-Carrel

Everyday from 7 am to 11 pm in summer and from 7 am to 9 pm in winter.

26-48-60-75

Rue de Belleville

It is the main street of a district that was attached to Paris in 1860. With Menilmontant, it symbolises the popular side of Paris sang by Maurice Chevalier, Edith Piaf and Charles Trenet. The area is still very lively, but has become much more cosmopolitan.

Parc de Belleville

The park was opened in 1988. Set on a hill it offers wonderful views over Paris, especially from the belvedere built at the top of the park. The landscaping makes the most of the sloping grounds with many winding alleys leading to waterfalls, ponds and water jets that indicate the presence of many springs. The few vines reminds us of the wine that used to be produced here.

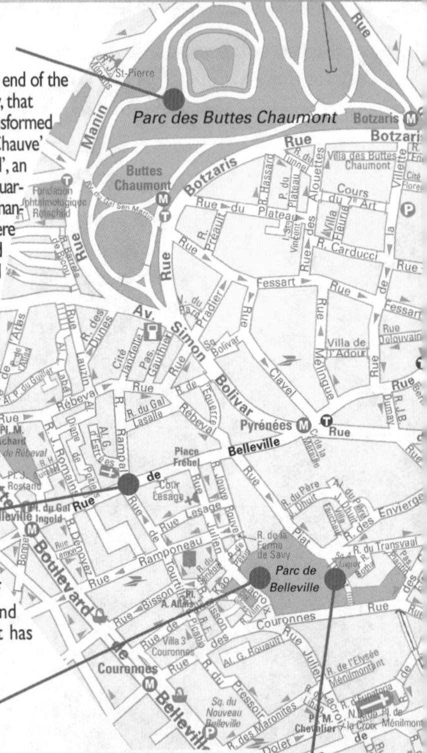

Maison de l'Air

A permanent exhibition and many children workshops help us discover air and how it behaves. We discover the instruments used to measure its quality and to forecast the weather.

Parc de Belleville -  *01 43 28 47 63*

 *Tuesdays to Sundays from 1 pm to 5 pm and 6 pm in summer*

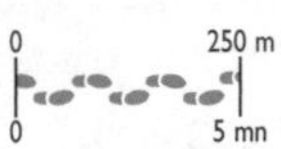

Ménilmontant - Père-Lachaise

Rue des Cascades, villa de l'Ermitage, passage de la Duée

These streets are picturesque and full of charm. Lined with small houses, the area looks like a village.

Cimetière du Père-Lachaise

It is named after the confessor of Louis XIV. The cemetery was built in the 19th century by Alexandre-Theodore Brongniart on the site of an old rest home owned by the Jesuits. As he kept the tree lined lanes, it made it look more like a park than a cemetery. Many well known personalities are buried there, turning the place into a museum and a history book. They include Heloise and Abelard, Alfred de Musset, Colette, Frederic Chopin, Balzac, La Fontaine, Molière, Delacroix, Edith Piaf, Jim Morrison.... At the back of the cemetery, the 'Mur des Fédérés' stands on the spot where the last rioters of the Paris Commune were shot.

Charonne

Another one of Paris's district that looks like a village, with its 15th century church (Saint-Germain-de-Charonne) and its graveyard. Charonne was attached to Paris in 1819.

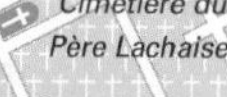

Metro (Underground)

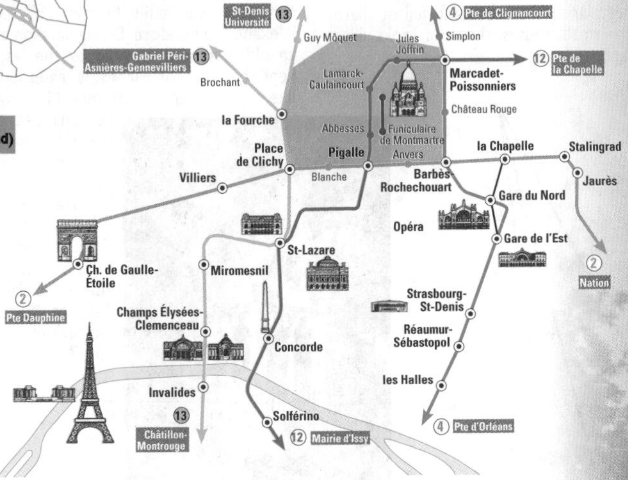

St-Denis Université 13
Gabriel Péri-Asnières-Gennevilliers 13
Guy Môquet
Brochant
la Fourche
Place de Clichy
Villiers
Ch. de Gaulle-Étoile
2 Pte Dauphine
Lamarck-Caulaincourt
Abbesses
Pigalle
Blanche
Jules Joffrin
Funiculaire de Montmartre
Anvers
4 Pte de Clignancourt
Simplon
Marcadet-Poissonniers
12 Pte de la Chapelle
Château Rouge
Barbès-Rochechouart
la Chapelle
Stalingrad
Jaurès
Gare du Nord
Gare de l'Est
Opéra
2 Nation
St-Lazare
Miromesnil
Champs Élysées-Clemenceau
Concorde
Strasbourg-St-Denis
Réaumur-Sébastopol
les Halles
4 Pte d'Orléans
Invalides
13 Châtillon-Montrouge
Solférino
12 Mairie d'Issy

Main access

Bd Bessières · Bd Ney · Bd Berthier · Boulevard Pereire · Av. de St-Ouen · R. Guy Môquet · Rue Championnet · Rue Ordener · Rue Riquet · R. de la Chapelle · Rue d'Aubervilliers · Rue de Crimée · Av. de Flandre · Bd Ornano · Bd Barbès · Avenue de Clichy · R. Pouchet · R. Cardinet · Rue Custine · Caulaincourt · R. Marx Dormoy

p. 124-125
p. 126-127

Moulin de la Galette
Cimetière de Montmartre
Moulin Rouge
Sacré-Cœur
Pl. du Gal Catroux
Pl. de Clichy
Bd de Clichy
Bd de Rochechouart
Bd de la Chapelle
Rotonde de la Villette
Gare du Nord
Rue de Villiers
Bd des Batignolles
Bd Malesherbes
Rue de Rome
R. d'Amsterdam
R. de Clichy
Ste-Trinité
Bd de Courcelles
Parc de Monceau
Rue Hoche
Av. de Friedland
R. de Londres
R. de Châteaudun
R. de Maubeuge
Rue La Fayette
R. du Fbg St-Denis
R. du Fbg St-Martin
Quai de Jemmapes
Rue de la Villette
Pl. du Col. Fabien
Av. Cl. Vellefaux
Gare St-Lazare
R.d.l. Ch. d'Antin
Bd Haussmann
Rue de Dunkerque
Gare de l'Est
Canal St-Martin
Bd de Magenta
Rue du Fbg Saint Honoré
Av. des Champs Élysées
Rd Point des Chps Élysées
Rue Tronchet
Opéra Garnier
Bd des Capucines
Bd des Italiens
Bd Poissonière
Bd de Bonne Nouvelle
Bd St-Martin
R. du 4 Septembre
Bourse
Bd de Strasbourg
Bd de Sébastopol
Place de la République
R. du Fbg du Temple
Bd J. Ferry
Ste-Marie Madeleine
Pl. de la Concorde
Jardin des Tuileries
Pl. Vendôme

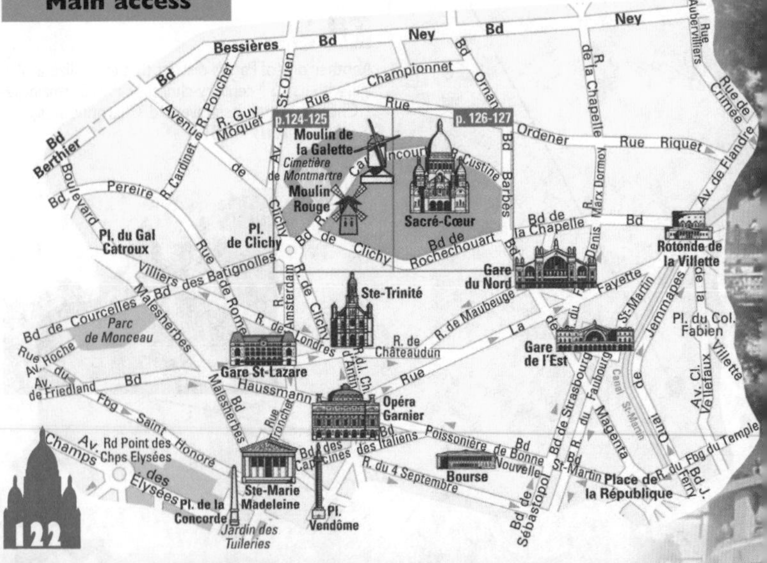

Montmartre

Cimetière de Montmartre

In 1825, a cemetery was opened over the old plaster quarries. During the French Revolution it had been used as a communal grave. Many artists are buried there: Degas, Alfred de Vigny, Jean Charcot, Louis Jouvet, Michel Berger and François Truffaut.

Le Moulin de la Galette

Vestige des moulins installés sur la butte, il fut transformé en bal musette par le meunier Debray au XIXe siècle et immortalisé par Auguste Renoir.

Bal du Moulin Rouge

It has been a place of fun and entertainment since it was opened. It gained its notoriety through its false windmill and the French Cancan. The tradition is kept up with dinners and shows.

82 boulevard de Clichy

01 53 09 82 82

30-54-68-74

www.moulinrouge.fr

Musée de l'Érotisme

The museum was opened in 1977 in one of Paris's hottest districts. It displays erotic works of art and other objects connected to the theme.

72 boulevard de Clichy - *01 42 58 28 73*

Everyday from 10 am to 2 am

Admission rate 7 euros, Reduced rate 5 euros

30-54-68-74

Musée de la Vie romantique

The painter Ary Scheffer lived in this early 19th century house where we find souvenirs of George Sand and the painter's work

16 rue Chaptal - *01 55 31 95 67*

From Tuesdays to Sundays from 10 am to 6 pm

Admission rate 4.50 euros, Reduced rate 3 euros

68-74

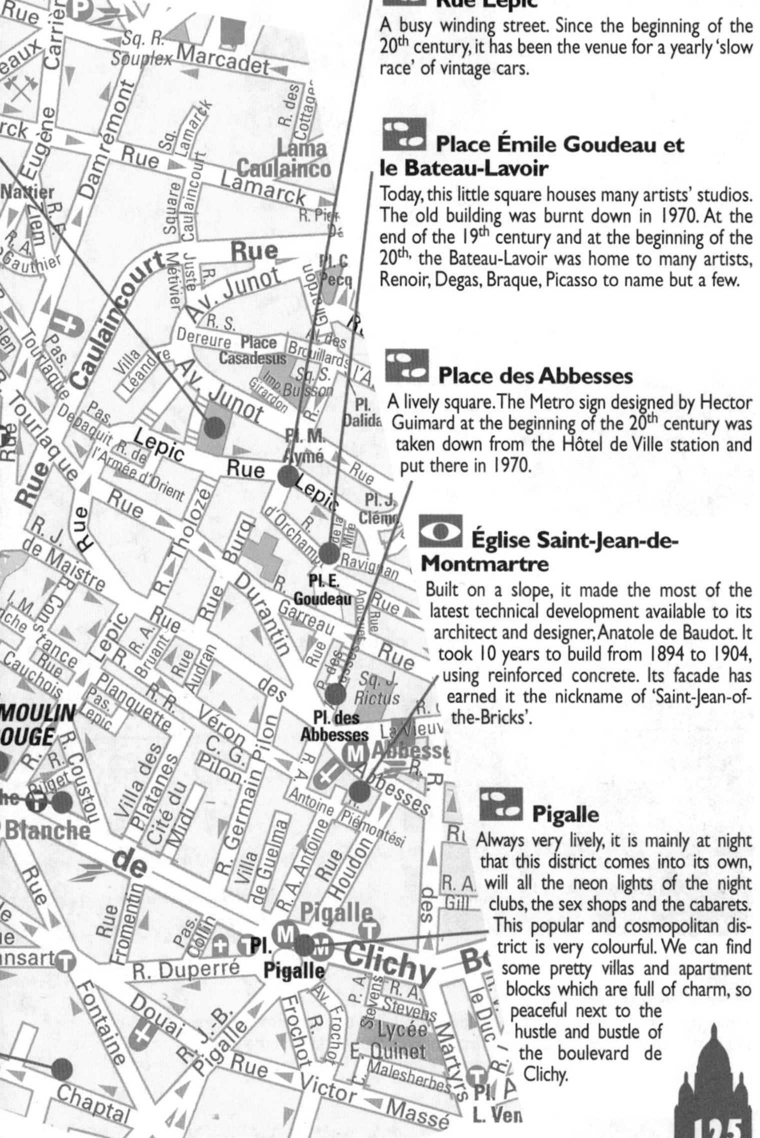

Rue Lepic

A busy winding street. Since the beginning of the 20th century, it has been the venue for a yearly 'slow race' of vintage cars.

Place Émile Goudeau et le Bateau-Lavoir

Today, this little square houses many artists' studios. The old building was burnt down in 1970. At the end of the 19th century and at the beginning of the 20th, the Bateau-Lavoir was home to many artists, Renoir, Degas, Braque, Picasso to name but a few.

Place des Abbesses

A lively square. The Metro sign designed by Hector Guimard at the beginning of the 20th century was taken down from the Hôtel de Ville station and put there in 1970.

Église Saint-Jean-de-Montmartre

Built on a slope, it made the most of the latest technical development available to its architect and designer, Anatole de Baudot. It took 10 years to build from 1894 to 1904, using reinforced concrete. Its facade has earned it the nickname of 'Saint-Jean-of-the-Bricks'.

Pigalle

Always very lively, it is mainly at night that this district comes into its own, will all the neon lights of the night clubs, the sex shops and the cabarets. This popular and cosmopolitan district is very colourful. We can find some pretty villas and apartment blocks which are full of charm, so peaceful next to the hustle and bustle of the boulevard de Clichy.

Rue Saint-Vincent et "Au Lapin Agile"

A picturesque street. The famous 'Au Lapin Agile' is on the corner of the rue des Saules. Its name is a pun on a drawing by a cartoonist, the 'Lapin à Gilles' (Gilles' Rabbit). The place was popular with painters and artists in the 1900s. Claude Brasseur and Georges Brassens started their career there. Young performers still appear on its stage.

Clos Montmartre

One of the last vineyards in Paris. Every year, when the grapes are picked, the locals gather for a great celebration.

Musée de Montmartre

This little museum is housed in a 17th century house where Renoir and Utrillo lived. It tells us the history of the district through documents, photos, paintings and other objects.

12 rue Cortot

01 46 06 61 11

Tuesdays to Sundays from 11 am to 6 pm

Admission rate 4 euros, Reduced rate 3 euros

54

Place du Tertre

In the past, this was the village square. Today it is full of café terraces, painters and portraitists and thousands of tourists from the four corners of the world.

0 250 m
0 5 mn

Église Saint-Pierre-de-Montmartre

The church dates back to the 12th century. It is what remains of the Montmartre Abbey. It is one of the oldest churches in Paris. Rebuilt in the 15th and in the 18th centuries, it became the Temple of Reason under the French Revolution. It was almost destroyed in the 19th century but was reprieved and restored in the 20th and new stained glass windows fitted in 1954.

Basilique du Sacré-Cœur

Dominating Montmartre and visible from a long way off, it is one of the city's landmarks. It is the symbol of a popular and bohemian Paris. After the terrible years of war in 1870 and of the Paris Commune, a promise was made to build a basilica which would be a place of pilgrimage. As the project was deemed to be of public interest, a competition was organised in 1873. It was won by Paul Abadie, and a national subscription launched to fund the project. The work started in 1875. The construction, which was finished by Louis Jean Hulot in 1914, was difficult as the church required deep foundations. The architecture is of Byzantine and Roman inspiration and there are several chapels. A large dome covers the choir. The 19 tonnes 'Savoyarde' bell hangs in the belfry.

Halle Saint-Pierre - Musée d'Art naïf Max Fourny

It is an old covered market, built at the end of the 19th century and restored in 1986. It is now the Max Fourny Museum of Naive Art (contemporary paintings and sculptures). There is also a gallery for temporary exhibitions. Art workshops are organised for children.

2 rue Ronsard - *01 42 58 72 89*

Everyday from 10 am to 6 pm

Admission 5 euros, Reduced rate 6 euros

54

Web *www.hallesaintpierre.org*

Funiculaire

pened in 1900, it gives easy access to the top of e hill.

Metro (Underground)

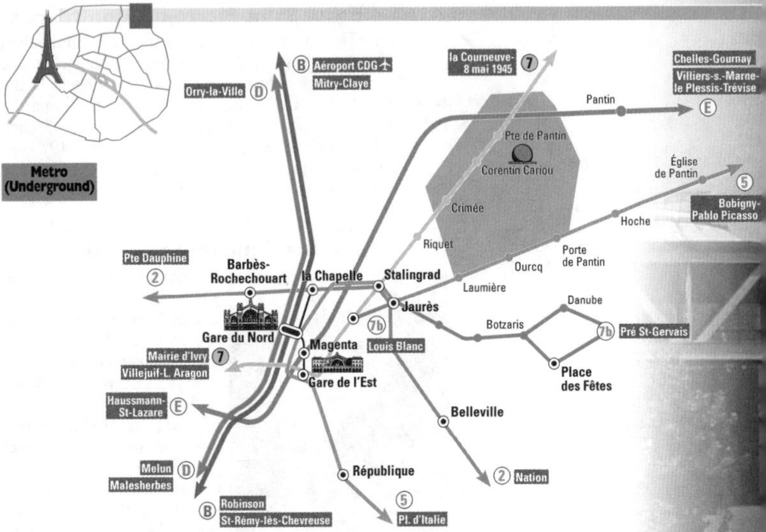

Main access

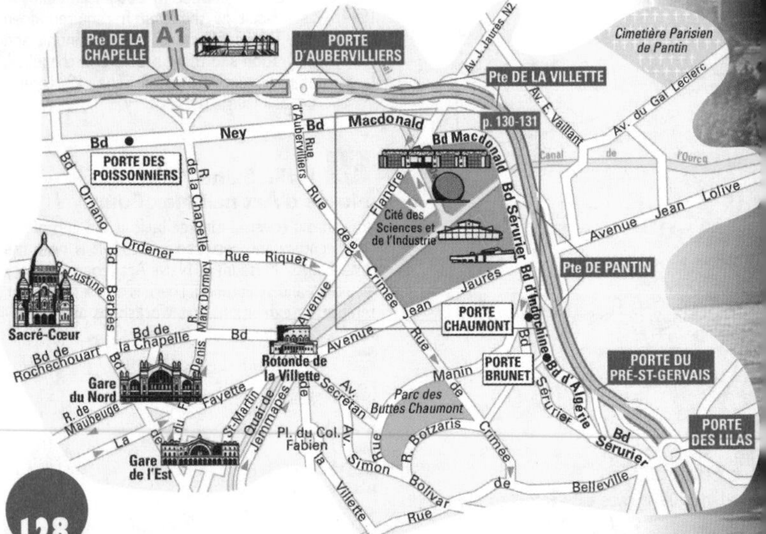

La Villette

La Cité des Sciences et de l'Industrie

The City of Science and Industry is housed in a gigantic building over 250 m long which was initially meant to be a meat market. It was later transformed into a museum. Inaugurated in 1986, it consists in several exhibition areas, workshops, a mediatheque, a planetarium and a cinema. Explora is undoubtedly the heart of the city, a series of permanent and temporary exhibitions on man and nature. They help us understand our body and our environment and discover the great scientific and technological revolutions. Workshops focus on a series of special themes.

30 avenue Corentin-Cariou - *01 42 58 28 73* - *75-139-150-152-PC*

Tuesdays to Sundays from 10 am to 6 pm - *Admission 7.50 euros, Reduced rate 5.50 euros*

www.cite-sciences.fr

La Cité des enfants

The city of children offers a hands-on way of discovering science and technologies. The children are encouraged to take part into activities that will satisfy the curiosity of young children (3 to 5 years old) and older ones (5 to 12 years old).

Tuesdays to Sundays, 90 minute sessions

Admission 5 euros

Le Cinaxe

It is more than a cinema. The screen and the room move in synchrony with the projected pictures to give a more realistic impression.

Tuesdays to Sundays, shows every 15 minutes from 11 am to 1 pm and from 2 pm to 5 pm

Admission 5.20 euros, Reduced rate 4.50 euros

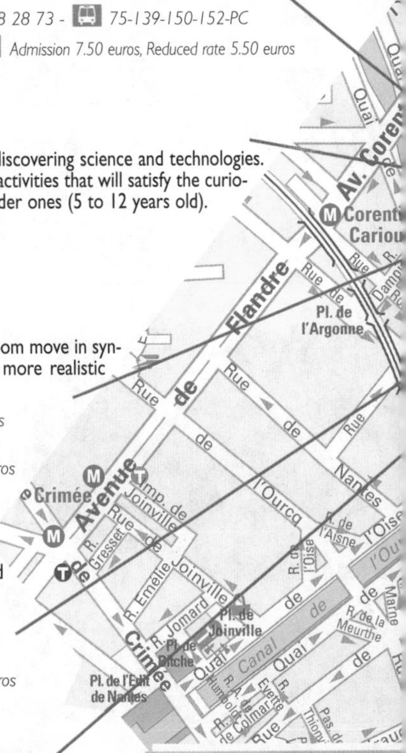

La Géode

It is a cinema and a projection room with a circular screen. It is striking and spectacular.

Tuesdays to Sundays from 10.30 am to 9.30 pm (7.30 pm on Sundays)

Admission 8.75 euros, Reduced rate 6.75 euros

www.lageode.fr

L'Argonaute

It was a real submarine that was decommissioned and transported here. It is a way of discovering and understanding life on board these vessels.

Tuesdays to Fridays from 10.30 am to 5.30 pm

Admission 3 euros

0 250 m
0 5 mn

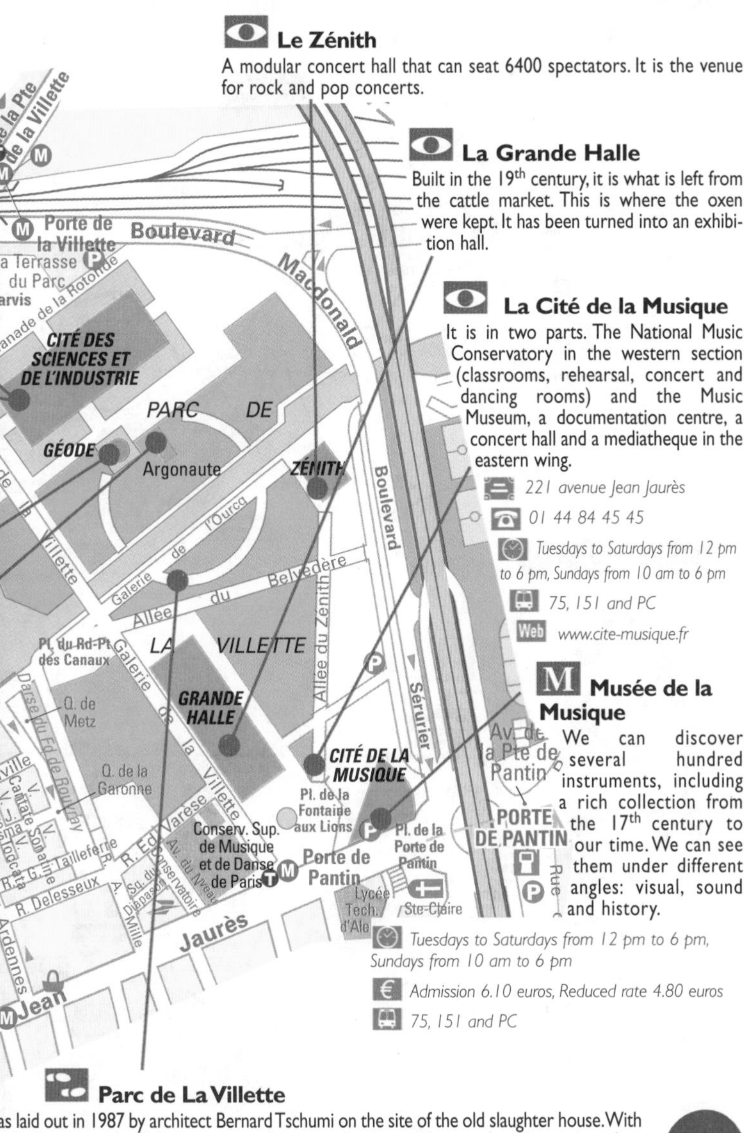

Le Zénith

A modular concert hall that can seat 6400 spectators. It is the venue for rock and pop concerts.

La Grande Halle

Built in the 19th century, it is what is left from the cattle market. This is where the oxen were kept. It has been turned into an exhibition hall.

La Cité de la Musique

It is in two parts. The National Music Conservatory in the western section (classrooms, rehearsal, concert and dancing rooms) and the Music Museum, a documentation centre, a concert hall and a mediatheque in the eastern wing.

221 avenue Jean Jaurès

01 44 84 45 45

Tuesdays to Saturdays from 12 pm to 6 pm, Sundays from 10 am to 6 pm

75, 151 and PC

www.cite-musique.fr

Musée de la Musique

We can discover several hundred instruments, including a rich collection from the 17th century to our time. We can see them under different angles: visual, sound and history.

Tuesdays to Saturdays from 12 pm to 6 pm, Sundays from 10 am to 6 pm

Admission 6.10 euros, Reduced rate 4.80 euros

75, 151 and PC

Parc de La Villette

was laid out in 1987 by architect Bernard Tschumi on the site of the old slaughter house. With red milestones (the Folies), its elevated promenades, its meadows and gardens, it is a place here people can relax, stroll and play. It is a garden with a futuristic atmosphere.

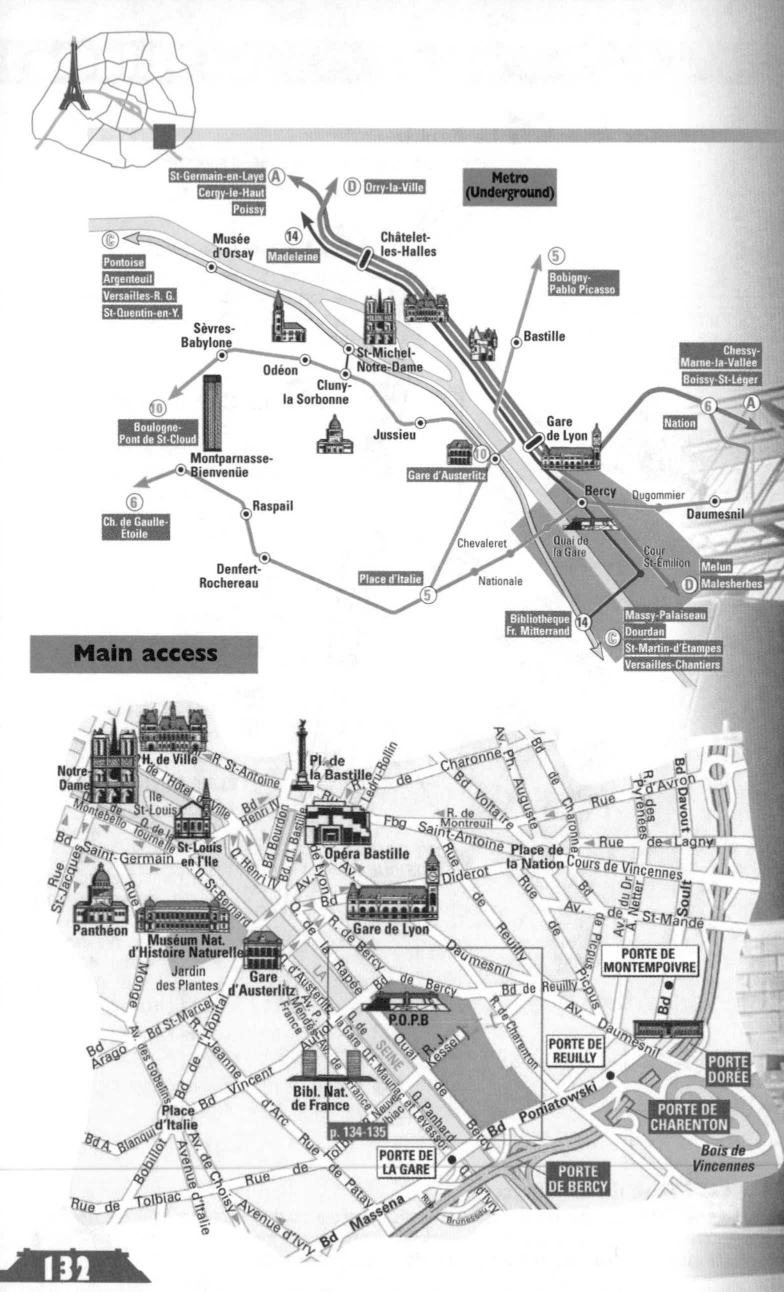

Metro (Underground)
St-Germain-en-Laye
Cergy-le-Haut
Poissy
Orry-la-Ville
Musée d'Orsay
Madeleine
Châtelet-les-Halles
Pontoise
Argenteuil
Versailles-R. G.
St-Quentin-en-Y.
Bobigny-Pablo Picasso
Bastille
Sèvres-Babylone
Odéon
St-Michel-Notre-Dame
Cluny-la Sorbonne
Chessy-Marne-la-Vallée
Boissy-St-Léger
Nation
Boulogne-Pont de St-Cloud
Jussieu
Gare de Lyon
Gare d'Austerlitz
Montparnasse-Bienvenüe
Bercy
Dugommier
Daumesnil
Raspail
Ch. de Gaulle-Étoile
Chevaleret
Quai de la Gare
Cour St-Émilion
Melun
Malesherbes
Denfert-Rochereau
Place d'Italie
Nationale
Bibliothèque Fr. Mitterrand
Massy-Palaiseau
Dourdan
St-Martin-d'Étampes
Versailles-Chantiers
Notre-Dame
H. de Ville
Pl. de la Bastille
Opéra Bastille
St-Louis en l'Ile
Place de la Nation
Panthéon
Muséum Nat. d'Histoire Naturelle
Jardin des Plantes
Gare d'Austerlitz
Gare de Lyon
P.O.P.B
Bibl. Nat. de France
Place d'Italie
PORTE DE MONTEMPOIVRE
PORTE DE REUILLY
PORTE DORÉE
PORTE DE CHARENTON
Bois de Vincennes
PORTE DE LA GARE
PORTE DE BERCY
p. 134-135
Bd Poniatowski
Bd Masséna
Cours de Vincennes
Fbg Saint-Antoine
Bd Saint-Germain
Rue de Tolbiac
Avenue d'Italie
Avenue d'Ivry

Main access

Bercy

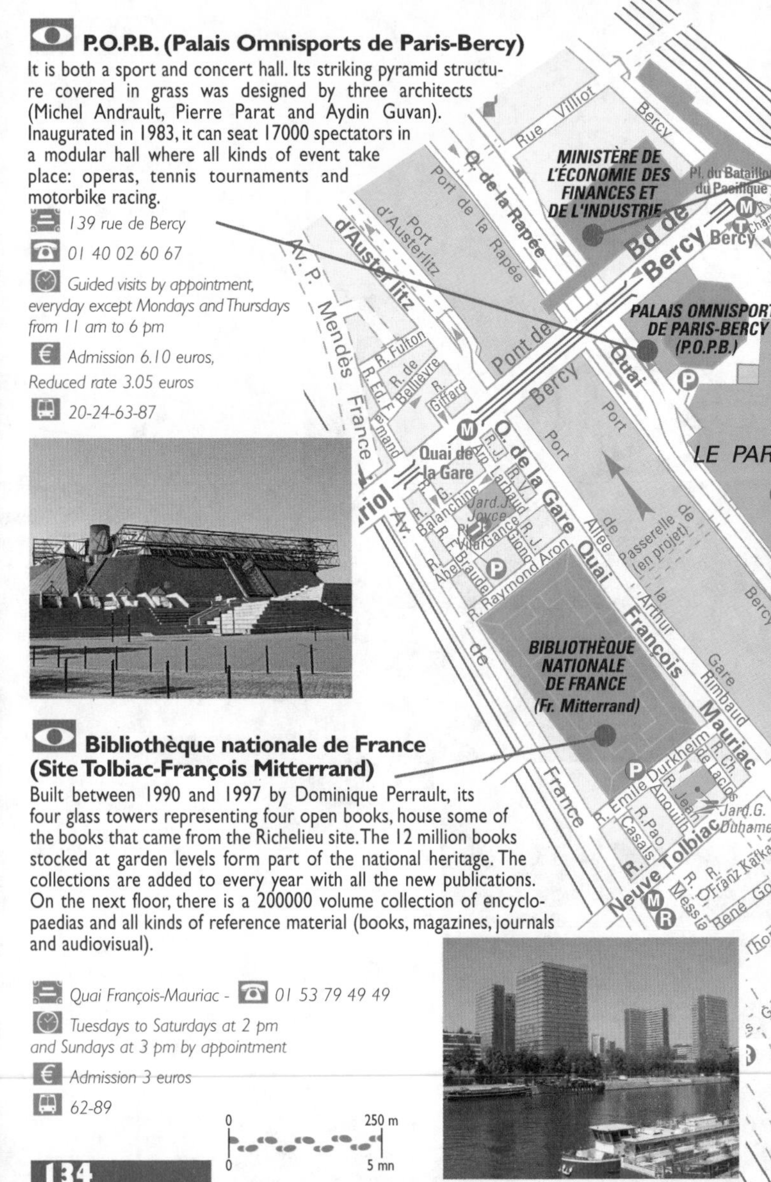

P.O.P.B. (Palais Omnisports de Paris-Bercy)

It is both a sport and concert hall. Its striking pyramid structure covered in grass was designed by three architects (Michel Andrault, Pierre Parat and Aydin Guvan). Inaugurated in 1983, it can seat 17000 spectators in a modular hall where all kinds of event take place: operas, tennis tournaments and motorbike racing.

139 rue de Bercy

01 40 02 60 67

Guided visits by appointment, everyday except Mondays and Thursdays from 11 am to 6 pm

Admission 6.10 euros, Reduced rate 3.05 euros

20-24-63-87

Bibliothèque nationale de France (Site Tolbiac-François Mitterrand)

Built between 1990 and 1997 by Dominique Perrault, its four glass towers representing four open books, house some of the books that came from the Richelieu site. The 12 million books stocked at garden levels form part of the national heritage. The collections are added to every year with all the new publications. On the next floor, there is a 200000 volume collection of encyclopaedias and all kinds of reference material (books, magazines, journals and audiovisual).

Quai François-Mauriac - 01 53 79 49 49

Tuesdays to Saturdays at 2 pm and Sundays at 3 pm by appointment

Admission 3 euros

62-89

Ministère de l'Économie, des Finances et de l'Industrie

When the Ministry abandoned its previous premises in one of the wings of the Louvre, all the services were regrouped in this 350 m long building which was inaugurated in 1989. A motorboat allows the minister and his cabinet to reach the centre of Paris quickly.

139 rue de Bercy - 01 40 04 04 04 - 24-87

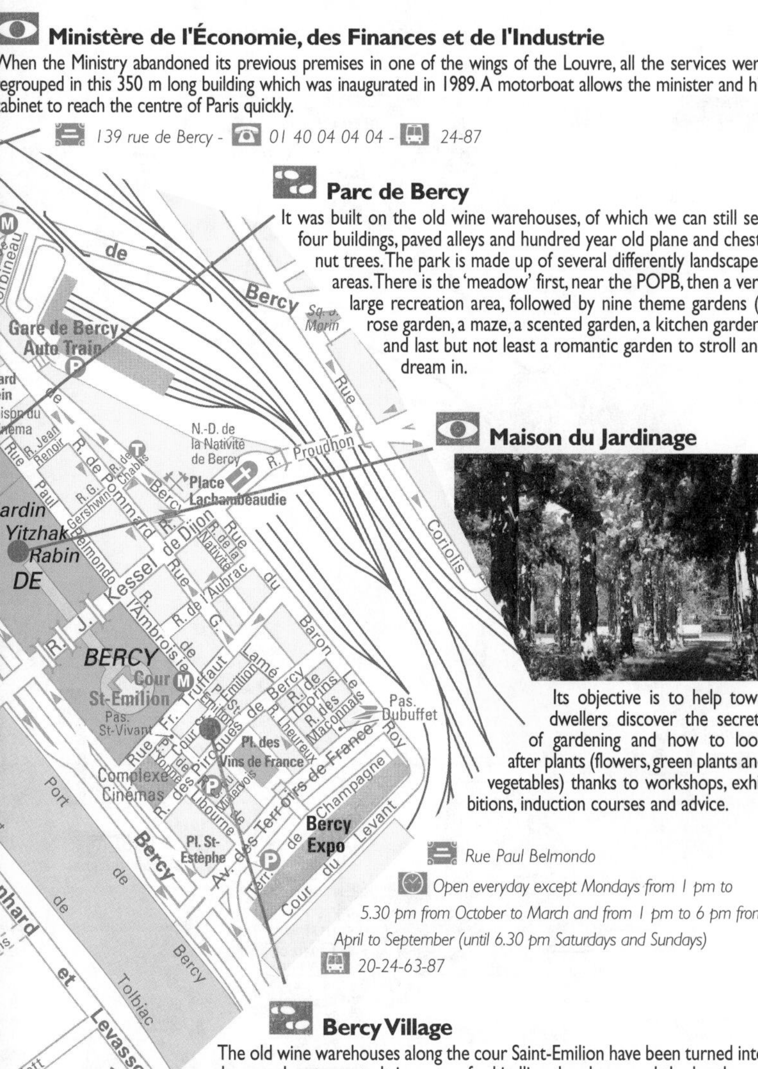

Parc de Bercy

It was built on the old wine warehouses, of which we can still see four buildings, paved alleys and hundred year old plane and chestnut trees. The park is made up of several differently landscaped areas. There is the 'meadow' first, near the POPB, then a very large recreation area, followed by nine theme gardens (a rose garden, a maze, a scented garden, a kitchen garden) and last but not least a romantic garden to stroll and dream in.

Maison du Jardinage

Its objective is to help town dwellers discover the secrets of gardening and how to look after plants (flowers, green plants and vegetables) thanks to workshops, exhibitions, induction courses and advice.

Rue Paul Belmondo

Open everyday except Mondays from 1 pm to 5.30 pm from October to March and from 1 pm to 6 pm from April to September (until 6.30 pm Saturdays and Sundays)

20-24-63-87

Bercy Village

The old wine warehouses along the cour Saint-Emilion have been turned into shops and restaurants. It is a way of rekindling the charm and the hustle and bustle of the past.

24-62 - Web www.bercyvillage.com

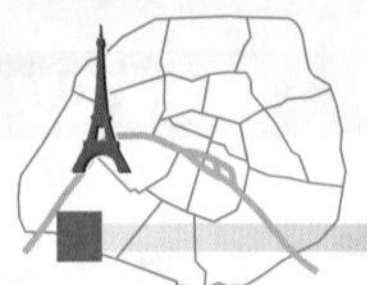

Metro (Underground)

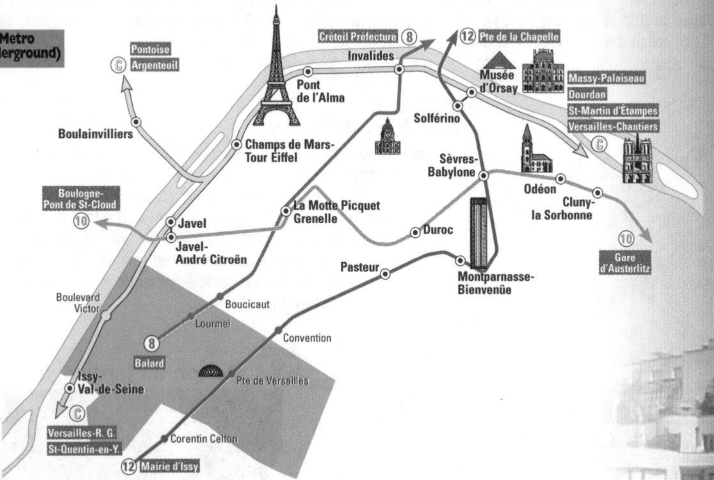

C Pontoise
Argenteuil
Boulainvilliers
Pont de l'Alma
Champs de Mars-Tour Eiffel
Créteil Préfecture 8
Invalides
12 Pte de la Chapelle
Musée d'Orsay
Solférino
Massy-Palaiseau
Dourdan
St-Martin d'Étampes
Versailles-Chantiers
C
Sèvres-Babylone
Odéon
Cluny-la Sorbonne
Boulogne-Pont de St-Cloud
10
Javel
Javel-André Citroën
La Motte Picquet Grenelle
Duroc
10
Gare d'Austerlitz
Pasteur
Montparnasse-Bienvenüe
Boulevard Victor
Boucicaut
Lourmel
8
Balard
Convention
Issy-Val-de-Seine
Pte de Versailles
C
Versailles-R. G.
St-Quentin-en-Y.
Corentin Celton
12 Mairie d'Issy

Main access

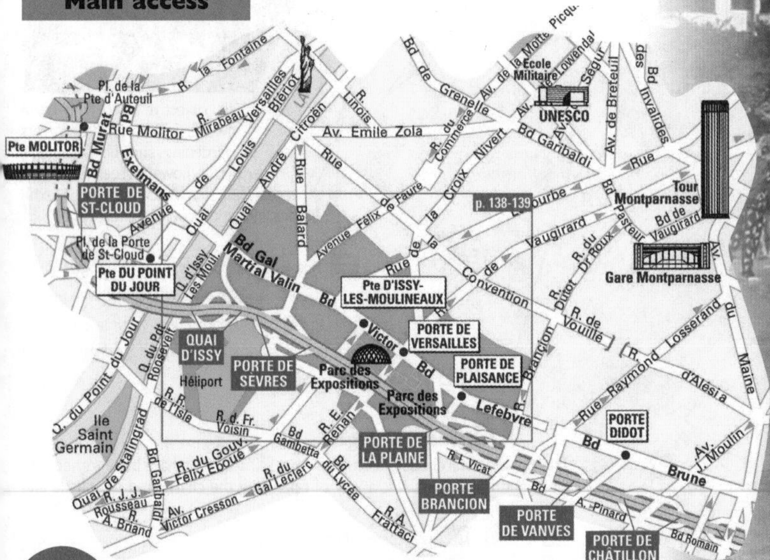

Pl. de la Pte d'Auteuil
R. la Fontaine
Pte MOLITOR
Rue Molitor
Bd Murat
R. Mirabeau
Versailles
Blériot
Av. Emile Zola
R. Linois
Bd de Grenelle
Av. de la Motte Picqu.
Ecole Militaire
Av. de Lowendal
Av. de Ségur
Av. de Breteuil
Bd des Invalides
UNESCO
Bd Exelmans
PORTE DE ST-CLOUD
Avenue de
Quai Louis
Quai André Citroën
Rue Balard
R. du Commerce
Croix Nivert
Bd Garibaldi
Rue Lecourbe
Bd Pasteur
Tour Montparnasse
Bd de Vaugirard
p. 138-139
Avenue Félix de Faure
Rue de la
Vaugirard
R. du Dr Roux
Pl. de la Porte de St-Cloud
Pte DU POINT DU JOUR
Q. d'Issy Les Moul.
Bd Gal Martial Valin
Pte D'ISSY-LES-MOULINEAUX
Rue de la Convention
R. Dutot
Gare Montparnasse
Av. du Maine
R. de Vouillé
Rue Losserand
Bd Victor
PORTE DE VERSAILLES
R. Brancion
Q. du Point du Jour
Q. du Pdt Roosevelt
QUAI D'ISSY
Héliport
PORTE DE SEVRES
Parc des Expositions
PORTE DE PLAISANCE
R. Raymond
Rue d'Alésia
Parc des Expositions
Bd Lefebvre
R. R. de l'Isle
R. d. Fr. Voisin
Ile Saint Germain
R. E. Renan
Bd Gambetta
PORTE DIDOT
Bd Brune
Av. J. Moulin
Bd Garibaldi
R. du Gouv. Félix Eboué
R. du Gal Leclerc
Bd du Lycée
PORTE DE LA PLAINE
R. L. Vicat
Quai de Stalingrad
R. J. J. Rousseau
R. A. Briand
Av. Victor Cresson
R. A. Frattaci
PORTE BRANCION
PORTE DE VANVES
Bd
A. Pinard
PORTE DE CHÂTILLON
Bd Romain

Porte de Versailles

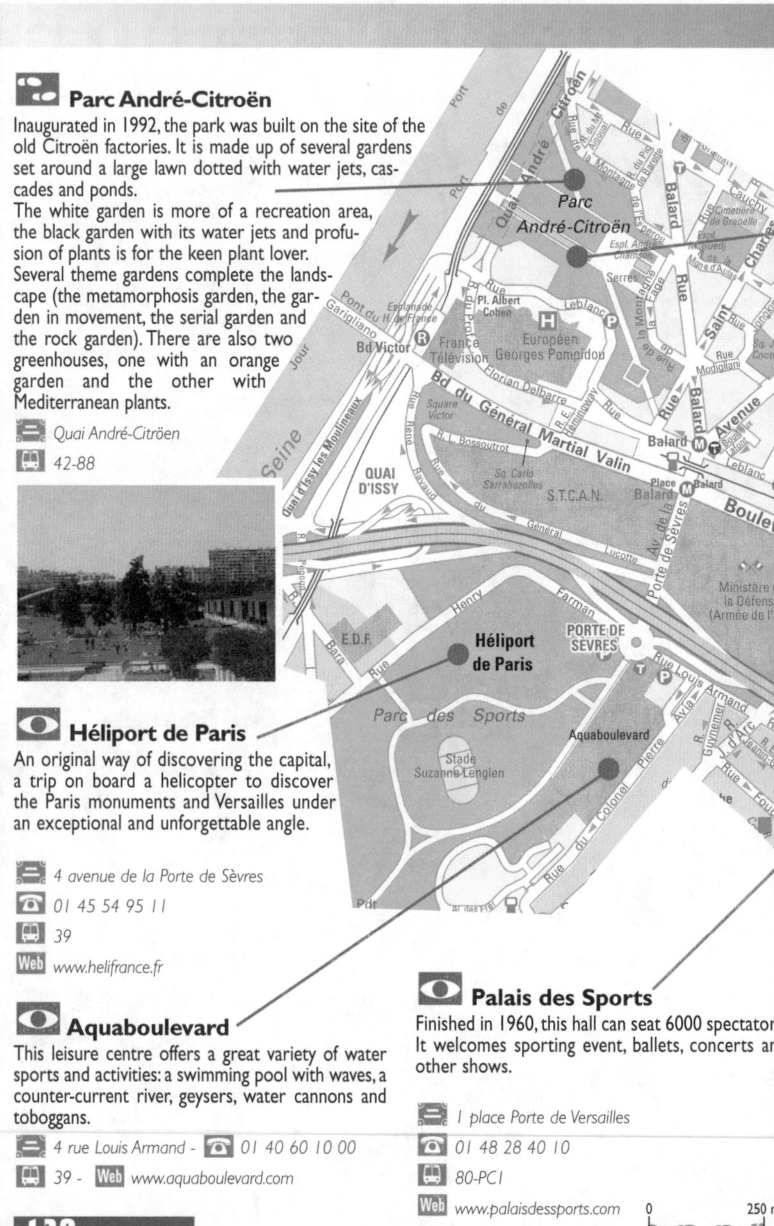

Parc André-Citroën

Inaugurated in 1992, the park was built on the site of the old Citroën factories. It is made up of several gardens set around a large lawn dotted with water jets, cascades and ponds.

The white garden is more of a recreation area, the black garden with its water jets and profusion of plants is for the keen plant lover. Several theme gardens complete the landscape (the metamorphosis garden, the garden in movement, the serial garden and the rock garden). There are also two greenhouses, one with an orange garden and the other with Mediterranean plants.

Quai André-Citröen

42-88

Héliport de Paris

An original way of discovering the capital, a trip on board a helicopter to discover the Paris monuments and Versailles under an exceptional and unforgettable angle.

4 avenue de la Porte de Sèvres

01 45 54 95 11

39

Web *www.helifrance.fr*

Aquaboulevard

This leisure centre offers a great variety of water sports and activities: a swimming pool with waves, a counter-current river, geysers, water cannons and toboggans.

4 rue Louis Armand - *01 40 60 10 00*

39 - Web *www.aquaboulevard.com*

Palais des Sports

Finished in 1960, this hall can seat 6000 spectator! It welcomes sporting event, ballets, concerts an other shows.

1 place Porte de Versailles

01 48 28 40 10

80-PC1

Web *www.palaisdessports.com*

Ballon Captif Eutelsat

Veather permitting, it is possible to discover Paris y going 150 m up in the balloon.

Quai André-Citröen - 42-88

Parc Georges Brassens

This was a vineyard in the 18th century. Later, in the 19th century, it became a market garden before becoming a slaughterhouse in 1894.
It was pulled down in 1975, except for the auction tower and two bronze bulls. The park was landscaped between 1975 and 1983. The alleys take the visitor round scented gardens, a rose garden, bee hives and a mini vineyard, reminiscent of the past.

2 place Jacques Marette

01 48 45 51 80 - 89-95

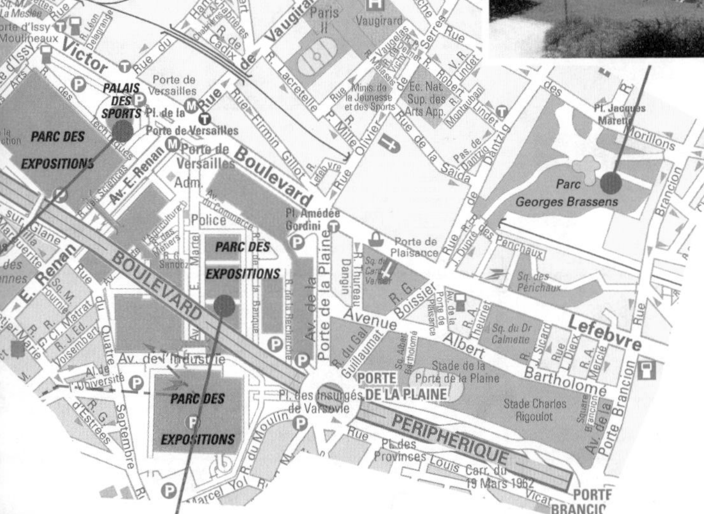

Paris Expo

n 1923, it was decided to built an exhibition centre to welcome the Paris Fair that had until now been held at the Champs-de-Mars. The exhibition halls cover a surface of 35 hectares and straddle three areas (Paris, Issy-les-Moulineaux and Vanves). Regularly modernised, it is Europe's fourth exhibition hall with an area of 220 000 m^2.

1 place Porte de Versailles - 01 43 95 37 00

39-49-80-PC1 - Web www.parisexpo.fr

Metro (Underground)

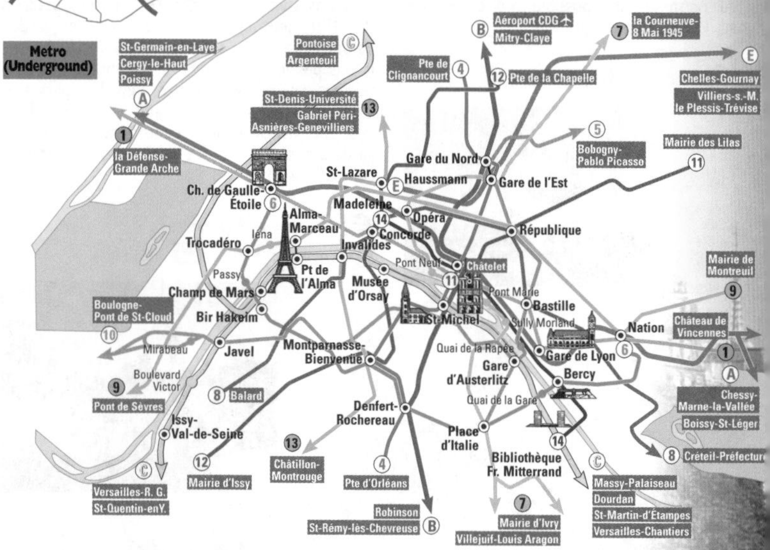

St-Germain-en-Laye
Cergy-le-Haut
Poissy
A
1
la Défense-Grande Arche
Pontoise C
Argenteuil
St-Denis-Université
Gabriel Péri-Asnières-Genevilliers
13
B Aéroport CDG
Mitry-Claye
Pte de Clignancourt 4
12 Pte de la Chapelle
7 la Courneuve-8 Mai 1945
E
Chelles-Gournay
Villiers-s.-M. le Plessis-Trévise
5
Bobogny-Pablo Picasso
Mairie des Lilas
11
Gare du Nord
Gare de l'Est
St-Lazare
E
Haussmann
Ch. de Gaulle-Étoile
6
Madeleine
14
Opéra
Alma-Marceau
Concorde
République
Iéna
Trocadéro
Invalides
Passy
Pt de l'Alma
Pont Neuf
Châtelet
11
Musée d'Orsay
Champ de Mars
Pont Marie
Mairie de Montreuil
9
Bastille
Boulogne-Pont de St-Cloud
10
Bir Hakeim
St-Michel
Sully Morland
Nation
Château de Vincennes
Mirabeau
Javel
Montparnasse-Bienvenüe
Quai de la Rapée
Gare de Lyon
6
1
A
Boulevard Victor
Gare d'Austerlitz
Bercy
9
Pont de Sèvres
8 Balard
Quai de la Gare
Chessy-Marne-la-Vallée
Boissy-St-Léger
Denfert-Rochereau
Issy-Val-de-Seine
Place d'Italie
13
14
8 Créteil-Préfecture
C
12
Châtillon-Montrouge
4
Bibliothèque Fr. Mitterrand
C
Versailles-R. G.
St-Quentin-enY.
Mairie d'Issy
Pte d'Orléans
Massy-Palaiseau
Dourdan
St-Martin-d'Étampes
Versailles-Chantiers
Robinson
St-Rémy-lès-Chevreuse B
7
Mairie d'Ivry
Villejuif-Louis Aragon

Main access

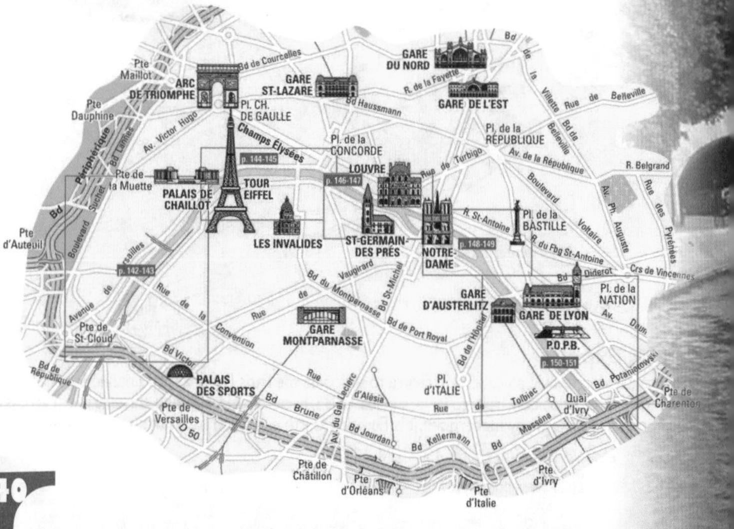

Bd de Courcelles
Pte Maillot
ARC DE TRIOMPHE
GARE ST-LAZARE
GARE DU NORD
R. de la Fayette
GARE DE L'EST
Bd Haussmann
Pte Dauphine
Pl. CH. DE GAULLE
Rue de Belleville
Bd de la Villette
Bd de Belleville
Périphérique
Bd Lannes
Av. Victor Hugo
Champs Élysées
Pl. de la CONCORDE
Pl. de la RÉPUBLIQUE
p. 144-145
Av. de la République
Rue de Turbigo
R. Belgrand
Pte de la Muette
p. 146-147
LOUVRE
Bd Suchet
PALAIS DE CHAILLOT
TOUR EIFFEL
Boulevard Voltaire
Av. Ph. Auguste
Rue des Pyrénées
R. St-Antoine
Pl. de la BASTILLE
Pte d'Auteuil
Boulevard
LES INVALIDES
ST-GERMAIN-DES PRÉS
NOTRE-DAME
p. 148-149
R. du Fbg St-Antoine
Bd Diderot
Crs de Vincennes
p. 142-143
Bd de Versailles
Vaugirard
Bd St-Michel
Bd du Montparnasse
Pl. de la NATION
GARE D'AUSTERLITZ
GARE DE LYON
Av. Daun
Avenue de
Rue de la Convention
Rue de
Bd de Port Royal
Pte de St-Cloud
GARE MONTPARNASSE
P.O.P.B.
Bd de l'Hôpital
p. 150-151
Bd Poniatowski
Bd Victor
Bd de République
PALAIS DES SPORTS
Pl. d'ITALIE
Rue d'Alésia
Av. du Gal Leclerc
Bd Brune
Rue de Tolbiac
Quai d'Ivry
Pte de Charenton
Pte de Versailles
D 50
Bd Jourdan
Bd Kellermann
Bd Masséna
Pte de Châtillon
Pte d'Orléans
Pte d'Italie
Pte d'Ivry

La Seine

Pont Mirabeau

This bridge was made famous by a poem by Guillaume Appollinaire. It was built in 1893. It spans the river in three metal arches. It boasts several bronze statues.

Pont RER

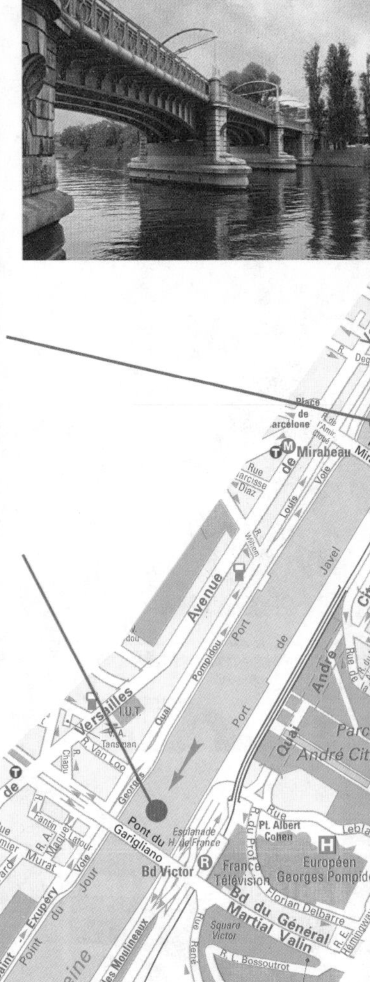

Pont du Garigliano

This existing bridge was built in 1963-66. It replaced a double stone viaduct built in 1865, which consisted of a road with the Paris circular railway above.

Pont de Bir Hakeim

This bridge replaced the Passy footbridge built for the 1878 Universal Exhibition. It was finished in time for the exhibition held in 1900. It has a vehicle track and a rail viaduct. In 1949, it was renamed after General Koening's victory at Bir Hakeim in 1942. It consists in two metal structures on a concrete base resting on the Ile des Cygnes (the island of swans). It is very ornate with many cast iron statues. The rail bridge it supported by a series of small columns

Pont de Grenelle

e wooden bridge built in 1827, collapsed in 1873 spite of being repaired several times in the mean-ne. It was replaced by a cast iron structure, which supported in the middle by the Ile des Cygnes. It is the tip of this island that we can find a small-scale plica of the New York Statue of Liberty designed Bartoldi.

hen this bridge deteriorated and became too nar-w, a new one was built (1966-68). This new bridge made up of two metal spans, 85 metres long each.

Pont Aval

Built between 1964 and 1968, it is, at 312.5 m, the longest bridge in Paris (four spans). It takes the west circular road (boulevard périphérique) across the Seine.

Passerelle Debilly

This footbridge was built in line with avenue Albert de Mun for the 1900 Universal Exhibition and was called the Military Exhibition Footbridge. In 1906, the City of Paris decided to move it to its present location and renamed it after one of Napoleon's generals, de Billy, who had died in 1806.

Pont de l'Alma

The modern bridge finished in 1974 replaced a first bridge built in the 19th century to commemorate Napoleon III's victories in the Crimean war. It boasts the famous 'Zouave', a statue by Georges Diébot, often used as a marker to check the level of river.

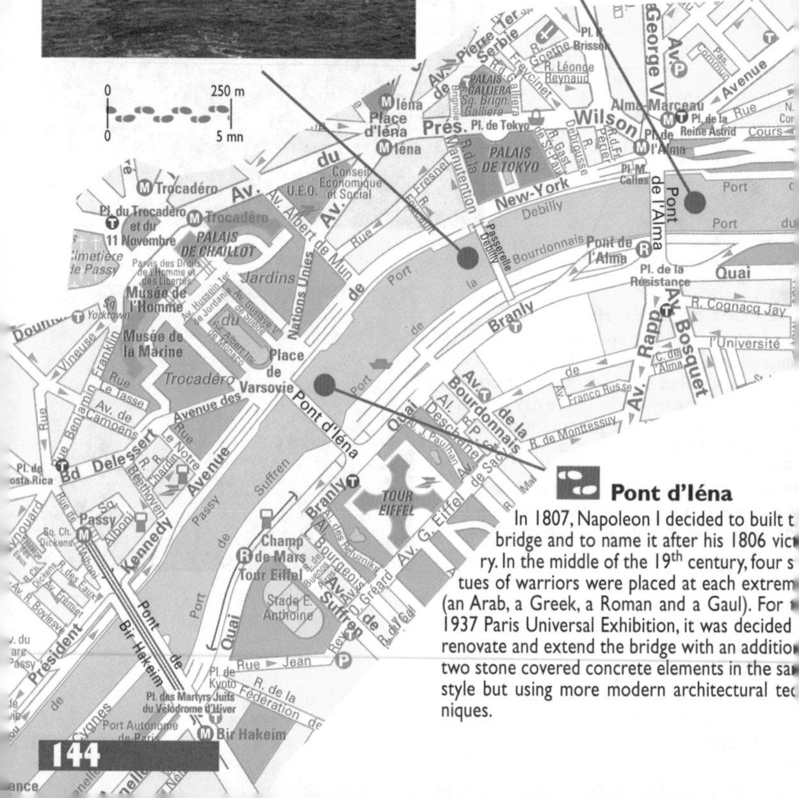

Pont d'Iéna

In 1807, Napoleon I decided to built t bridge and to name it after his 1806 vic ry. In the middle of the 19th century, four s tues of warriors were placed at each extrem (an Arab, a Greek, a Roman and a Gaul). For t 1937 Paris Universal Exhibition, it was decided renovate and extend the bridge with an additio two stone covered concrete elements in the sa style but using more modern architectural tec niques.

Pont des Invalides

It was first decided to build a suspension bridge a little further upstream, but it collapsed in 1824 before being finished because of a ruptured suspension cable. To preserve the perspective of the Esplanade of the Invalides, a new suspension bridge was built where the present one stands. Finished in 1829, it quickly became extremely dangerous for traffic and it was decided to replace it with a masonry bridge in 1854. The piles are decorated with statues and military trophies. Damaged, it was restored in 1880.

Pont de la Concorde

Started in 1786, it was finished five years later using stones from the Bastille. It was originally going to be called the Louis XVI bridge, but the 1789 events changed the course of history and it was called the Bridge of the Revolution and finally the Pont de la Concorde in 1830. It had many statues that had to be taken off because of their weight. The bridge was widened in 1930.

Passerelle Solferino

The original cast iron bridge was removed in 1960, as it had become too dangerous. In 1961, it was replaced by a new temporary footbridge, which was only removed in 1992 to build the new permanent footbridge. Its original design makes it accessible from both the banks of the river and from the road with the two levels joining in the middle.

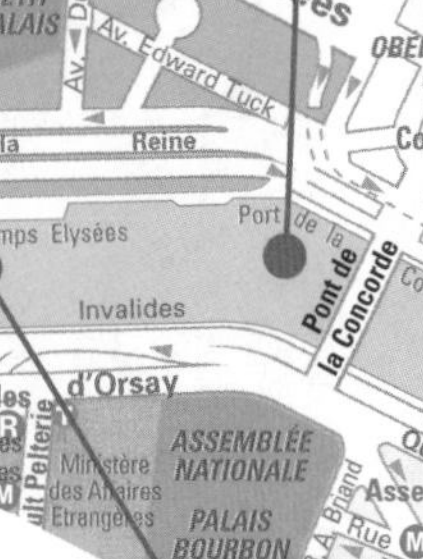

Pont Alexandre III

t is the first of the Paris bridges to have been built n a single span. It was inaugurated for the 1900 Universal Exhibition. With all ts decorations, it is without a doubt, Paris's most beautiful bridge.

Each angle pillar is topped with an equestrian statue representing Sciences and Arts on the Right Bank and Trade and Industry on the Left Bank. The keystones are decorated with nymphs, the Seine and the arms of Paris upstream, and the Neva and the arms of Russia downstream.

Pont du Carrousel

The first bridge built on this spot was called the Pont des Saint-Pères before being renamed the Pont du Carousel for its inauguration in 1834. But its structure was too lightweight for the increasing traffic, and it was decided to build a new bridge in 1930, further to the west level with the ticket offices of the Louvre museum.

Pont Royal

Built in stone at the end of the 17th century and financed by Louis XIV (hence its name), it replaced a wooden bridge built in 1632 (the Pont Sainte-Anne or Pont Rouge) which itself had replaced a ferry boat. In the 18th century, it was the venue for celebrations, but Bonaparte placed his cannons there to defend the Convention that sat in the Tuileries. At each end, marks indicates the high water levels reached by the Seine.

Pont des Arts

The existing footbridge was installed between 1982 and 1984. It replaced the one built at the beginning of the 19th century, which had been damaged by a boat in 1979.

Pont Neuf

It is the most famous and the oldest of the bridges of Paris. Started under the reign of Henri III in 1570 it was finished in 1607 and inaugurated by Henri IV. Built in two parts, the central section leans on two small islands. Built without any houses, its pavements were quickly filled by merchants and peddlers of all sorts.

A first equestrian statue of Henri IV was erected in 1614. However this was destroyed during the French Revolution and was replaced by the present Louis XVIII statue.

The bridge has been restored twice, once in the 19th century and again in the 20th.

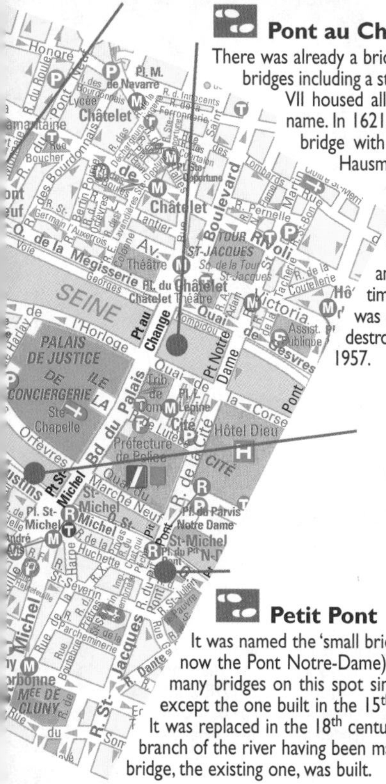

Pont au Change

There was already a bridge there in Roman times, followed by a succession of bridges including a stone bridge in the 9th century. In the 15th century, Louis VII housed all the moneychangers on the bridge, which gave it its name. In 1621, the bridge was destroyed and replaced by a masonry bridge with the permission to build houses too. In 1860, with Hausmann's new plans a new bridge became necessary.

Pont Saint-Michel

The first bridge on this site was built in the 14th century and was lined with houses. It was built and rebuilt several times before a stone bridge was built in the 17th century. It was one of the rare bridges to keep its houses, which were destroyed, in the 19th century. The existing bridge was built in 1957.

Petit Pont

It was named the 'small bridge' in opposition to the 'big bridge' (the Grand-Pont, now the Pont Notre-Dame) over the other branch of the river. There have been many bridges on this spot since antiquity. Most were destroyed by the river flow except the one built in the 15th century, which was burnt down in the 17th century. It was replaced in the 18th century by a stone bridge without any houses. The smaller branch of the river having been made navigable in the middle of the 19th century, a new bridge, the existing one, was built.

Pont Notre-Dame

There was a bridge on this site since antiquity, it was known as the Grand-Pont. In the Middle Ages, it was replaced by the Pont des Planches Milbray, which was carried off by floods at the beginning of the 15th century. It took its present name in 1413 when a wooden bridge with houses was built. Rebuilt in 1507, it continued to have houses until 1786. In the middle of the 19th century, a masonry bridge was built. But with five arches, it was considered dangerous for navigation, it was altered at the beginning of the 20th century and the three central arches replaced with a single metal span.

Pont d'Arcole

A footbridge was built on this spot in 1828. It was repla ced by a metal bridge in the middle of the 19t century. But it was rather flimsy and light weight and had to be reinforced i 1888. It was refurbished whe the Georges Pompido Road was built an restored in 1995

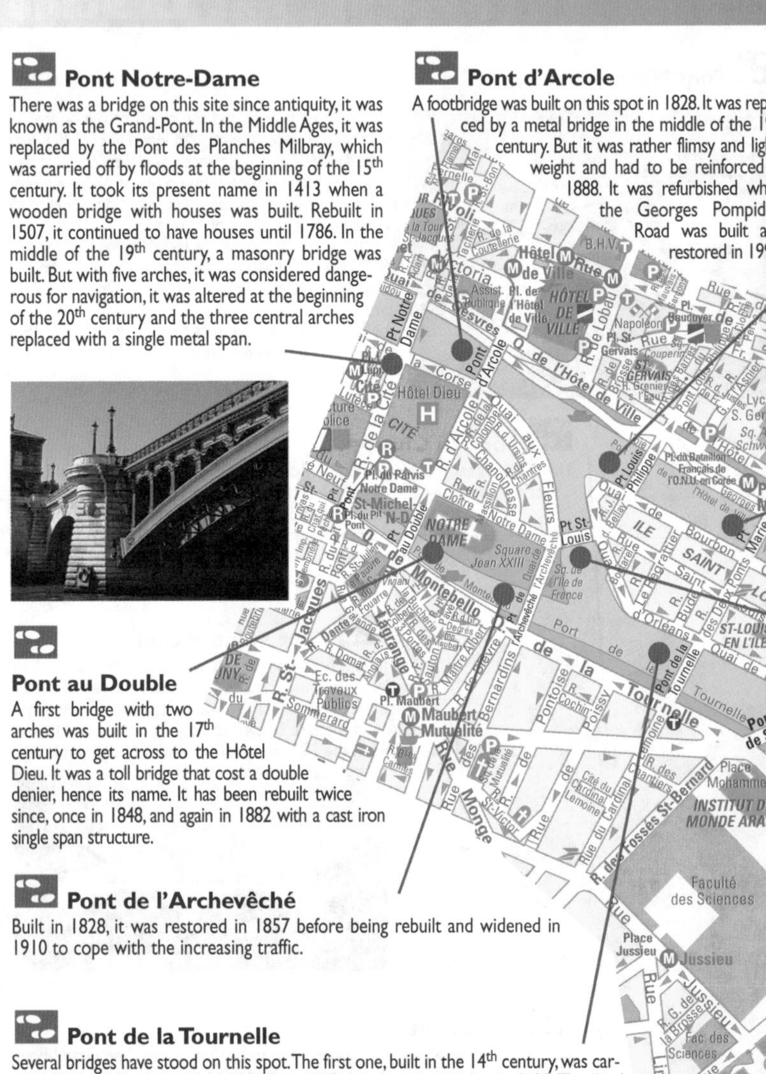

Pont au Double

A first bridge with two arches was built in the 17th century to get across to the Hôtel Dieu. It was a toll bridge that cost a double denier, hence its name. It has been rebuilt twice since, once in 1848, and again in 1882 with a cast iron single span structure.

Pont de l'Archevêché

Built in 1828, it was restored in 1857 before being rebuilt and widened in 1910 to cope with the increasing traffic.

Pont de la Tournelle

Several bridges have stood on this spot. The first one, built in the 14th century, was carried off by the flows, the second built in 1620 was destroyed by ice in 1637. The third bridge was built in stone in the middle of the 17th century and resisted until 1918 when, because of general wear and tear and accumulated flood damage, it had to be destroyed. The existing bridge was finished in 1928. The left pile is extended by a 14 m column topped by the statue of Saint Genevieve.

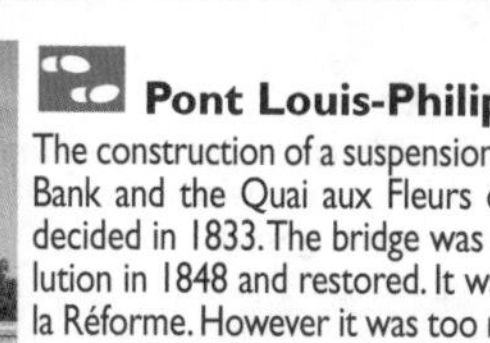

Pont Louis-Philippe

The construction of a suspension bridge between the Right Bank and the Quai aux Fleurs on the Ile de la Cité was decided in 1833. The bridge was damaged during the revolution in 1848 and restored. It was then called the Pont de la Réforme. However it was too narrow and had to be destroyed in 1860 and replaced by the present bridge which links the Right Bank with the Ile Saint-Louis in the axe of the rue du Pont Louis-Philippe.

Pont Marie

Ilt was built when the Ile Saint-Louis was rebuilt in the 17th century by Christophe Marie. In 1658, the river carried off part of the bridge and the houses that stood on it. It was replaced by a wooden bridge until 1670 before being rebuilt. It was restored in the 19th century.

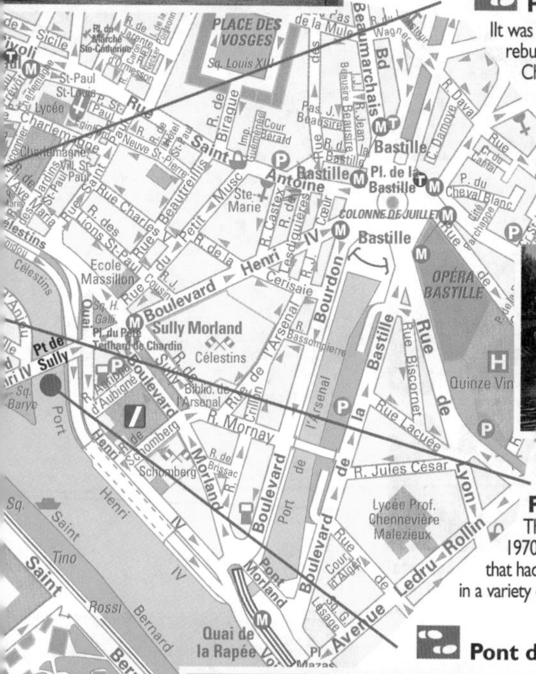

Pont Saint-Louis

The present bridge was built in 1970 and replaced a number of bridges that had been built since the 17th century in a variety of styles to connect the islands.

Pont de Sully

The metal bridge is in tow parts with the central section resting on the Ile Saint-Louis. It was built in 1876 to replace two footbridges.

0 250 m
0 5 mn

Pont d'Austerlitz

A first bridge was built in the 19th century, but deemed too dangerous it was rebuilt and widened in 1854. It had to be widened again at the end of the 19th century because of the increasing traffic.

Pont de Tolbiac

Built at the end of the 19th century, it was immortalised by Léo Mallet. It has five elliptic arches and measures 168 m.

Pont National

Built at the end of the 19th century, It continues in the axe of the boulevards des Maréchaux. It was called Pont Napoleon III until 1870 and was used by the railway line. It was later widened and doubled in size in the 20th century.

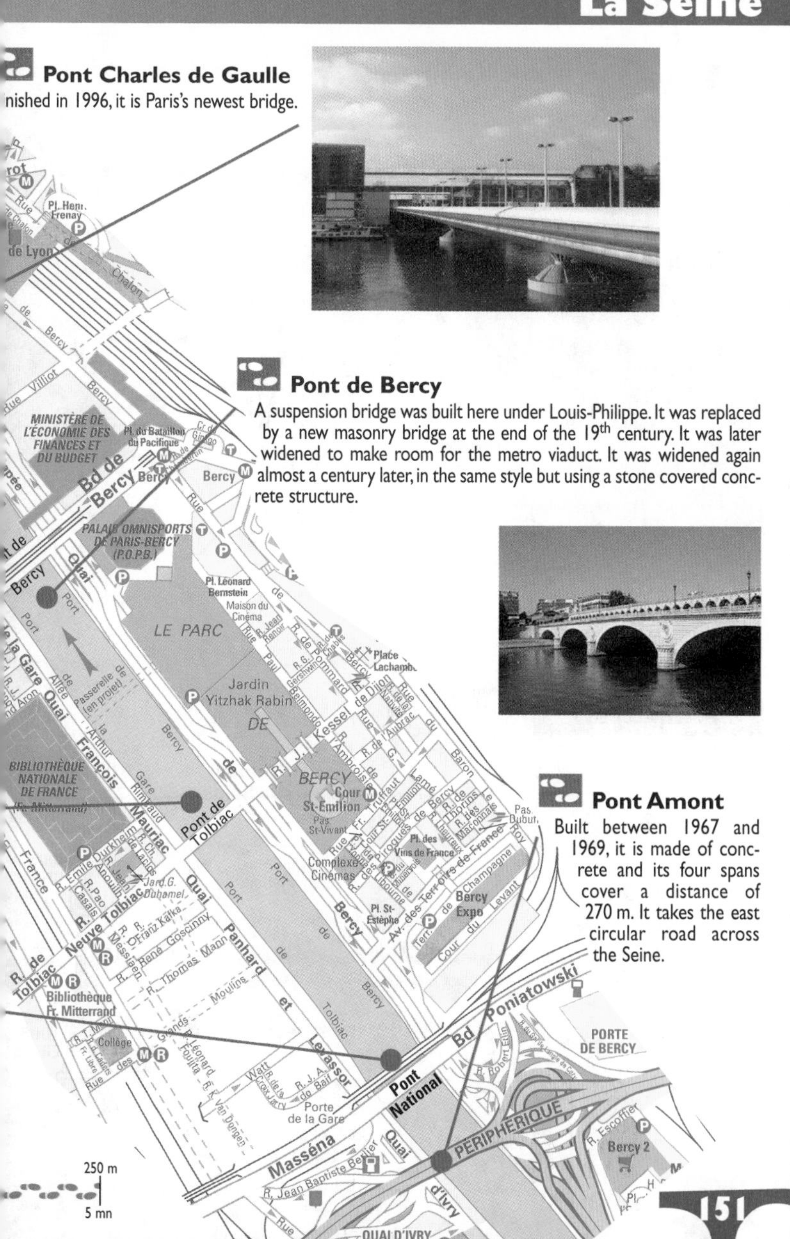

Pont Charles de Gaulle

nished in 1996, it is Paris's newest bridge.

Pont de Bercy

A suspension bridge was built here under Louis-Philippe. It was replaced by a new masonry bridge at the end of the 19th century. It was later widened to make room for the metro viaduct. It was widened again almost a century later, in the same style but using a stone covered concrete structure.

Pont Amont

Built between 1967 and 1969, it is made of concrete and its four spans cover a distance of 270 m. It takes the east circular road across the Seine.

250 m

5 mn

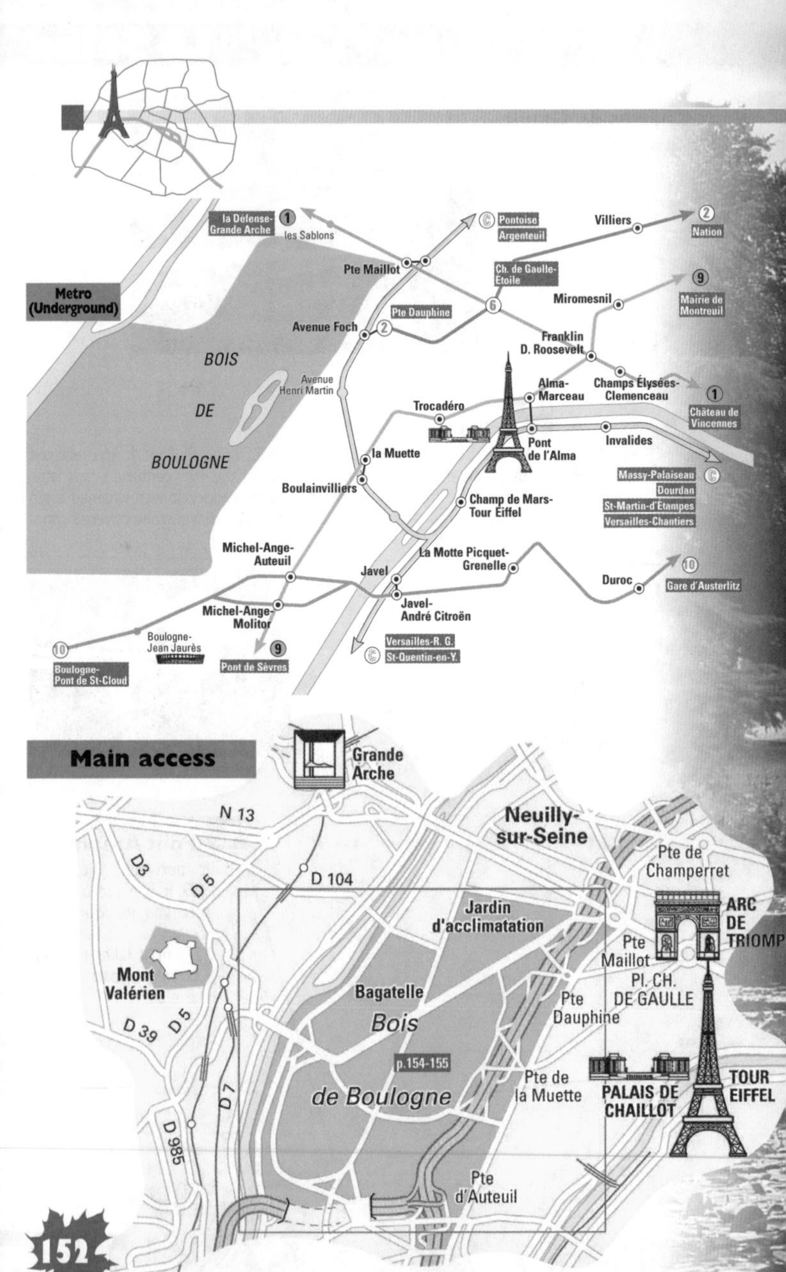

Metro (Underground)
la Défense-Grande Arche
1
les Sablons
Pontoise
Argenteuil
Villiers
2
Nation
Pte Maillot
Ch. de Gaulle-Etoile
6
Miromesnil
9
Mairie de Montreuil
Pte Dauphine
Avenue Foch
2
Franklin D. Roosevelt
BOIS
DE
BOULOGNE
Avenue Henri Martin
Alma-Marceau
Champs Élysées-Clemenceau
1
Château de Vincennes
Trocadéro
Pont de l'Alma
Invalides
la Muette
Boulainvilliers
Massy-Palaiseau
Dourdan
St-Martin-d'Étampes
Versailles-Chantiers
Champ de Mars-Tour Eiffel
Michel-Ange-Auteuil
La Motte Picquet-Grenelle
10
Javel
Duroc
Gare d'Austerlitz
Michel-Ange-Molitor
Javel-André Citroën
Boulogne-Jean Jaurès
10
Boulogne-Pont de St-Cloud
9
Pont de Sèvres
Versailles-R. G.
St-Quentin-en-Y.
Main access
Grande Arche
N 13
Neuilly-sur-Seine
Pte de Champerret
D3
D5
D 104
Jardin d'acclimatation
ARC DE TRIOMP
Pte Maillot
Mont Valérien
Bagatelle
Pl. CH. DE GAULLE
Pte Dauphine
Bois
D 39
D5
p.154-155
de Boulogne
Pte de la Muette
PALAIS DE CHAILLOT
TOUR EIFFEL
D7
D 985
Pte d'Auteuil

Bois de Boulogne

Jardin d'acclimatation

It was once a place of discovery and when it first opened in 1860, it showed the animals and plants it had received from the four corners of the world. Today, it is more of a recreation park where children can enjoy train rides, bumper cars, theatre plays, Punch and Judy shows, golf etc... There is also discovery workshops and a farm with animals and a kitchen garden.

3 entrances: Carrefour des Sablons, near the Porte de Neuilly and near the Bowling (avenue du Mahatma Gandhi)

01 40 67 90 82

June to September from 10 am to 7 pm, October to May 10 am to 6 pm

Admission 2.30 euros, Reduced rate 1.15 euros, Free for children under 3

Web *www.jardindacclimatation.fr*

Parc de Bagatelle

The Château is situated in the middle of the park. It was built in less than two months following a bet taken by the Count d'Artois and Marie-Antoinette. The park was landscaped at the same time with several grottoes, ponds, a belvedere and a rose garden. There is also a large collection of plants.

Route de Sèvres à Neuilly

01 40 67 97 00

From 9 am to 5 pm

Admission 0.75 euro

244

Stade Roland Garros

Built in 1928, it is the venue for the French Tennis Open Championship which takes place at the end of May and beginning of June. The Tenniseum, the tennis museum should open in time for the 2003 championship.

2 av. Gordon-Bennett - 01 47 43 48 00

Guided visits at 2.30 and 4.30 (except during the Roland-Garos championship)

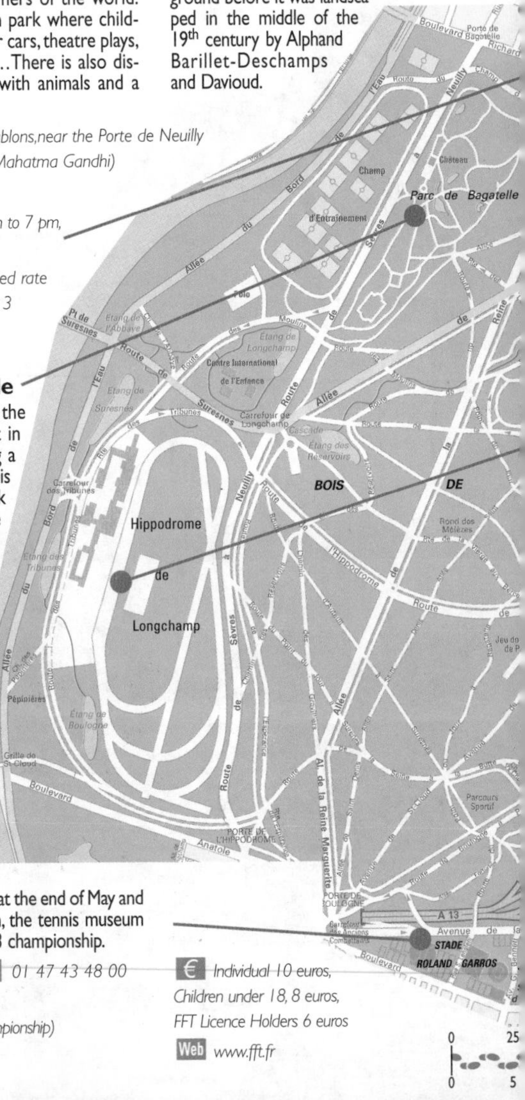

Individual 10 euros, Children under 18, 8 euros, FFT Licence Holders 6 euros

Web *www.fft.fr*

Bois de Boulogne

A large forest surrounded Paris once and the Bois Boulogne was part of it. At first it was a hunt ground before it was landscaped in the middle of the 19th century by Alphand Barillet-Deschamps and Davioud.

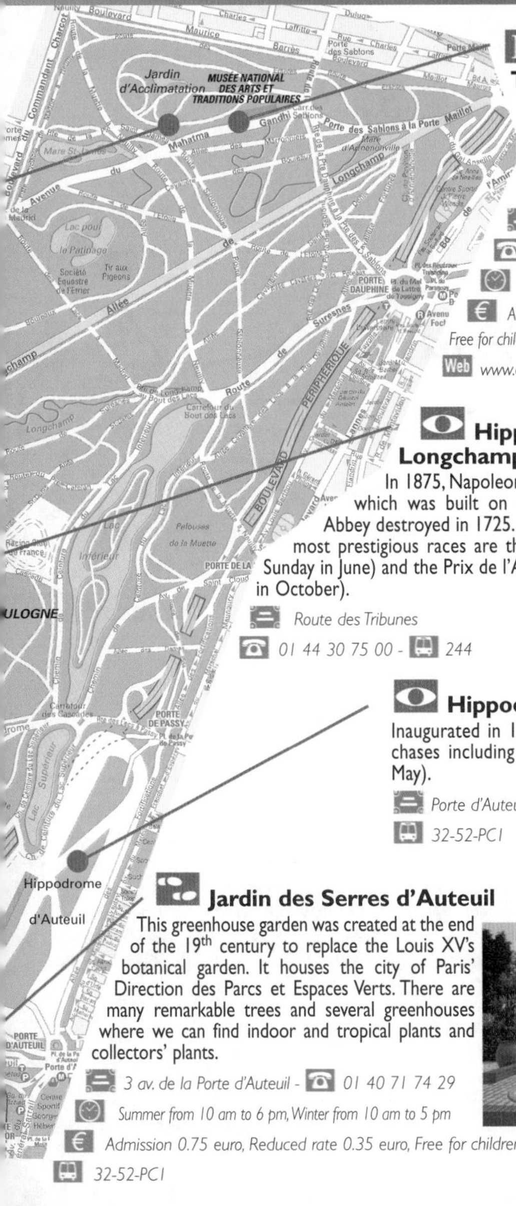

Musée des Arts et Traditions populaires

In a building completed in 1968, it houses collections of everyday objects from the past from all the regions of France.

6 av. du Mahatma Gandhi

01 44 17 60 00

From 9.30 am to 5 pm, closed on Tuesdays

Admission 4 euros, Reduced rate 2.60 euros, Free for children under 18

Web *www.culture.gouv.fr/culture/atp/mnatp*

Hippodrome de Longchamp

In 1875, Napoleon III inaugurated this hippodrome which was built on the site of the old Longchamp Abbey destroyed in 1725. It is a flat races racing course, its most prestigious races are the Grand Prix de Paris (the last Sunday in June) and the Prix de l'Arc de Triomphe (the first Sunday in October).

Route des Tribunes

01 44 30 75 00 - 244

Hippodrome d'Auteuil

Inaugurated in 1876, it is the venue for steeple-chases including the Grand Steeple de Paris (in May).

Porte d'Auteuil - 01 45 27 12 25

32-52-PC1

Jardin des Serres d'Auteuil

This greenhouse garden was created at the end of the 19th century to replace the Louis XV's botanical garden. It houses the city of Paris' Direction des Parcs et Espaces Verts. There are many remarkable trees and several greenhouses where we can find indoor and tropical plants and collectors' plants.

3 av. de la Porte d'Auteuil - 01 40 71 74 29

Summer from 10 am to 6 pm, Winter from 10 am to 5 pm

Admission 0.75 euro, Reduced rate 0.35 euro, Free for children under 3

32-52-PC1

Metro (Underground)

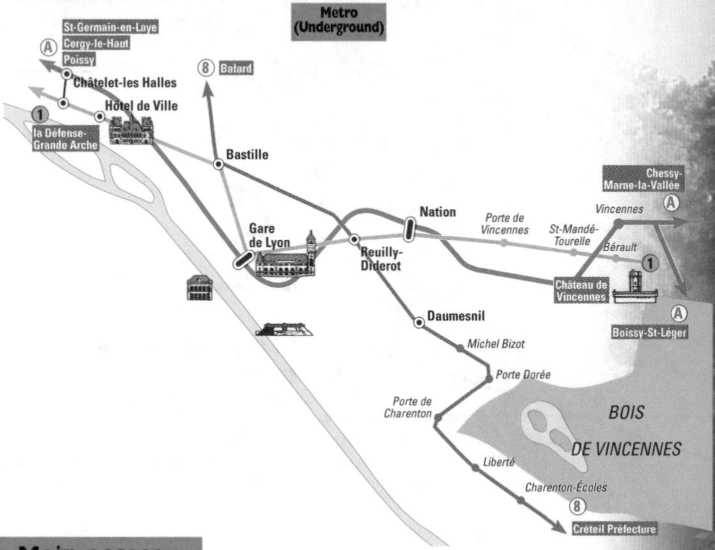

St-Germain-en-Laye
Cergy-le-Haut
Poissy
A
Châtelet-les Halles
Hôtel de Ville
1
la Défense-Grande Arche
8 Balard
Bastille
Gare de Lyon
Reuilly-Diderot
Nation
Porte de Vincennes
St-Mandé-Tourelle
Bérault
Vincennes
Chessy-Marne-la-Vallée
A
1
Château de Vincennes
A
Boissy-St-Léger
Daumesnil
Michel Bizot
Porte Dorée
Porte de Charenton
BOIS DE VINCENNES
Liberté
Charenton-Écoles
8
Créteil Préfecture

Main access

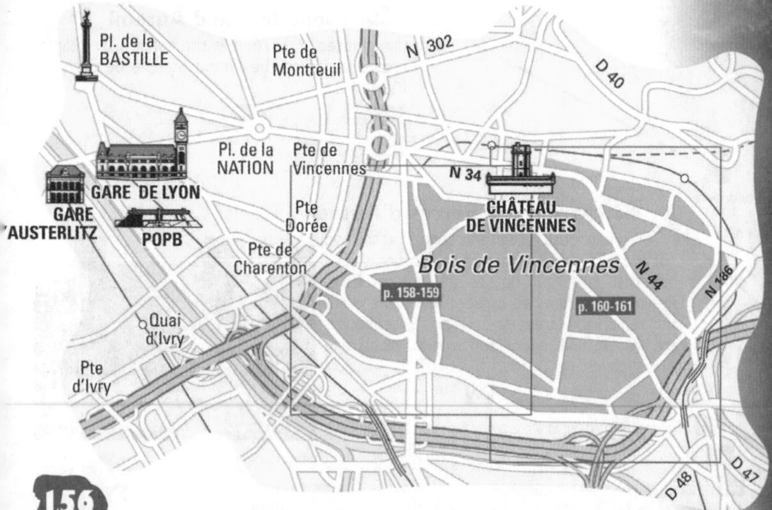

Pl. de la BASTILLE
Pte de Montreuil
N 302
D 40
GARE DE LYON
Pl. de la NATION
Pte de Vincennes
N 34
CHÂTEAU DE VINCENNES
GARE D'AUSTERLITZ
POPB
Pte Dorée
Pte de Charenton
Bois de Vincennes
N 44
N 186
p. 158-159
p. 160-161
Quai d'Ivry
Pte d'Ivry
D 48
D 47

Bois de Vincennes

Palais de la Porte Dorée (Ancien Musée des Arts d'Afrique et d'Océanie)

It was inaugurated in 1931, for the Colonial Exhibition. It was first called the Museum of the Colonies and Overseas France then the Museum of Overseas France (1935-1960). Behind the bas-reliefs of the facade, ionly the aquarium with tropical fish and terrarium with crocodiles and tortoises remain in the basement. The art collections from Oceania, Africa and North Africa wil be taken shortly to a new museum, the Musée du Quai Branly, wich is due to open in 2005.

293 avenue Daumesnil

01 43 46 51 61

Everyday except Tuesdays from 10 am to 5.15 pm

Admission 4 euros

Reduced rate 2,60 euros,

46-PC

Bois de Vincennes

With the Bois de Boulogne, it is Paris's second green belt. In the 12th century, it was a royal residence surrounded by hunting grounds. Legend has it that Saint-Louis dispensed justice there under an oak tree. After the French Revolution, it became a training ground for the militaries. It was Napoleon III who transformed it into a parc.

Foire du Trône

The fair's origins can be traced back to the Middle Ages when a fair was held around the Saint-Antoine Abbey. The abbey was destroyed during the French Revolution and in 1805 the fairground people came back to the Faubourg Saint-Antoine. The fair grew, spreading to nearby streets until it was moved in 1964. Today, with its 350 attractions, it welcomes over 5 million visitors during the eight weeks it lasts from the end of March to the end of May.

Pelouse de Reuilly - *Free entrance*

46-PC1-PC2 - Web *www.foiredutrone.com*

Zoo de Vincennes

It was also created for the 1931 Colonial Exhibition, it houses nearly 1200 species of animals including some rare species (ayes-ayes, Eld deer, okapis, pandas) and more familiar ones (elephants, giraffes, lions). The zoo is very proud of its breeding track record.

53 avenue Saint-Maurice

01 44 75 20 10

Winter from 9 am to 5 pm, Summer from 9 am to 6 or 6.30 pm

Admission 8 euros, Reduced rate 5 euros

46-86-325

Temple tibétain et Institut bouddhique

They have taken over two old pavilions dating from the Colonial Exhibition (the Cameroon and Togo Pavilions) which have been restored. The first one is used for worship and houses the largest Buddha in Europe, the second is a library with a collection of important traditional texts. There are also initiation session to Buddhism and meditation lessons.

40 rue de la Ceinture du Lac Daumesnil

01 43 41 54 48

46-325

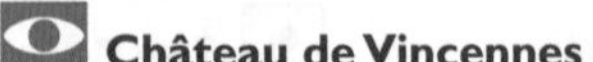

Château de Vincennes

It was Louis VII who first made use of the woods in the 12th century. In the 13th, Philippe Auguste and Saint-Louis built a manor and a Sainte-Chapelle. But it was not until Charles V, the Wise, that it became a castle with a dungeon and surrounding walls. In the 17th century, two pavilions were added by Louis XIV and Mazarin, they were designed by Le Vau. It was later abandoned and turned into a prison and then into an arsenal during the French Revolution. The seven watchtowers and the manor were pulled down at the beginning of the 19th century and it was only under Napoleon III that the castle was restored by Viollet-le-Duc. The dungeon (closed to the public for the time being), the Sainte-Chapelle, and the Village Tower (recently restored) are the castle's finest elements.

 *1 av. de Paris, Vincennes - 01 48 08 31 20*

1 April to 30 September from 10 am to 12 pm and from 1.15 pm to 6 pm – 1 October to 31 March from 10 am to 12 pm and from 1.15 pm to 5 pm

Long visit (guided visit of the walls, the moat and the Sainte-Chapelle in 75 minutes, Admission 5.50 euros, Reduced rate 3.50 euros

Short visit (guided visit of the Sainte-Chapelle and history of the Castle) in 45 minutes, Admission 4 euros, Reduced rate 2.50 euros

56-325

Ferme Georges Ville

Housed in a former nursery, it shows young town dwellers how vegetable, cereals and fruit grow and the farm animals.

 *Route du Pesage - 01 43 28 47 63*

Weekends and Public Holidays from 1.30 pm to 5 pm (November to February) and from 1.30 pm to 7 pm (Mars to October)

Admission 3.35 euros, Reduced rate 1.65 euros -  *112*

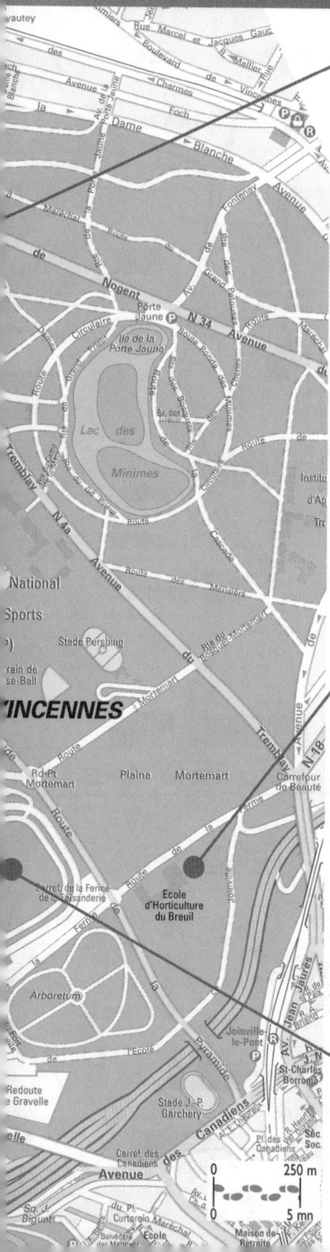

Parc Floral

This botanical garden was opened in 1969. It has hundreds of varieties of flowers and plants in its flower valleys, dahlia, four season and iris gardens and in its pavilions. It is also a large recreation area with a number of activities (car circuit, mini-golf, quadricycles, small train, climbing frames, a book and games library, a children's theatre and a Punch and Judy): a real paradise for children of all ages.

Esplanade du Château de Vincennes

01 55 94 20 20

1 April to 14 October from 9.30 am to 7 or 8 pm,
15 October to 31 March from 9.30 am to 5 or 6 pm

During horticultural shows,
Free for children under 6,
Adults 1.50 euros, 6 to 17 year-old
and over 60s 0.75 euro
At other times Admission 0.75 euro,
Reduced rate 0.35 euro

46-112

Web *www.parcfloraldeparis.com*

École d'horticulture du Breuil

The school was founded in 1867. In addition to its teaching mission, it is a way of discovering thanks to its arboretum, several hundred species of trees. It also runs gardening courses for the amateurs.

Route de la Ferme - 01 53 66 14 00

Mondays to Fridays from 8 am to 4 pm,
weekends and Bank Holidays from 10 am to 5 pm
(November to February), 10 am to 6 pm
(March to October), 10 am to 7 pm (April to September)

Admission 0.75 euro, Reduced rate 0.35 euro

112

Hippodrome de Vincennes

Inaugurated in 1879, it specialises in trotting and evening racing (since 1952).

2 route de la Ferme

01 49 77 17 17 - 112

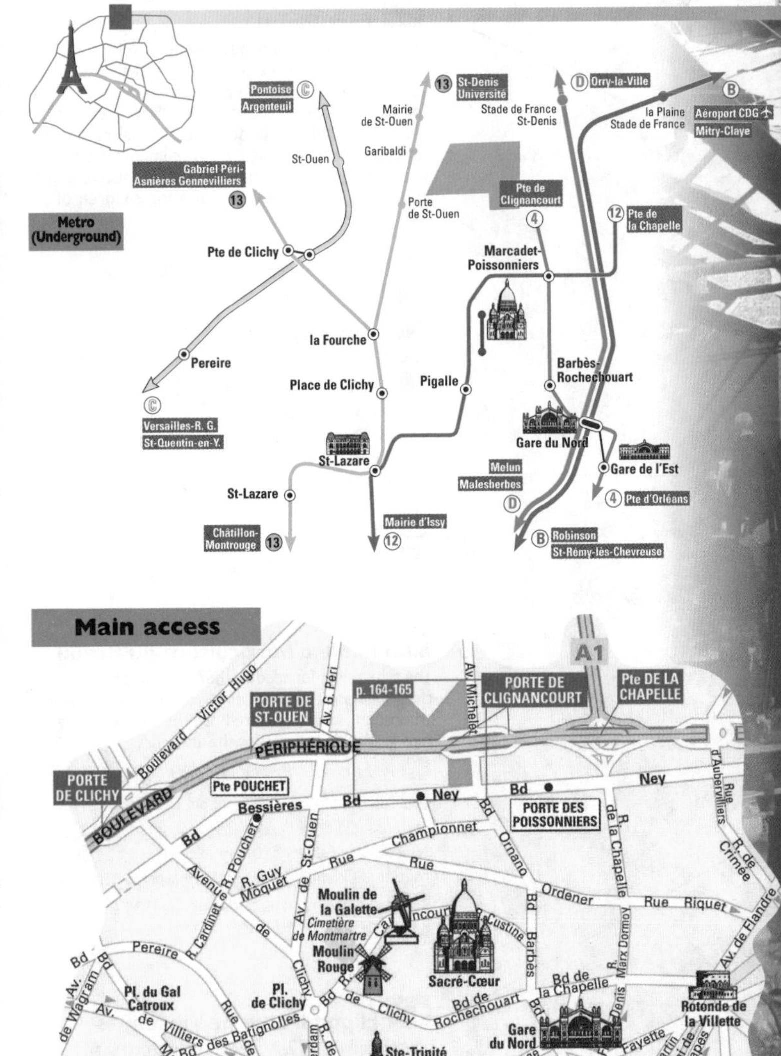
Metro (Underground)
Pontoise
Argenteuil
St-Ouen
Gabriel Péri-Asnières Gennevilliers
Pte de Clichy
Pereire
Versailles-R. G.
St-Quentin-en-Y.
St-Lazare
Châtillon-Montrouge
Mairie de St-Ouen
Garibaldi
Porte de St-Ouen
St-Denis Université
la Fourche
Place de Clichy
St-Lazare
Mairie d'Issy
Stade de France St-Denis
Orry-la-Ville
Pte de Clignancourt
Marcadet-Poissonniers
Pigalle
Barbès-Rochechouart
Gare du Nord
Melun
Malesherbes
la Plaine Stade de France
Aéroport CDG
Mitry-Claye
Pte de la Chapelle
Gare de l'Est
Pte d'Orléans
Robinson
St-Rémy-lès-Chevreuse
Main access
A1
PORTE DE ST-OUEN
p. 164-165
PORTE DE CLIGNANCOURT
Pte DE LA CHAPELLE
PÉRIPHÉRIQUE
PORTE DE CLICHY
Pte POUCHET
PORTE DES POISSONNIERS
Boulevard Victor Hugo
Av. G. Péri
Av. Michelet
Bd Ney
Bessières
R. de la Chapelle
Rue d'Aubervilliers
R. de Crimée
Bd Championnet
Rue Championnet
Av. de St-Ouen
R. Pouchet
R. Guy Moquet
Bd Ornano
Rue Ordener
Rue Riquet
Moulin de la Galette
Cimetière de Montmartre
Caulaincourt
Custine
Moulin Rouge
Sacré-Cœur
Bd Barbès
R. Marx Dormoy
Av. de Flandre
Avenue de Clichy
R. Cardinet
Bd Pereire
Bd Av. de Wagram
Pl. du Gal Catroux
Av. de Villiers
Pl. de Clichy
Bd de Clichy
Bd de Rochechouart
Bd de la Chapelle
Gare du Nord
Rotonde de la Villette
Bd des Batignolles
Rue de Rome
Bd Malesherbes
Bd de Courcelles
Parc de Monceau
R. d'Amsterdam
R. de Clichy
Ste-Trinité
R. de Londres
Gare St-Lazare
Bd Haussman
R. de Châteaudun
R. de Maubeuge
Rue La Fayette
R. du Fg St-Denis
R. du Faubourg St-Martin
Quai de Jemmapes
Pl. du Col Fabien
Gare de l'Est
Canal

Puces de Saint-Ouen

Marché aux puces

Arriving here in Paris's oldest and biggest market, it is like entering in a vast attic room with more than 3C traders in three different markets each offering a great variety of objects (rags, works of art, , furniture, pa tings…) where you can find almost everything. The market regularly overflows into nearby streets.

Marché Jules Vallès

The atmosphere and the setting must be very similar to the way the flea market looked when it first started. It is more of a junk and second hand market where you can find almost anything at a very low price.

Marché Dauphine

The market is more recent. Housed over two levels in a metallic structure, it welcomes 150 antique and second hand dealers of all sorts with many art specialists of old books, old toys and other collectors' items.

Marchés Serpette et Paul Bert

a traditional atmosphere, it regroups specialists of old paintings, sculptures and other works of art as well as ecialists of the 1950s.

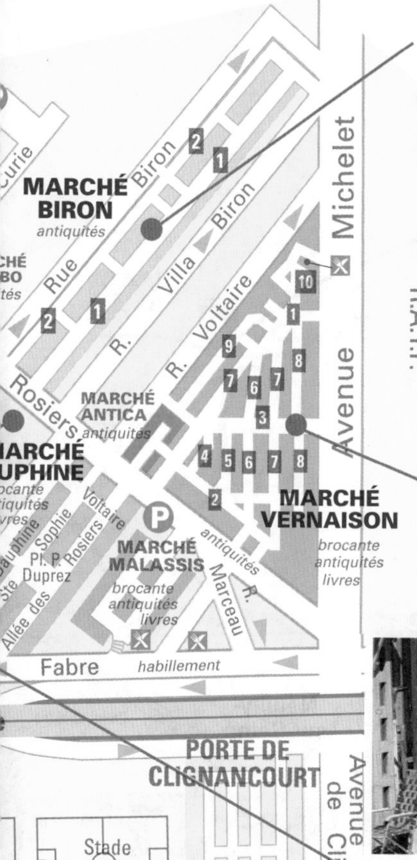

Marché Biron

In 1925, seventy second-hand dealers got together to create this market that gained an international reputation. There amateurs and professionals can make the most of a wide choice of quality objects and good bargains. Weapons, jewellery, paintings, furniture, pottery, instruments and tapestries…

Marché Vernaison

It is the first market you get to as you arrive (with 300 traders) and the oldest. It was the owner of the market gardens who, at the end of the 19th century, let the field to rag and bone people. We can still find furniture and second-hand clothes.

Marché Malik

It specialises in second-hand clothes and accessories. It is the temple of yesterday and tomorrow's fashion trends.

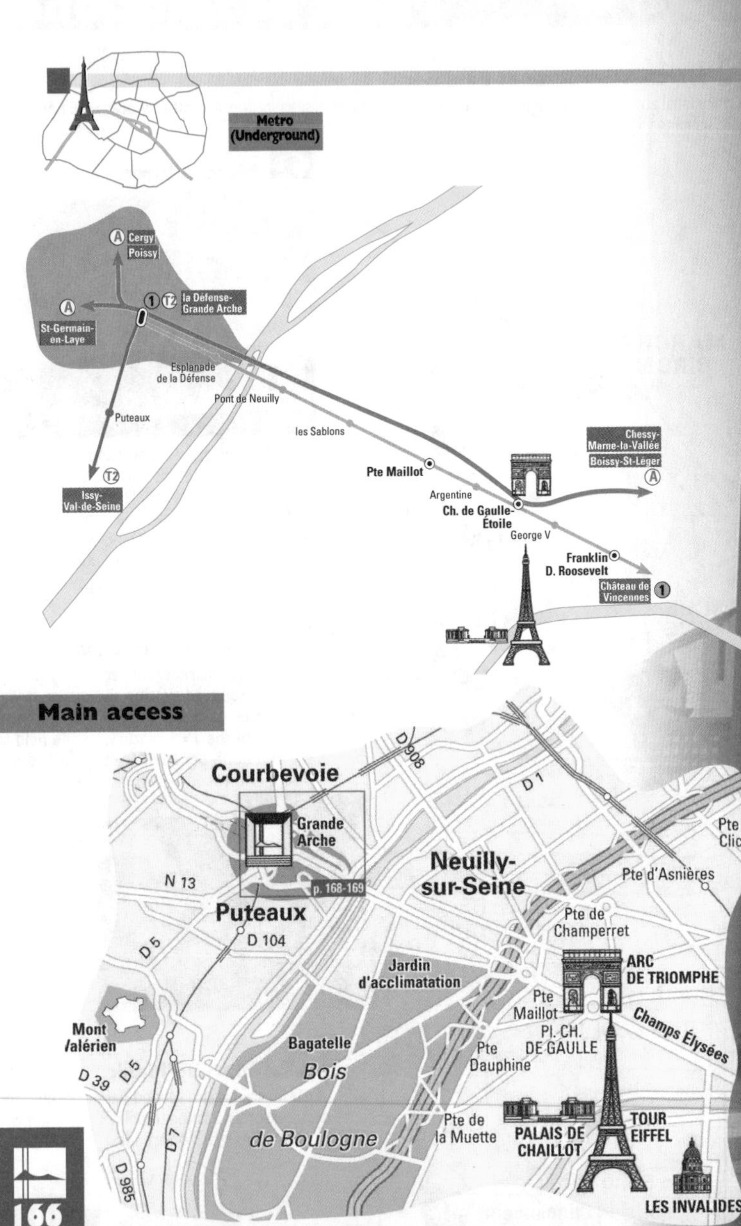
Metro (Underground)
Cergy
Poissy
la Défense-Grande Arche
St-Germain-en-Laye
Esplanade de la Défense
Pont de Neuilly
Puteaux
les Sablons
Issy-Val-de-Seine
Pte Maillot
Argentine
Ch. de Gaulle-Étoile
George V
Franklin D. Roosevelt
Chessy-Marne-la-Vallée
Boissy-St-Léger
Château de Vincennes
Main access
Courbevoie
D 908
D 1
Grande Arche
Neuilly-sur-Seine
N 13
p. 168-169
Puteaux
Pte d'Asnières
Pte de Champerret
D 5
D 104
Jardin d'acclimatation
ARC DE TRIOMPHE
Pte Maillot
Champs Élysées
PI. CH. DE GAULLE
Bagatelle
Bois de Boulogne
Pte Dauphine
D 39
D 5
D 7
D 985
Pte de la Muette
PALAIS DE CHAILLOT
TOUR EIFFEL
LES INVALIDES

La Défense

La Grande Arche

A monumental gate, it stands majestically at the end of the perspective and historical axe designed by Le Nôtre in the 17th century, in the line of the Tuileries Gardens, the place de la Concorde, the avenue of the Champs-Elysées, the Arc de Triomphe, the avenue de la Grande Armée, the avenue Charles de Gaulle and the Pont de Neuilly.

Designed by Danish architect Otto von Spreckelsen, it was finished by Paul Andreu and inaugurated for the bi-centenary of the French Revolution on 14 July 1989.

It is a hollow cube covered in white marble. Each side is almost 110 m, it is both an arch and an office building where we can find the International Foundation of Human Rights and the Ministry of Equipment, Transport, Housing, Tourism and the Sea. Through the 'clouds',(the canvass that stretches between the sides), several lifts take the visitors to the top to see the most of the spectacular view over Paris.

01 49 07 27 57

10 am to 7 pm

Admission 7 euros, Reduced rate 5.50 euros

73-Balabus

CNIT

Inaugurated in 1959 by General de Gaulle, it was designed by three architects: Zehrfuss, Camelot and Mailly. This wonderful 200 m long vault is a listed historical monument. It is an architectural and technical feat, the venue for 30 years for professional exhibitions. In 1989, it became an international business centre with a conference centre , a hotel, shops and a golf practice course.

L'Esplanade de la Défense

The central axe of the Defense district, it is a large walkway linking the different districts. T 'dalle' is reserved for pedestrians while cars a public transports are relegated to the lower leve

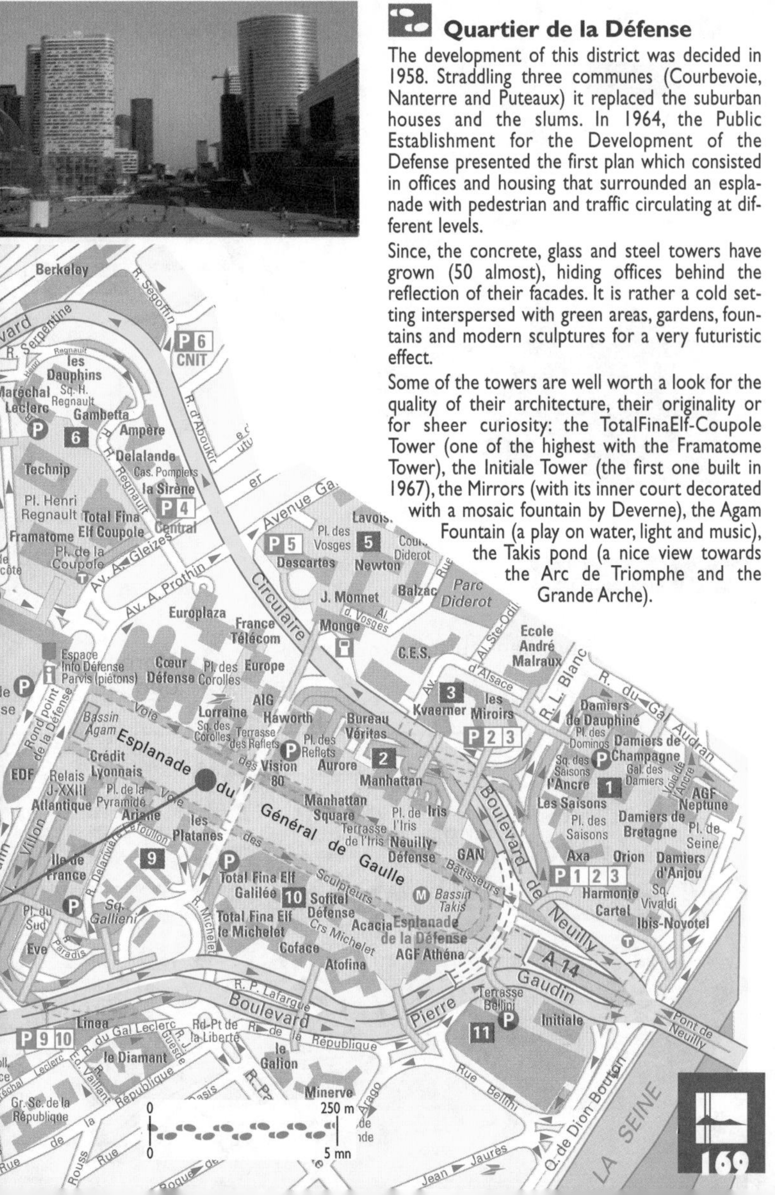

Quartier de la Défense

The development of this district was decided in 1958. Straddling three communes (Courbevoie, Nanterre and Puteaux) it replaced the suburban houses and the slums. In 1964, the Public Establishment for the Development of the Defense presented the first plan which consisted in offices and housing that surrounded an esplanade with pedestrian and traffic circulating at different levels.

Since, the concrete, glass and steel towers have grown (50 almost), hiding offices behind the reflection of their facades. It is rather a cold setting interspersed with green areas, gardens, fountains and modern sculptures for a very futuristic effect.

Some of the towers are well worth a look for the quality of their architecture, their originality or for sheer curiosity: the TotalFinaElf-Coupole Tower (one of the highest with the Framatome Tower), the Initiale Tower (the first one built in 1967), the Mirrors (with its inner court decorated with a mosaic fountain by Deverne), the Agam Fountain (a play on water, light and music), the Takis pond (a nice view towards the Arc de Triomphe and the Grande Arche).

RER C

Bois de Boulogne
Pont de l'Alma
Invalides
Champ de Mars-Tour Eiffel
Javel
Boulevard Victor
Issy-Val-de-Seine
Issy
Meudon-Val-Fleuri
Chaville-Vélizy
Viroflay-Rive gauche
Porchefontaine
Versailles-Rive Gauche
Versailles Chantiers
St-Quentin-en-Yvelines
Massy-Palaiseau
Dourdan
St-Martin d'Étampes
Versailles-Chantiers

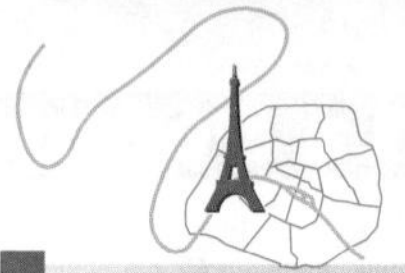

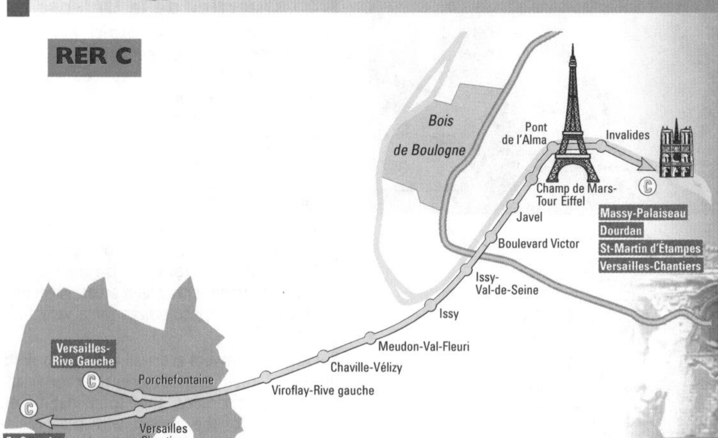

Main access

Rocquencourt
Arboretum
D 186
N 321
Marnes-la-Coquette
le Chesnay
D 985
Pte St-Antoine
Trianons
p. 172-173
Château de Versailles
p. 174-175
St-Cyr-l'École
D 10
D 183
D 10
N 186
Viroflay
D 938

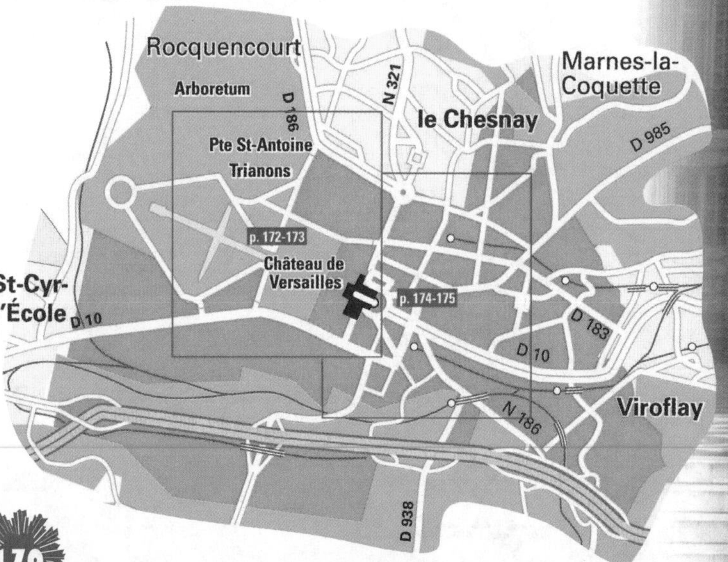

Château de Versailles

Le Hameau

Around the great lake, Marie-Antoinette had these little beamed houses built where, legend has it, she used to play at being a farmer.

Le grand Trianon

After 1687, it replaced the too fragile 'Porcelain Trianon' where Louis XIV used to come with Madame de Montespan. The new marble palace was built by Jules Hardouin-Mansart. Louis XIV used to stay there for short periods away from the court. The furniture disappeared during the French Revolution but was restored by Napoleon I. Since 1962, it has become the residence of visiting Heads of States and other foreign delegations.

November to March from 12 pm to 5.30 pm, April to October from 12 pm to 6.30 pm

Admission 5 euros, Reduced rate 3 euros, Free for children under 18 (tickets twinned with the Petit Trianon)

Grand Canal et petit Canal

A large cross-shaped water surface, surrounded b the woods that make the large park. The main ax of the water surface is in line with the castle and th setting sun. At the time of Louis XIV, it was th venue for great nautical feasts, with lots of littl boats sailing up and down like in Venice.

Le petit Trianon

›uis XV had this little palace built by Jacques-ıge Gabriel for Madame de Pompadour and to ɛtisfy his passion for plants. Louis XVI gave it to ıarie-Antoinette who transformed the garden and dded a theatre, a Love Temple, a music room and e hamlet.

November to March from 12 pm to 5.30, ›ril to October 12 pm to 6.30 pm

Admission 5 euros, Reduced rate 3 euros, ɛe for children under 18 (tickets twinned with the and Trianon)

L'Orangerie

is set in a privileged area, just beyond the arterre du Midi' and the two wings that support e 'hundred steps' stairs. More than 1000 trees ›range, lemon, pomegranate, palm, laurel trees and ›se bushes) shelter there away from the cold in ›nter (from mid October to mid May) and are ken out in the summer.

Les Grandes Eaux

32 ponds and more than 1000 water jets which are activated to create an enchanting water show. The night shows are the most spectacular. To bring water to these ponds, fountains and jets, there is a vast network of channels, pipes, aqueducts and reservoirs. The network and the equipment date mostly from the time of Louis XIV.

Les jardins

Planted over old marshes in front of the castle, the French style gardens were landscaped by Le Nôtre. The beds, alleys, ponds and statues (almost 300) form a perfect natural picture of plants, water and stones showing great creativity and vision. Although, the park has been well looked after and regularly replanted, the 1999 storm took its toll. The considerable damage caused has necessitated a restoration programme which will reproduce the garden as its was in 1700.

Open everyday except in bad weather conditions from 7 am (8 am in the winter) to sunset (5.30 or 9.30 depending on the season)

Admission 3 euros, Reduced rate (10 to 17 year-old) 3 euros

Le Château

At first it was a hunting lodge. Under Louis XII it became a small castle, but it was Louis XIV who after his accession to the throne in 1661, transformed it into this masterpiece known the world over. First the gardens were landscaped by Le Nôtre, then Le Vau started the improvement work on the castle to turn it into the theatre for so many royal celebrations. In 1668, further extension work was carried out by Le Vau and by Jules Hardouin-Mansart from 1678. The court and government moved there in 1682.

This is when an army of workers and artists led by Hardouin-Mansart, Charles Le Brun and André Le Nôtre gathered their talents to build an exceptional palace, adding new buildings (the southern wing, the north wing, the ministerial wings, the Orangerie, stables and the Trianon) and the Royal Chapel.

Although each room is richly decorated, it is the King's and Queen's apartments and the hall of mirrors that are the castle's unchallenged masterpieces.

In the 18th century, Louis XV asked Jacques-Ange Gabriel to change the layout of the palace, and build the Little Trianon and the royal opera. It was emptied of its treasures during the French Revolution and was turned into a museum by Louis-Philippe in 1830 to save it from destruction. Restored at the beginning of the 20th century, it is the venue for the meetings of the deputies and senators when the constitution needs changing.

01 30 84 76 18

May to September from 9 am to 6.30 pm, October to April from 9 am to 5.30 pm

Admission 7.50 euros, Reduced rate 5.30 euros Free for children under 18

www.chateauversailles.fr

Parterre du Midi, parterre du Nord

Designed to be seen from the King's and Queen's apartments, these flower beds are delicately laced with boxwood, lawns, ponds and statues.

Musée Lambinet

Housed in an 18th century Hôtel, it displays many 18th and 19th century works of art (ceramic, porcelain, paintings, collections dating from the French Revolution and weapons).

54 boulevard de la Reine

01 39 50 30 32

Tuesdays, Thursdays, Saturdays and Sundays from 2 pm to 6 pm, Wednesdays from 1 pm to 6 pm, Fridays from 2 pm to 5 pm, closed on Mondays

Admission 5 euros, Reduced rate 2.50 euros

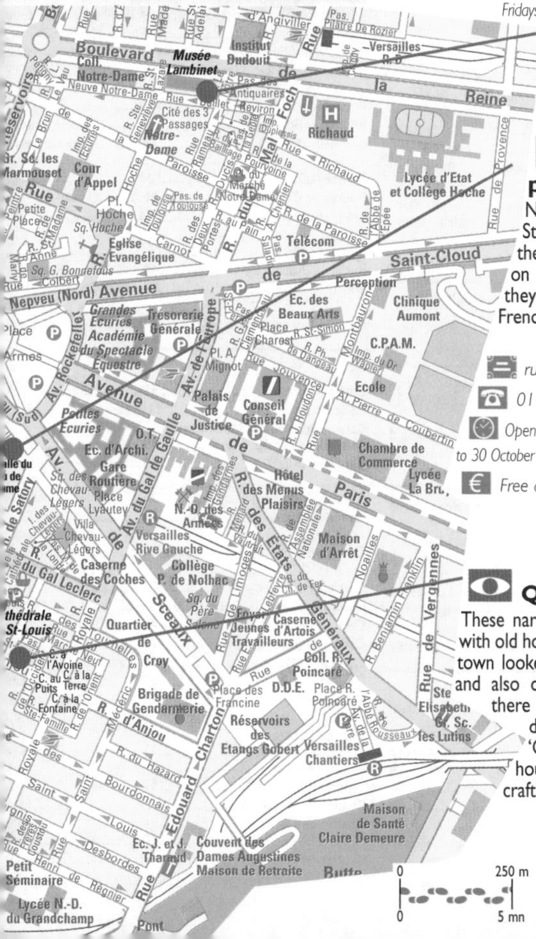

Salle du Jeu de paume

Not being able to get into the State Generals, the deputies of the Tiers Etat gathered in this hall on 20 June 1789 and swore that they would not leave until the French Constitution was written.

rue du Jeu de Paume

01 39 83 77 88

Open Saturdays and Sundays from 1 April to 30 October from 12.30 pm to 6.30 pm

Free admission

Quartier Saint-Louis

These narrow peaceful little lanes, lined with old houses reminds us of the way the town looked in the 18th century. Nearby and also dating from the 18th century, there is the cathedral whose towers dominate the district and the 'Carrés' built by Louis XV to house a market. They now house craft and antique shops.

0 250 m
0 5 mn

Site..Arrdt	page	Métro

P

Q

R

S

ite..Arrdt...............page.............Métro

Site..Arrdt...............page.............Métro

V

Z

■ BERCY VILLAGE
Cour St-Émilion
75012 Paris
Metro : Cour St-Émilion

■ BHV
52-64 rue de Rivoli
75004 Paris
Tél : 01 42 74 90 00
Métro : Hôtel de Ville

■ BHV
119 avenue de Flandre
75019 Paris
Tél : 01 42 74 99 00
Métro : Crimée

■ BON MARCHÉ
24 rue de Sèvres
75007 Paris
Tél : 01 44 39 80 00
Métro : Sèvres-Babylone

■ CARROUSEL DU LOUVRE
Rue de Rivoli, cour Napoléon
75001 Paris
Métro : Palais Royal-Musée du Louvre

■ FORUM DES HALLES
Rue Berger, rue Pierre Lescot
75001 Paris
Métro : Châtelet-Les Halles

■ GALERIES LAFAYETTE
40 bd Haussmann
75009 Paris
Tél : 01 42 82 34 56
Métro : Chaussée-d'Antin

■ GALERIES LAFAYETTE
22 rue du Départ
75015 Paris
Tél : 01 45 38 52 87
Métro : Montparnasse-Bienvenüe

■ LES QUATRE TEMPS
15 le Parvis de la Défense
92800 Puteaux
Métro : La Défense-Grande Arche

■ PRINTEMPS-GALAXIE
30 avenue d'Italie
75013 Paris
Tél : 01 40 78 17 17
Métro : Place d'Italie

■ PRINTEMPS-HAUSSMANN
64 boulevard Haussmann
75009 Paris
Tél : 01 42 82 50 00
Métro : Havre-Caumartin

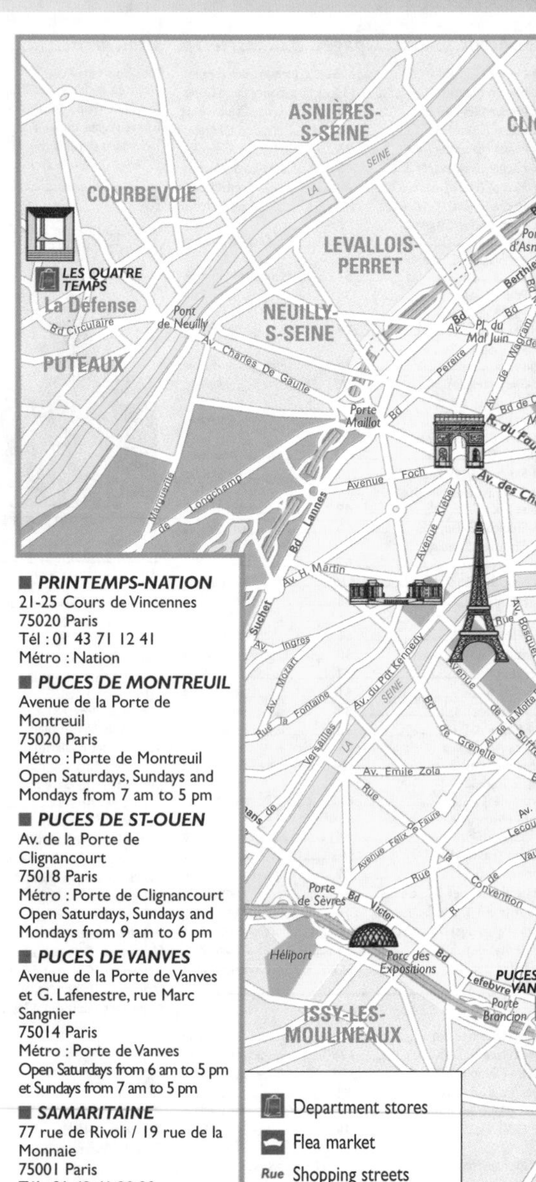

■ PRINTEMPS-NATION
21-25 Cours de Vincennes
75020 Paris
Tél : 01 43 71 12 41
Métro : Nation

■ PUCES DE MONTREUIL
Avenue de la Porte de Montreuil
75020 Paris
Métro : Porte de Montreuil
Open Saturdays, Sundays and Mondays from 7 am to 5 pm

■ PUCES DE ST-OUEN
Av. de la Porte de Clignancourt
75018 Paris
Métro : Porte de Clignancourt
Open Saturdays, Sundays and Mondays from 9 am to 6 pm

■ PUCES DE VANVES
Avenue de la Porte de Vanves et G. Lafenestre, rue Marc Sangnier
75014 Paris
Métro : Porte de Vanves
Open Saturdays from 6 am to 5 pm et Sundays from 7 am to 5 pm

■ SAMARITAINE
77 rue de Rivoli / 19 rue de la Monnaie
75001 Paris
Tél : 01 40 41 20 20
Métro : Pont Neuf

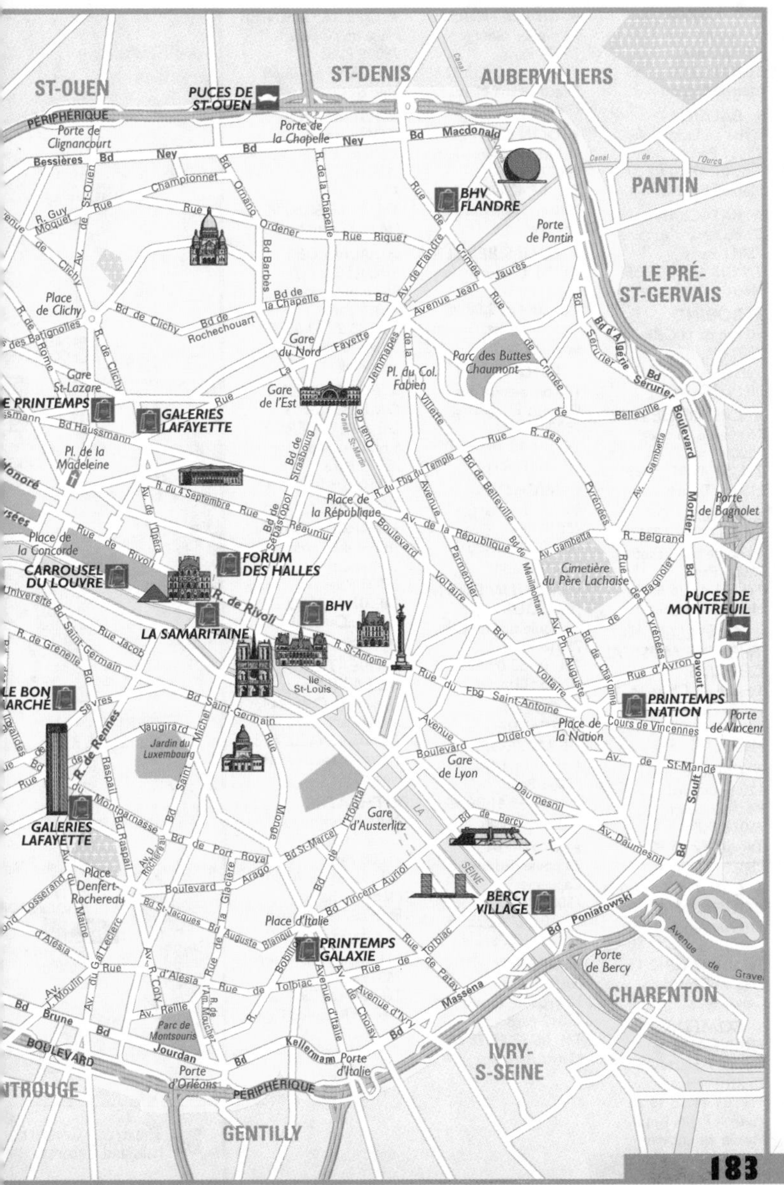
ST-OUEN
PUCES DE ST-OUEN
ST-DENIS
AUBERVILLIERS
PÉRIPHÉRIQUE
Porte de Clignancourt
Porte de la Chapelle
Bd Macdonald
Bd Ney
Bessières
Canal de l'Ourcq
PANTIN
BHV FLANDRE
Porte de Pantin
LE PRÉ-ST-GERVAIS
Rue Championnet
Bd Ornano
Rue Ordener
R. de la Chapelle
Rue Riquet
Rue de Crimée
Av. de Flandre
Avenue Jean Jaurès
Bd Barbès
Bd de la Chapelle
Place de Clichy
Bd de Clichy
Bd de Rochechouart
Gare du Nord
Gare St-Lazare
Gare de l'Est
Pl. du Col. Fabien
Parc des Buttes Chaumont
Bd d'Algérie
Bd Sérurier
PRINTEMPS
GALERIES LAFAYETTE
Bd Haussmann
Pl. de la Madeleine
Bd de Strasbourg
Quai de Jemmapes
Canal St-Martin
Rue de Belleville
R. des Pyrénées
Av. Gambetta
Boulevard Mortier
Porte de Bagnolet
R. du 4 Septembre
Rue Réaumur
Place de la République
R. du Fbg du Temple
Bd de Belleville
Av. de la République
R. Belgrand
Place de la Concorde
Rue de Rivoli
CARROUSEL DU LOUVRE
FORUM DES HALLES
Bd de Sébastopol
Boulevard Voltaire
Avenue Parmentier
Cimetière du Père Lachaise
Bd de Ménilmontant
Rue de Bagnolet
PUCES DE MONTREUIL
BHV
LA SAMARITAINE
R. de Rivoli
Rue Jacob
R. de Grenelle
Bd Saint-Germain
R. St-Antoine
Ile St-Louis
Rue du Fbg Saint-Antoine
Rue d'Avron
Bd Davout
Bd de Charonne
Av. Ph. Auguste
LE BON MARCHÉ
Sèvres
Vaugirard
Jardin du Luxembourg
Bd Saint-Michel
Rue Monge
PRINTEMPS NATION
Place de la Nation
Cours de Vincennes
Porte de Vincennes
Avenue Diderot
Gare de Lyon
Av. de St-Mandé
Bd Soult
R. de Rennes
Bd Raspail
Bd du Montparnasse
GALERIES LAFAYETTE
Daumesnil
Gare d'Austerlitz
Bd de l'Hôpital
Bd de Bercy
Av. Daumesnil
LA SEINE
Bd de Port Royal
Bd Arago
Bd St-Marcel
Rue de la Glacière
Place Denfert-Rochereau
Boulevard Bd St-Jacques
Bd Auguste Blanqui
Bd Vincent Auriol
Place d'Italie
BERCY VILLAGE
Bd Poniatowski
PRINTEMPS GALAXIE
Rue de Tolbiac
Rue de Patay
Porte de Bercy
Avenue de Gravelle
CHARENTON
Av. du Gal Leclerc
Av. du Maine
Rue d'Alésia
Av. R. Coty
Av. Reille
Parc de Montsouris
Avenue d'Italie
Avenue de Choisy
Avenue d'Ivry
Bd Masséna
Bd Brune
BOULEVARD Jourdan
Porte d'Orléans
Bd Kellermann
Porte d'Italie
PÉRIPHÉRIQUE
IVRY-S-SEINE
GENTILLY

★ **ALCAZAR**
62 rue Mazarine
75006 Paris
Tél : 01 53 10 19 99
Métro : Odéon

★ **BALAJO**
9 rue de Lappe
75011 Paris
Tél : 01 47 00 07 87
Métro : Bastille

★ **BATACLAN**
50 boulevard Voltaire
75011 Paris
Tél : 01 43 14 35 35
Métro : Oberkampf

★ **BOBINO**
20 rue de la Gaîté
75014 Paris
Tél : 01 43 27 75 75
Métro : Gaîté

★ **CASINO DE PARIS**
16 rue de Clichy
75009 Paris
Tél : 01 49 95 99 99
Métro : Trinité

★ **CAVEAU DE LA HUCHETTE**
5 rue de la Huchette
75005 Paris
Tél : 01 43 26 65 05
Métro : Saint-Michel

★ **CHÂTELET THÉÂTRE MUSICAL DE PARIS**
1 place du Châtelet
75001 Paris
Tél : 01 40 28 28 40
Métro : Châtelet

★ **CIGALE**
120 boulevard Rochechouart
75018 Paris
Tél : 01 49 25 89 99
Métro : Pigalle

★ **CIRQUE D'HIVER BOUGLIONE**
110 rue Amelot
75011 Paris
Tél : 01 47 00 12 15
Métro : Filles-du-Calvaire

★ **COMÉDIE FRANÇAISE**
1 place Colette
75001 Paris
Tél : 01 44 58 15 15
Métro : Palais Royal-Musée du Louvre

★ **CRAZY HORSE**
12 avenue George V
75008 Paris
Tél : 01 47 23 32 32
Métro : Alma-Marceau, George V

★ **DON CAMILO**
10 rue des Saints-Pères
75007 Paris
Tél : 01 42 60 82 84
Métro : Saint-Germain des Prés

★ **FOLIES BERGÈRE**
32 rue Richer
75009 Paris
Tél : 01 44 79 98 98
Métro : Cadet, Grands Boulevards

★ **LIDO**
116 bis avenue des Champs Elysées
75008 Paris
Tél : 01 40 76 56 10
Métro : George V

★ **MICHOU**
80 rue des Martyrs
75018 Paris
Tél : 01 42 57 20 37
Métro : Pigalle

★ **MOULIN ROUGE (BAL DU)**
82 boulevard de Clichy
75018 Paris
Tél : 01 53 09 82 82
Métro : Blanche

★ **ODÉON (THÉÂTRE DE L'EUROPE)**
1 place Paul Claudel
75006 Paris
Tél : 01 44 41 36 36
Métro : Odéon

★ **OLYMPIA**
28 boulevard des Capucines
75009 Paris
Tél : 01 47 42 25 49
Métro : Madeleine

★ **OPÉRA BASTILLE**
120 rue de Lyon
75012 Paris
Tél : 08 92 69 78 68
Métro : Bastille

★ **OPÉRA GARNIER**
Place de l'Opéra
75009 Paris
Tél : 08 92 69 78 68
Métro : Opéra

★ **PALAIS DES CONGRÈS**
2 place de la Porte Maillot
75017 Paris
Tél : 01 40 68 00 05
Métro : Porte Maillot

★ **PALAIS DES SPORTS**
Porte de Versailles
75015 Paris
Tél : 08 25 03 80 39
Métro : Porte de Versailles

★ **POPB (PALAIS OMNISPORTS DE PARIS-BERCY)**
8 boulevard de Bercy
75012 Paris
Tél : 08 03 03 00 31
Métro : Bercy

★ **PARADIS LATIN**
28 rue du Cardinal Lemoine
75005 Paris
Tél : 01 43 25 28 28
Métro : Cardinal Lemoine

★ **THÉÂTRE DE LA VILLE**
2 place du Châtelet
75001 Paris
Tél : 01 42 74 22 77
Métro : Châtelet-Les Halles

★ **THÉÂTRE MARIGNY**
Carré Marigny
75008 Paris
Tél : 01 53 96 70 00
Métro : Champs Elysées-Clemenceau

★ **ZÉNITH**
211 avenue Jean Jaurès
75019 Paris
Tél : 01 42 08 60 00
Métro : Porte de Pantin

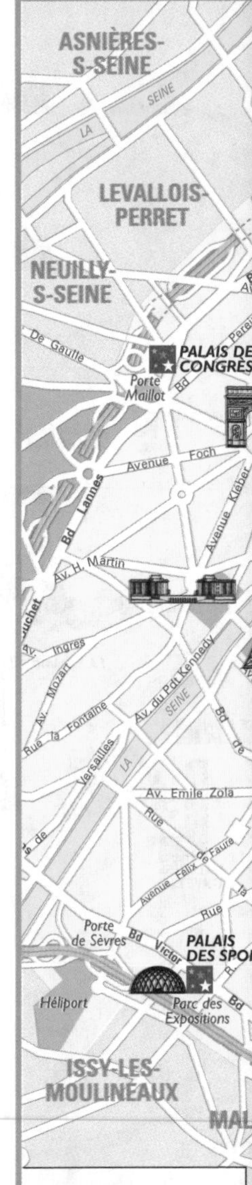

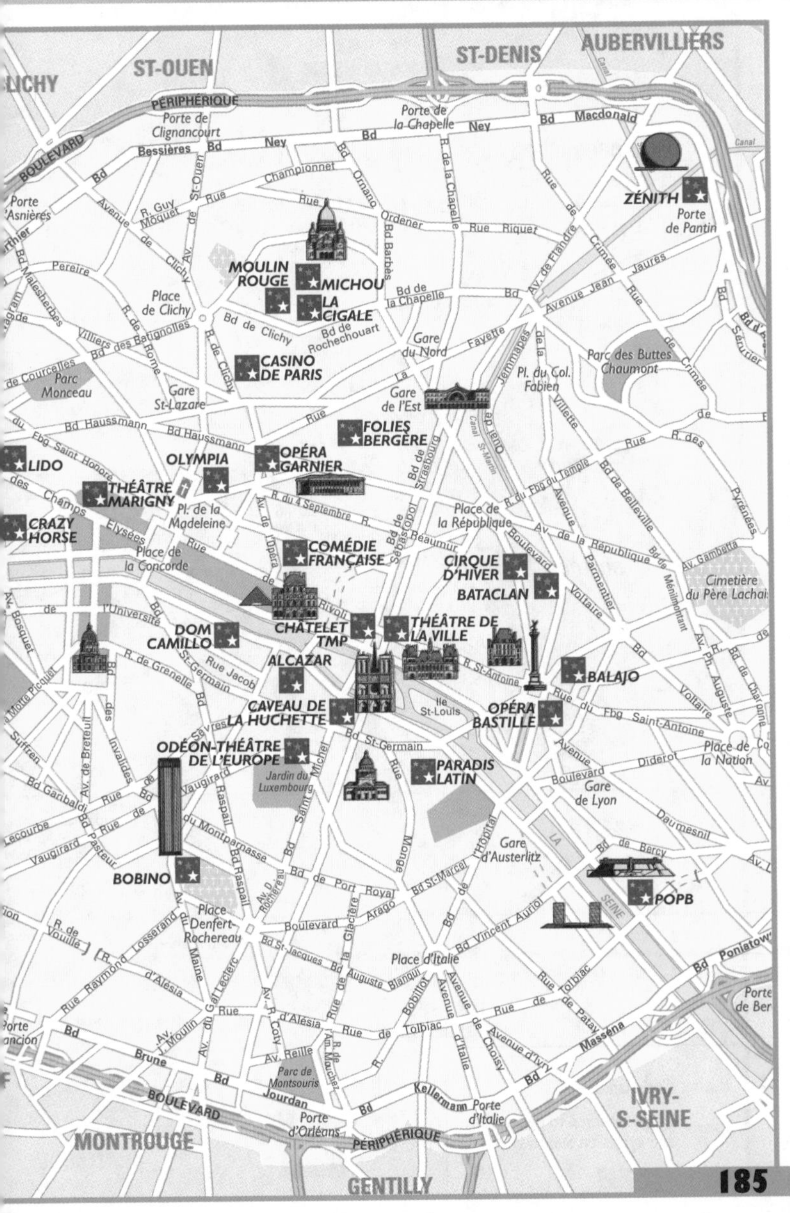
ST-OUEN
ST-DENIS
AUBERVILLIERS
CLICHY
PÉRIPHÉRIQUE
Porte de Clignancourt
Porte de la Chapelle
Porte d'Asnières
ZÉNITH
Porte de Pantin
MOULIN ROUGE
MICHOU
LA CIGALE
Place de Clichy
CASINO DE PARIS
Gare du Nord
Parc des Buttes Chaumont
Pl. du Col. Fabien
Parc Monceau
Gare St-Lazare
Gare de l'Est
Canal St-Martin
FOLIES BERGÈRE
LIDO
OLYMPIA
OPÉRA GARNIER
THÉATRE MARIGNY
Pl. de la Madeleine
Place de la République
CRAZY HORSE
COMÉDIE FRANÇAISE
Place de la Concorde
CIRQUE D'HIVER
BATACLAN
Cimetière du Père Lachaise
DOM CAMILLO
CHATELET TMP
THÉATRE DE LA VILLE
ALCAZAR
BALAJO
CAVEAU DE LA HUCHETTE
Ile St-Louis
OPÉRA BASTILLE
ODÉON-THÉATRE DE L'EUROPE
Jardin du Luxembourg
PARADIS LATIN
Place de la Nation
Gare de Lyon
Gare d'Austerlitz
BOBINO
POPB
Place Denfert-Rochereau
Place d'Italie
Parc de Montsouris
Porte d'Orléans
Porte d'Italie
MONTROUGE
IVRY-S-SEINE
GENTILLY
LA SEINE

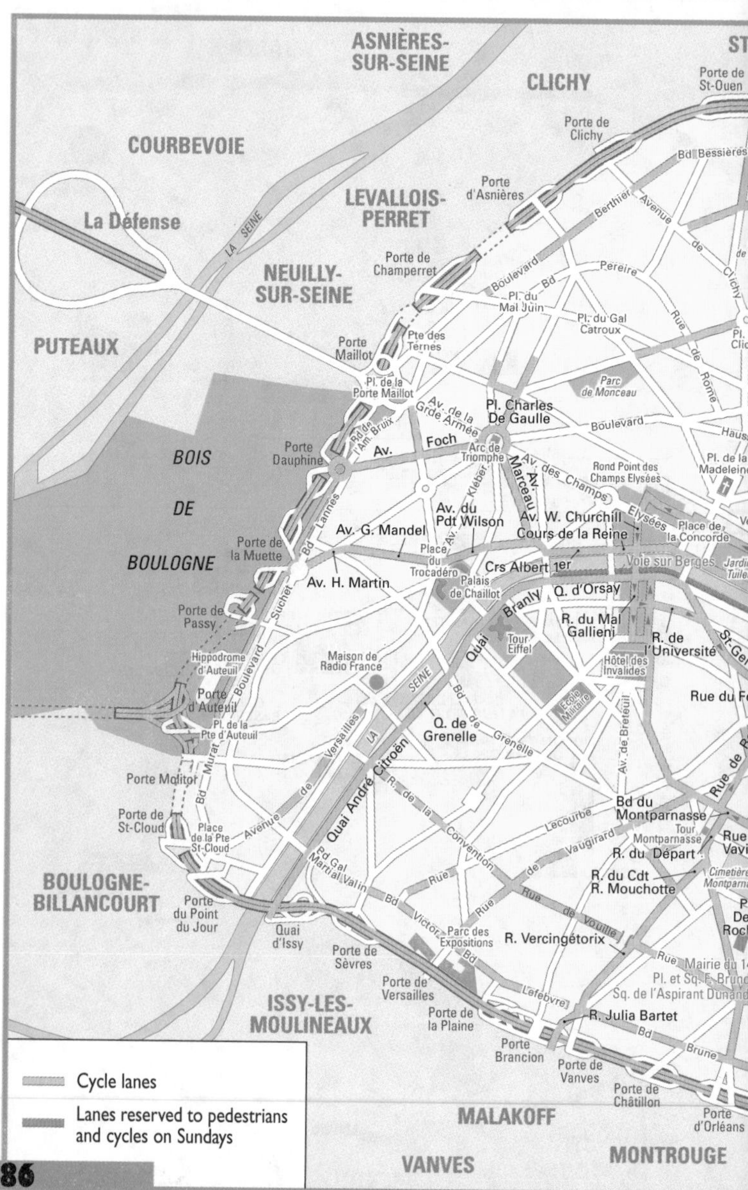
ASNIÈRES-SUR-SEINE
CLICHY
Porte de St-Ouen
Porte de Clichy
Bd Bessières
COURBEVOIE
Porte d'Asnières
LEVALLOIS-PERRET
La Défense
LA SEINE
Berthier
Avenue de Clichy
Porte de Champerret
NEUILLY-SUR-SEINE
Boulevard
Bd
Pereire
Pl. du Mal Juin
Pl. du Gal Catroux
Rue de Rome
PUTEAUX
Porte Maillot
Pte des Ternes
Pl. de la Porte Maillot
Parc de Monceau
Av. de la Grde Armée
Pl. Charles De Gaulle
Boulevard
Bd de l'Am. Bruix
Av. Foch
Arc de Triomphe
BOIS DE BOULOGNE
Porte Dauphine
Av. des Champs Elysées
Rond Point des Champs Elysées
Pl. de la Madeleine
Av. Marceau
Av. Kleber
Lannes
Av. du Pdt Wilson
Av. W. Churchill
Place de la Concorde
Av. G. Mandel
Cours de la Reine
Porte de la Muette
Place du Trocadéro
Voie sur Berges
Bd
Av. H. Martin
Crs Albert 1er
Palais de Chaillot
Q. d'Orsay
Branly
Porte de Passy
Suchet
R. du Mal Gallieni
R. de l'Université
Quai
Tour Eiffel
Hippodrome d'Auteuil
Maison de Radio France
Hôtel des Invalides
Rue du F
Boulevard
Porte d'Auteuil
SEINE
Bd
Ecole Militaire
Q. de Grenelle
de Grenelle
Pl. de la Pte d'Auteuil
Versailles
LA
Av. de Breteuil
Murat
Quai André Citroën
Porte Molitor
Bd
Avenue de
R. de la Convention
Bd du Montparnasse
Porte de St-Cloud
Place de la Pte St-Cloud
Lecourbe
Tour Montparnasse
Vaugirard
R. du Départ
Bd Gal Martial Valin
Rue de
BOULOGNE-BILLANCOURT
R. du Cdt
R. Mouchotte
Porte du Point du Jour
Bd Victor
Rue
Rue de Vouillé
Parc des Expositions
R. Vercingétorix
Quai d'Issy
Porte de Sèvres
Mairie du 14
Pl. et Sq. F. Brunot
Sq. de l'Aspirant Dunand
Porte de Versailles
Lefebvre
ISSY-LES-MOULINEAUX
Porte de la Plaine
R. Julia Bartet
Bd Brune
Porte Brancion
Porte de Vanves
Porte de Châtillon
Porte d'Orléans
Cycle lanes
Lanes reserved to pedestrians and cycles on Sundays
MALAKOFF
VANVES
MONTROUGE

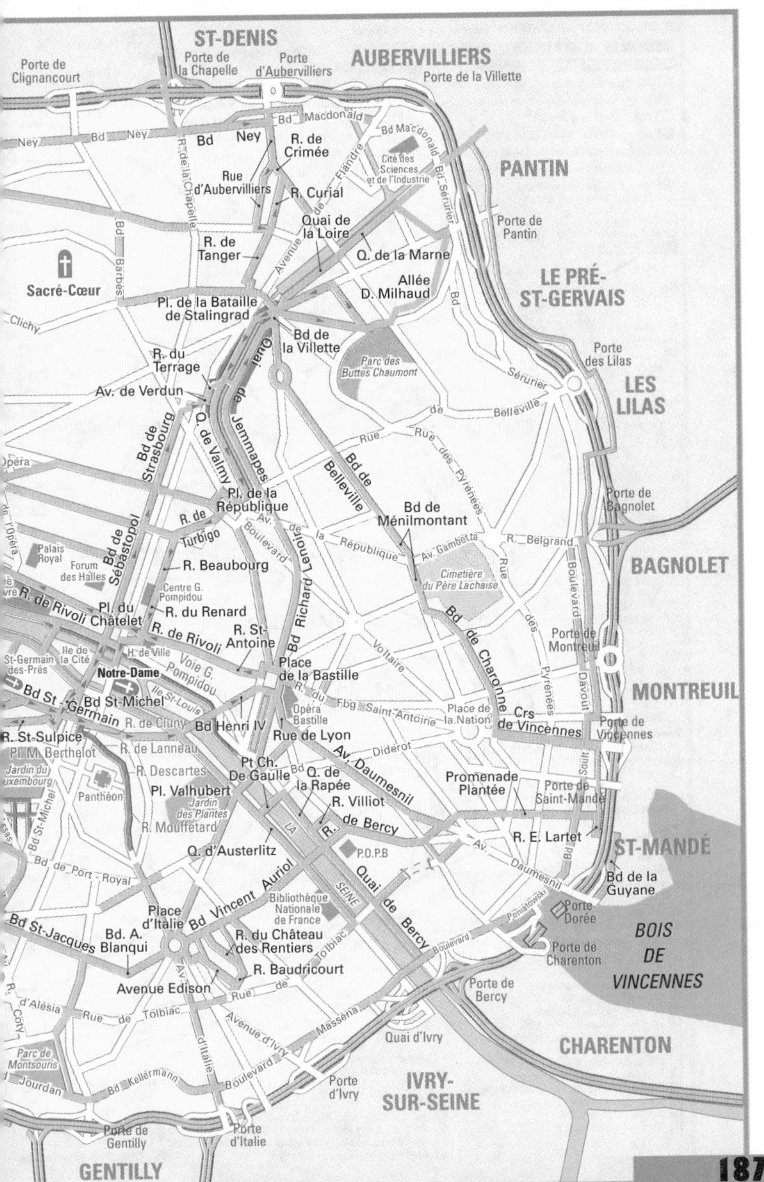
ST-DENIS
Porte de Clignancourt
Porte de la Chapelle
Porte d'Aubervilliers
AUBERVILLIERS
Porte de la Villette
Bd Macdonald
Bd Ney
R. de Crimée
Rue d'Aubervilliers
R. Curial
R. de la Chapelle
Cité des Sciences et de l'Industrie
Avenue de Flandre
Bd Sérurier
PANTIN
Porte de Pantin
Quai de la Loire
Q. de la Marne
R. de Tanger
Bd Barbès
Sacré-Cœur
Allée D. Milhaud
LE PRÉ-ST-GERVAIS
Pl. de la Bataille de Stalingrad
Clichy
Bd de la Villette
Quai de Jemmapes
Parc des Buttes Chaumont
R. du Terrage
Porte des Lilas
LES LILAS
Av. de Verdun
Rue de Belleville
Bd de Strasbourg
Q. de Valmy
Rue des Pyrénées
Opéra
Bd de Belleville
Pl. de la République
Porte de Bagnolet
R. de Turbigo
Bd de Ménilmontant
Palais Royal
Forum des Halles
Bd de Sébastopol
Boulevard Richard Lenoir
Av. de la République
Av. Gambetta
R. Belgrand
BAGNOLET
R. Beaubourg
Cimetière du Père Lachaise
Centre G. Pompidou
R. de Rivoli
Pl. du Châtelet
R. du Renard
Bd de Charonne
Boulevard Davout
R. St-Antoine
Voltaire
Porte de Montreuil
Ile de la Cité
St-Germain des-Prés
H. de Ville
Voie G. Pompidou
Place de la Bastille
Notre-Dame
Ile St-Louis
MONTREUIL
Bd St-Germain
Bd St-Michel
R. du Fbg Saint-Antoine
Place de la Nation
Opéra Bastille
Crs de Vincennes
Porte de Vincennes
R. de Cluny
Bd Henri IV
R. St-Sulpice
Rue de Lyon
Pl. M. Berthelot
R. de Lanneau
Diderot
Av. Daumesnil
Jardin du Luxembourg
R. Descartes
Pt Ch. De Gaulle
Bd Q. de la Rapée
Promenade Plantée
Porte de Saint-Mandé
Bd Soult
Panthéon
Pl. Valhubert
Jardin des Plantes
R. Villiot
R. de Bercy
R. Mouffetard
Bd St-Michel
R. E. Lartet
Q. d'Austerlitz
P.O.P.B
LA SEINE
ST-MANDÉ
Bd de Port-Royal
Quai de Bercy
Bd de la Guyane
Bibliothèque Nationale de France
Bd Vincent Auriol
Porte Dorée
Place d'Italie
Bd Poniatowski
Bd St-Jacques
Bd. A. Blanqui
R. du Château des Rentiers
R. de Tolbiac
Porte de Charenton
BOIS DE VINCENNES
R. Baudricourt
Avenue Edison
Porte de Bercy
R. d'Alésia
Rue de Tolbiac
Avenue d'Ivry
Bd Masséna
Quai d'Ivry
Parc de Montsouris
Av. d'Italie
CHARENTON
Bd Jourdan
Bd Kellermann
Porte d'Ivry
IVRY-SUR-SEINE
Porte de Gentilly
Porte d'Italie
GENTILLY

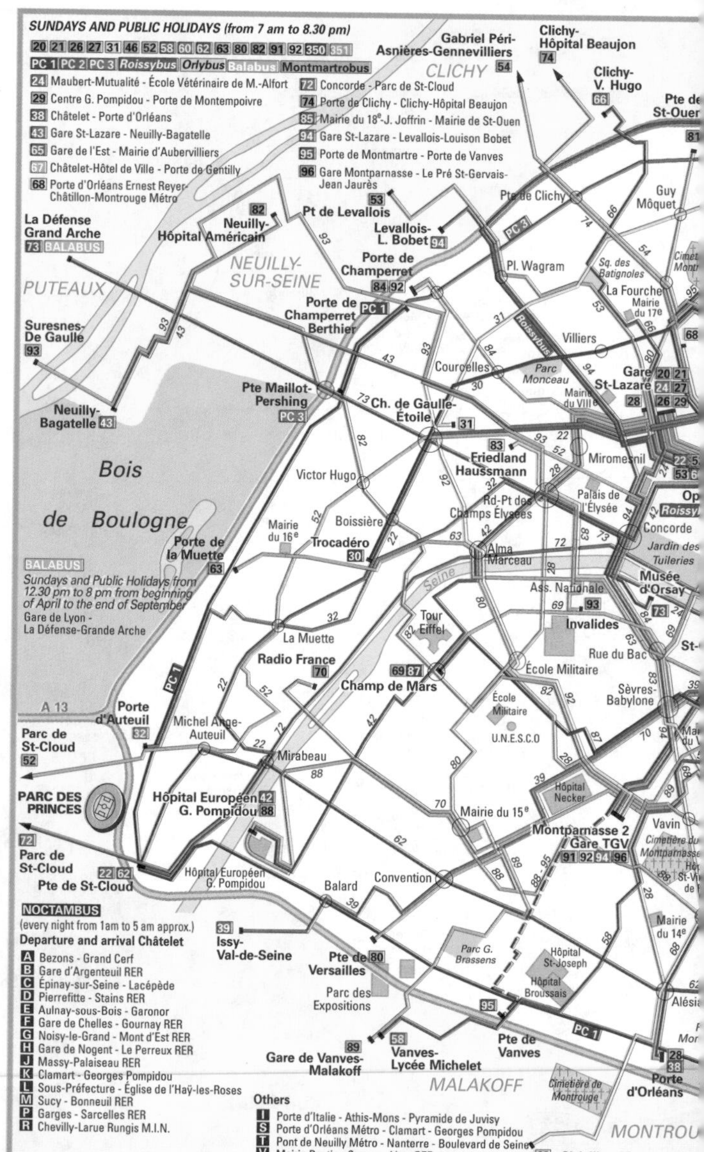

SUNDAYS AND PUBLIC HOLIDAYS (from 7 am to 8.30 pm)
20 21 26 27 31 46 52 58 60 62 63 80 82 91 92 350 351
PC 1 PC 2 PC 3 Roissybus Orlybus Balabus Montmartrobus
24 Maubert-Mutualité - École Vétérinaire de M.-Alfort
29 Centre G. Pompidou - Porte de Montempoivre
38 Châtelet - Porte d'Orléans
43 Gare St-Lazare - Neuilly-Bagatelle
65 Gare de l'Est - Mairie d'Aubervilliers
67 Châtelet-Hôtel de Ville - Porte de Gentilly
68 Porte d'Orléans Ernest Reyer-Châtillon-Montrouge Métro
72 Concorde - Parc de St-Cloud
74 Porte de Clichy - Clichy-Hôpital Beaujon
85 Mairie du 18e-J. Joffrin - Mairie de St-Ouen
94 Gare St-Lazare - Levallois-Louison Bobet
95 Porte de Montmartre - Porte de Vanves
96 Gare Montparnasse - Le Pré St-Gervais-Jean Jaurès
BALABUS
Sundays and Public Holidays from 12.30 pm to 8 pm from beginning of April to the end of September
Gare de Lyon - La Défense-Grande Arche
NOCTAMBUS
(every night from 1am to 5 am approx.)
Departure and arrival Châtelet
A Bezons - Grand Cerf
B Gare d'Argenteuil RER
C Épinay-sur-Seine - Lacépède
D Pierrefitte - Stains RER
E Aulnay-sous-Bois - Garonor
F Gare de Chelles - Gournay RER
G Noisy-le-Grand - Mont d'Est RER
H Gare de Nogent - Le Perreux RER
J Massy-Palaiseau RER
K Clamart - Georges Pompidou
L Sous-Préfecture - Église de l'Haÿ-les-Roses
M Sucy - Bonneuil RER
P Garges - Sarcelles RER
R Chevilly-Larue Rungis M.I.N.
Others
I Porte d'Italie - Athis-Mons - Pyramide de Juvisy
S Porte d'Orléans Métro - Clamart - Georges Pompidou
T Pont de Neuilly Métro - Nanterre - Boulevard de Seine
V Mairie Pantin - Sevran - Livry RER
Gabriel Péri-Asnières-Gennevilliers
Clichy-Hôpital Beaujon
CLICHY
Clichy-V. Hugo
La Défense Grande Arche
Neuilly-Hôpital Américain
Pt de Levallois
Levallois-L. Bobet
NEUILLY-SUR-SEINE
PUTEAUX
Porte de Champerret
Porte de Champerret Berthier
Suresnes-De Gaulle
Neuilly-Bagatelle
Pte Maillot-Pershing
Ch. de Gaulle-Étoile
Pte de Clichy
Pl. Wagram
Sq. des Batignoles
La Fourche
Mairie du 17e
Guy Môquet
Villiers
Courcelles
Parc Monceau
Gare St-Lazare
Friedland Haussmann
Miromesnil
Palais de l'Élysée
Rd-Pt des Champs Élysées
Concorde
Jardin des Tuileries
Musée d'Orsay
Bois de Boulogne
Victor Hugo
Boissière
Mairie du 16e
Trocadéro
Porte de la Muette
Alma Marceau
Seine
Ass. Nationale
Invalides
Tour Eiffel
La Muette
Radio France
Champ de Mars
Rue du Bac
École Militaire
Sèvres-Babylone
U.N.E.S.C.O
A 13
Porte d'Auteuil
Michel Ange-Auteuil
Parc de St-Cloud
Mirabeau
PARC DES PRINCES
Hôpital Européen G. Pompidou
Hôpital Necker
Mairie du 15e
Montparnasse 2 Gare TGV
Vavin
Pte de St-Cloud
Balard
Convention
Issy-Val-de-Seine
Pte de Versailles
Parc des Expositions
Parc G. Brassens
Hôpital St-Joseph
Hôpital Broussais
Mairie du 14e
Gare de Vanves-Malakoff
Vanves-Lycée Michelet
Pte de Vanves
MALAKOFF
Cimetière de Montrouge
Porte d'Orléans
Châtillon-Montrouge-Métro

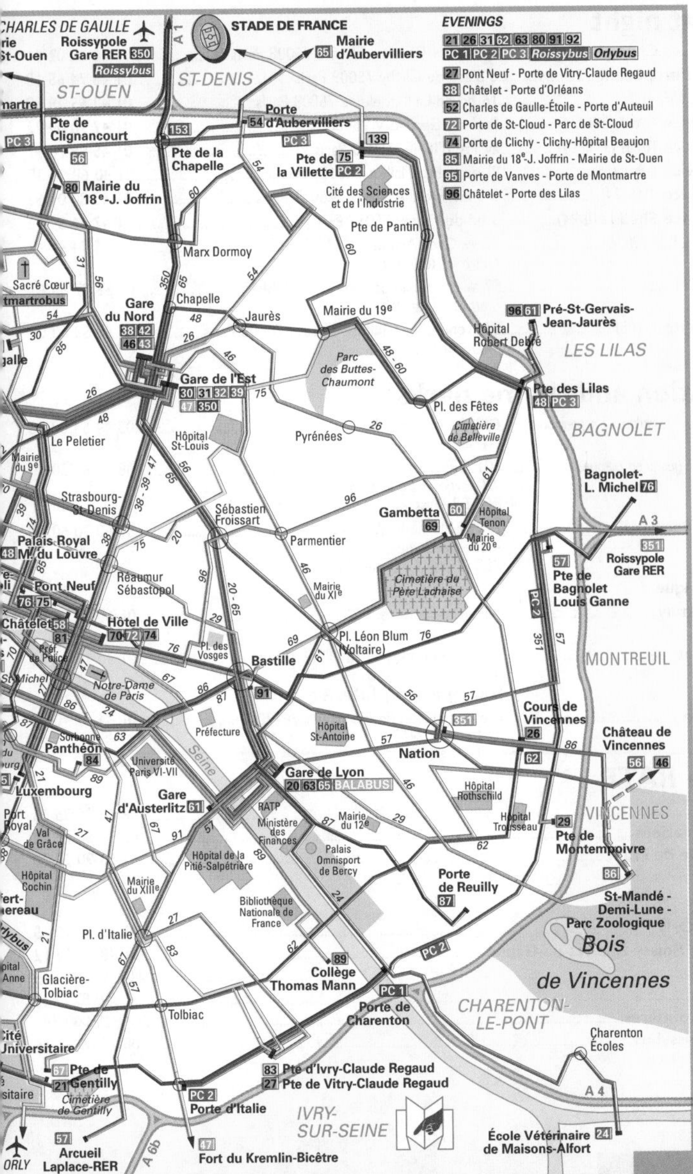
EVENINGS
21 26 31 62 63 80 91 92
PC 1 PC 2 PC 3 Roissybus Orlybus
27 Pont Neuf - Porte de Vitry-Claude Regaud
38 Châtelet - Porte d'Orléans
52 Charles de Gaulle-Étoile - Porte d'Auteuil
72 Porte de St-Cloud - Parc de St-Cloud
74 Porte de Clichy - Clichy-Hôpital Beaujon
85 Mairie du 18e-J. Joffrin - Mairie de St-Ouen
95 Porte de Vanves - Porte de Montmartre
96 Châtelet - Porte des Lilas
STADE DE FRANCE
Roissypole Gare RER 350
Mairie d'Aubervilliers
ST-DENIS
ST-OUEN
Pte de Clignancourt
Porte d'Aubervilliers
Pte de la Chapelle
Pte de la Villette
Cité des Sciences et de l'Industrie
Mairie du 18e-J. Joffrin
Pte de Pantin
Marx Dormoy
Sacré Cœur
Chapelle
Gare du Nord
Jaurès
Mairie du 19e
Pré-St-Gervais-Jean-Jaurès
Hôpital Robert Debré
LES LILAS
Parc des Buttes-Chaumont
Gare de l'Est
Pte des Lilas
Pl. des Fêtes
Cimetière de Belleville
BAGNOLET
Hôpital St-Louis
Pyrénées
Le Peletier
Bagnolet-L. Michel
Strasbourg-St-Denis
Sébastien Froissart
Gambetta
Hôpital Tenon
Mairie du 20e
Parmentier
Palais Royal M. du Louvre
Roissypole Gare RER
Pont Neuf
Réaumur Sébastopol
Mairie du XIe
Cimetière du Père Lachaise
Pte de Bagnolet Louis Ganne
Châtelet
Hôtel de Ville
Pl. Léon Blum (Voltaire)
Préf. de Police
Pl. des Vosges
Bastille
MONTREUIL
St Michel
Notre-Dame de Paris
Préfecture
Hôpital St-Antoine
Cours de Vincennes
Château de Vincennes
Panthéon
Nation
Université Paris VI-VII
Gare de Lyon
BALABUS
Seine
Luxembourg
Gare d'Austerlitz
Hôpital Rothschild
RATP
Ministère des Finances
Mairie du 12e
Hôpital Trousseau
VINCENNES
Pte de Montempoivre
Port Royal
Val de Grâce
Palais Omnisport de Bercy
Hôpital de la Pitié-Salpêtrière
Hôpital Cochin
Porte de Reuilly
Mairie du XIIIe
St-Mandé - Demi-Lune - Parc Zoologique
Bibliothèque Nationale de France
Bois de Vincennes
Pl. d'Italie
Collège Thomas Mann
Glacière-Tolbiac
Porte de Charenton
CHARENTON-LE-PONT
Tolbiac
Cité Universitaire
Charenton Écoles
Pte de Gentilly
Pte d'Ivry-Claude Regaud
Pte de Vitry-Claude Regaud
A 4
Cimetière de Gentilly
Porte d'Italie
IVRY-SUR-SEINE
École Vétérinaire de Maisons-Alfort
Arcueil Laplace-RER
Fort du Kremlin-Bicêtre
ORLY
A 1
A 3
A 6b

Open at night

Pharmacie Les Champs *(24h/24)*........84 av. des Champs-Elysées 75008 Paris 01 45 62 02 41
Pharmacie Européenne *(24h/24)*.........6 place de Clichy 75009 Paris 01 48 74 65 18
Journaux *(24h/24)*..........................16 bd de La Madeleine 75008 Paris.............................. 01 42 65 29 19
Station-service Total *(24h/24)*..............Parking George-V 75008 Paris.. 01 47 20 09 22
Station-service Total *(24h/24)*..............av. Pte d'Italie 75013 Paris 01 45 88 78 91
Station-service BP *(1h)*..........................Pl. de la Pte Maillot 75017 Paris 01 40 68 92 35
Station-service *(24h/24)*..........................3-5 av. Pte d'Asnières 75017 Paris 01 43 80 01 53
Station-service Shell *(24h/24)*..............3 bd de l'Yser 75017 Paris 01 47 66 54 92
Tabac Le Maillot *(0h30)*.........................78 av. Grde Armée 75017 Paris... 01 45 74 41 42
métro Porte Maillot
Monoprix *(0h)*...52 av. des Champs-Elysées 75008Paris............................01 53 77 65 65
métro : George-V
Virgin Megastore *(0h)*............................52 avenue des Champs-Elysées 75008 Paris................ 01 49 53 50 00
métro George-V

Recreation and theme parks

Mer de Sable *(jusqu'au 27 septembre)*........60950 Ermenonville 03 44 54 00 96
A1 sortie n°7
Parc Astérix *(jusqu'en octobre)* ....60128 Plailly 08 36 68 30 10
A1 sortie «Parc Astérix»
RER B3 Roissy-Ch.-de-Gaulle + bus
Disneyland Paris ....77990 Marne-la-Vallée- 01 60 30 60 30
A Chessy-Marne-La-Vallée
RER Chessy A4 sortie n°14
Parc Zoologique
du Bois d'Attilly ....Ozoir-La-Ferrière, ...01 60 02 70 80
N4
France Miniature ....25 route du Mesnil, 78990 Elancourt 01 30 16 16 30
A13 puis A12 et A86
SNCF ligne La Déf.-La Verrière
Parc de Thoiry ....rue du Pavillon de Montreuil, 78770 Thoiry..................01 34 87 40 67
A13 et A12, N12

SNCF - RATP

SNCF..08 36 35 35 35
RATP Informations 08 92 68 77 14
SNCF Info Ile de France...01 53 90 20 20

Planes

Aéroport d'Orly...01 49 75 15 15
Aéroport de Roissy-Charles-de-Gaulle.. 01 48 62 12 12
Vols du jour 0 836 681 515
Air France...0 820 820 820
Nouvelles Frontières..0 825 000 747
Orlybus - Roissybus...08 92 68 77 14

Taxis - Bike hire

lpha Taxis 01 45 85 85 85
7 .... 01 47 39 47 39
es Taxis Bleus 01 49 36 10 10
aris à Vélo c'est sympa ! 01 48 87 60 01
aris Vélo 01 43 37 59 22
Escapade Nature 01 53 17 03 18
Maison Roue Libre 08 10 44 15 34
Vélo Taxi
(bikes and motorbikes) 01 42 72 70 12

Car rental

.D.A. 08 25 16 91 69
vis 08 20 05 05 05
xeco 01 43 14 78 87
udget
utomobiles et motocyclettes) 0 800 10 00 01
Citer 01 44 38 61 61
Europcar 08 25 35 23 52
Hertz 01 39 38 38 38
Rent a Car 08 91 70 02 00
Sixt 01 44 38 55 55

Boat trips

ateaux-Mouches 01 42 25 96 10
ateaux Parisiens-Tour Eiffel 01 44 11 33 44
atobus Paris 01 44 11 33 99
anauxrama
canal Saint-Martin et canal de l'Ourcq) 01 42 39 15 00
Les Vedettes du Pont Neuf 01 46 33 98 38
Paris Canal
(Seine et canal Saint-Martin) 01 42 40 96 97
Vedettes de Paris 01 44 18 08 03
Yachts de Paris 01 44 54 14 70

Guided tours and Bus Tours

ssociation des Guides
nterprêtes et conférenciers 01 41 31 25 25
entre d'Information
es Monuments Nationaux 01 44 61 21 50
Cityrama 01 44 55 60 00
Les Cars Rouges 01 53 953 953
Paris Vision 01 42 86 95 36
Touringscope 01 53 34 11 91

Textes : Jean-Luc Pottier
Photography : D. Ogeret - C. Chemin
Design : Moviken

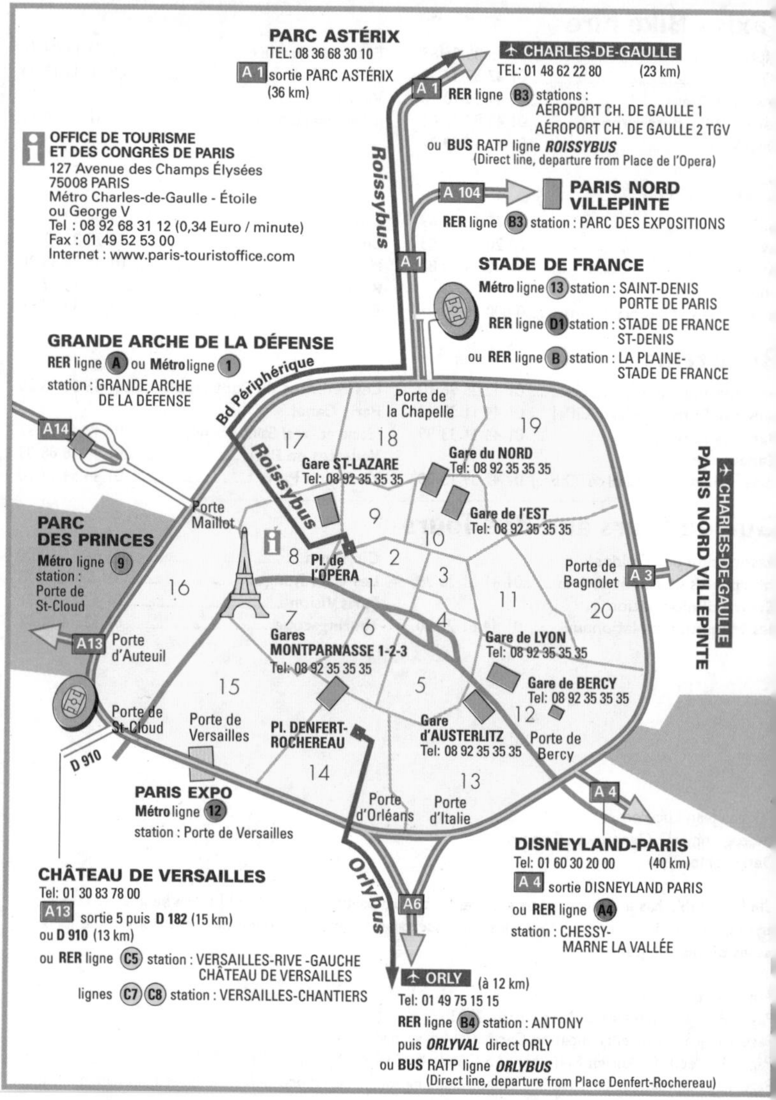

From Paris to...

PARC ASTÉRIX
TEL: 08 36 68 30 10
A 1 sortie PARC ASTÉRIX
(36 km)

✈ CHARLES-DE-GAULLE
TEL: 01 48 62 22 80 (23 km)
A 1 **RER** ligne B3 stations :
AÉROPORT CH. DE GAULLE 1
AÉROPORT CH. DE GAULLE 2 TGV
ou **BUS** RATP ligne ***ROISSYBUS***
(Direct line, departure from Place de l'Opera)

OFFICE DE TOURISME
ET DES CONGRÈS DE PARIS
127 Avenue des Champs Élysées
75008 PARIS
Métro Charles-de-Gaulle - Étoile
ou George V
Tel : 08 92 68 31 12 (0,34 Euro / minute)
Fax : 01 49 52 53 00
Internet : www.paris-touristoffice.com

A 104
PARIS NORD VILLEPINTE
RER ligne B3 station : PARC DES EXPOSITIONS

Roissybus
A 1

STADE DE FRANCE
Métro ligne 13 station : SAINT-DENIS PORTE DE PARIS
RER ligne D1 station : STADE DE FRANCE ST-DENIS
ou **RER** ligne B station : LA PLAINE-STADE DE FRANCE

GRANDE ARCHE DE LA DÉFENSE
RER ligne A ou **Métro** ligne 1
station : GRANDE ARCHE DE LA DÉFENSE

Bd Périphérique
Porte de la Chapelle
A14
17
18
19
Roissybus
Gare ST-LAZARE
Tel: 08 92 35 35 35
Gare du NORD
Tel: 08 92 35 35 35
Gare de l'EST
Tel: 08 92 35 35 35
Porte Maillot
9
10

PARC DES PRINCES
Métro ligne 9
station : Porte de St-Cloud

8
Pl. de l'OPÉRA
2
3
Porte de Bagnolet
A 3
✈ CHARLES-DE-GAULLE
PARIS NORD VILLEPINTE
16
1
11
20
7
6
4
A13
Porte d'Auteuil
Gares MONTPARNASSE 1-2-3
Tel: 08 92 35 35 35
Gare de LYON
Tel: 08 92 35 35 35
15
5
Gare de BERCY
Tel: 08 92 35 35 35
Porte de St-Cloud
Porte de Versailles
Pl. DENFERT-ROCHEREAU
Gare d'AUSTERLITZ
Tel: 08 92 35 35 35
12
Porte de Bercy
D 910
14
13
A 4

PARIS EXPO
Métro ligne 12
station : Porte de Versailles

Porte d'Orléans
Porte d'Italie

DISNEYLAND-PARIS
Tel: 01 60 30 20 00 (40 km)
A 4 sortie DISNEYLAND PARIS
ou **RER** ligne A4
station : CHESSY-MARNE LA VALLÉE

Orlybus
A6

CHÂTEAU DE VERSAILLES
Tel: 01 30 83 78 00
A13 sortie 5 puis **D 182** (15 km)
ou **D 910** (13 km)
ou **RER** ligne C5 station : VERSAILLES-RIVE -GAUCHE CHÂTEAU DE VERSAILLES
lignes C7 C8 station : VERSAILLES-CHANTIERS

✈ ORLY (à 12 km)
Tel: 01 49 75 15 15
RER ligne B4 station : ANTONY
puis ***ORLYVAL*** direct ORLY
ou **BUS** RATP ligne ***ORLYBUS***
(Direct line, departure from Place Denfert-Rochereau)

© ÉDITIONS L'INDISPENSABLE 16-18 rue de l'Amiral Mouchez - 75014 Paris • Tel : 01 45 65 48 48
Internet : www.massin.fr • All rights reserved• No part of this publication may be reproduced • ISBN 2 7072 0468 4
Map MOVIKEN • Printed by G. Canale & C. S. p.A.-Borgaro T.se (TO)